How to get to
THE NORTH POLE

How to get to
THE NORTH POLE
...and other iconic adventures

Tim Moss

howtobooks

To my wife, and an idea.

Published by How To Books Ltd.
Spring Hill House, Spring Hill Road
Begbroke, Oxford OX5 1RX
United Kingdom
Tel: (01865) 375794
Fax: (01865) 379162
info@howtobooks.co.uk
www.howtobooks.co.uk

First published 2012

How To Books greatly reduce the carbon footprint of their books
by sourcing their typesetting and printing in the UK.

British Library Cataloguing in Publication Data
A catalogue record of this book is available from the British Library.

ISBN: 978 1 84528 490 9

Chapter opening artwork by www.jimshannon.co.uk
Illustrations by Firecatcher Creative
Maps by Ted Hatch

Produced for How To Books by Deer Park Productions, Tavistock, Devon
Designed and typeset by Mousemat Design Ltd
Printed and bound in Great Britain by Bell & Bain Ltd, Glasgow

NOTE: The material contained in this book is set out in good faith for general
guidance and no liability can be accepted for loss or expense incurred as a result of
relying in particular circumstances on statements made in the book. Laws and
regulations are complex and liable to change, and readers should check the current
position with relevant authorities before making personal arrangements.

Contents

List of Illustrations

Illustrations

Maps

About the Author

Tim Moss has organised expeditions to all seven continents. He has run expeditions to climb new mountains in Siberia, Bolivia and Kyrgyzstan, walked across the tiny Wahiba Sands Desert of Oman and travelled around the world using 80 different methods of transport.

In 2009, he left his nine-to-five job organising expeditions for the British Schools Exploring Society to work for himself. Operating under the banner of 'The Next Challenge', Tim has helped over 100 different individuals and expeditions including an all-female South Pole expedition, a human-powered trip from London to Tokyo, and several large-scale ventures in the Arctic.

Tim is now joined on most of his expeditions by his wife, Laura, with whom he lives in London. For now.

Visit: www.thenextchallenge.org.

About the Illustrators

Jim Shannon

Jim Shannon produced the illustrations for the start of each chapter. Jim was an illustrator for clients like Harper Collins, *The London Evening Standard* and *The Spectator*. He has since moved into creative direction for advertising, working with companies such as Google, ITV, John Lewis, Lonely Planet and YouTube.
www.jimshannon.co.uk

Rebecca Peacock

The diagrams within each chapter and the maps in the sailing, cycling, desert, mountain and rowing chapters were produced by Rebecca Peacock. Rebecca founded illustration company Firecatcher with best friend Sam Tickner in 2005. Since then she has drawn everything from potatoes to mountains to skeletons riding a bicycle. She works in Rawtenstall, Lancashire. She is also the author of *Make and Mend: a guide to recycling clothes and fabrics* and *Sweets and Treats to Give Away*.
www.firecatcher.co.uk

Ted Hatch

The maps of Antarctica and the Arctic Ocean, in the South and North Pole chapters respectively, are unique, hand drawn pieces by Ted Hatch. There is a lot more that I would like to write about all that Ted has done over the years but the only thing he's allowed me to say is that he is a draughtsmen who works in the Royal Geographical Society.

Foreword

When I entered the expedition world there was no instruction manual. I had to learn my lessons the hard way.

It took seven years of non-stop hard work to drum up the necessary support for my Trans Globe Expedition, the first circumpolar navigation of the globe. On my attempt to walk solo to the Geographic North Pole, I lost the tips of all the fingers on my left hand after hauling my sled from the icy water. And, after three months dragging all of my own supplies across the Antarctic continent, I lost a large proportion of my body weight.

The world of expeditions can be a difficult place to navigate. To a newcomer, its language can sound utterly foreign. It can be daunting at first and there is a risk that some will fail at the first hurdle simply through a lack of understanding and not knowing where to start. And this is where Tim's book can help.

In demystifying so many aspects of some of the world's greatest challenges – laying out the options and explaining what is involved with each – a book like this should both encourage and enable more people to lace their boots and get out there.

Remember, however, that no book will ever get you to the North Pole any more than it will pedal a bike around the world for you. You cannot cross an ocean on words alone. There will come a point when what is needed is action. A first step.

So read this book, soak up its information and its inspiration. But don't sit there for too long because reading is no substitute for doing.

Sir Ranulph Fiennes

Ranulph Fiennes is a veteran of over 30 expeditions around the globe and is described by Guinness World Records as 'the world's greatest living adventurer'. He completed the first unsupported crossing of the Antarctic continent, has climbed both the North Face of the Eiger and Mount Everest despite suffering from vertigo, has travelled to both Poles and is credited with discovering the Lost City of Ubar in the Empty Quarter Desert of Oman.

Preface

I first decided I wanted to go to the North Pole in 2008.

I travelled to the Arctic to spend a week learning to ski, dragging a heavy sled and camping in the snow looking out for polar bears.

Some things I learned during my research surprised me. Like the fact that if you want to go to the 'true' Geographic North Pole then your expedition will *start* further north than the Magnetic North Pole to which Jeremy Clarkson so famously drove.

I had to piece together this sort of information from trawling the internet and picking the brains of those who had been on North Pole expeditions. I was lucky, of course, because I worked in the Royal Geographical Society where such people were ten a penny.

The following year, I led an expedition to climb new peaks in the Russian Altai mountains – a consolation of sorts for my North Pole plans never coming to fruition.

During planning, I was struck by the amount of conflicting information. An experienced climber told us in no uncertain terms that we were going at the wrong time of year; the rivers would be too high and the snow conditions would be unclimbable. We faltered and almost went cycling instead.

But we stuck to our guns and flew to Russia where we made several first and first-British ascents without getting wet above the knees or having any difficulty with the snow.

Finally, I moved to Oman for a few months where the desert both enticed and intimidated. An initial foray resulted in a thirsty march back to a car I had to dig out of the sand using the lid of a coolbox. But following that experience, my wife and I walked the width of the tiny Wahiba Sands Desert carrying all of our own food and water. And suddenly I had gone from no experience to feeling comfortable in the desert.

So I decided to write this book for the following reasons:

1. To demystify what can be a confusing world, and break down some of the perceived barriers to such expeditions and explain them in simple terms.
2. To filter the information and separate fact from opinion.
3. To encourage people to try to get out there and have a go.

I am not offering advice based on personal experience (I have invited those with more experience to do that instead). Rather, I have tried to use my experience to explain what the different expeditions involve and present the options and information as impartially as possible.

This book cannot teach you everything that you need to know – you will need to load a rucksack and get out into the world for that – but, I hope, it is a good place to start.

Tim Moss FRGS

Introduction

This book contains seven chapters, each one dedicated to a different adventure. Below is a brief section about the contents of the book and expeditions in general.

General Notes on Expeditions

Options – guided vs independent
No expedition is 'better' than another and certain approaches will simply suit some more than others. However, there are a variety of options for any given expedition and some of them will clearly be easier. The following are a few approaches which broadly tend to be easier:

- hiring a guide;
- joining an organised event;
- relying on significant technological assistance (e.g. driving across a desert);
- completing a shorter itinerary (e.g. skiing to the Magnetic rather than Geographic North Pole).

These contrast with independently organised and led expeditions that tackle a task in its entirety.

Each chapter defines a 'purest method'. Purity in an expedition is an intangible measure at best and a silly term at worst but its use in this context serves to highlight the simple fact that having someone guide you up a mountain is not the same as climbing that same mountain yourself.

This need not have any influence on your decision making process – you should, of course, simply opt for whichever expedition appeals most. It is important, however, to remember that although the end result may be the same – a mountain climbed, an ocean crossed – the means by which they are achieved can be very different.

Costs

The figures given are accurate where possible but there are so many variables with any given expedition that grand totals will always have to be taken with a pinch of salt. The length of the trip, the quality of equipment you buy and your willingness to 'make do' will all make a difference.

There will always be expedition budgets that sit outside the indicated amounts. Many trips can be completed very cheaply if you already have the equipment – a fully stocked offshore cruiser or a cupboard filled with climbing gear – and if you happen to live near your destination. I walked across the Wahiba Sands for less than £20 because it was only a few hours' drive from my flat and I didn't need any new kit.

Equally, there is no upper limit to the cost of an expedition. There are undoubtedly many smaller expenses that I have not factored into my calculations – notably training costs and insurance, something which you would be wise to obtain for any expedition – and costs for larger scale, more complicated trips can easily spiral out of control.

Communications and emergencies

It is possible to communicate with the outside world from almost anywhere on the planet. Satellite phones have global coverage and an emergency beacon will send a distress signal wherever you are.

However, whilst this can bring many benefits including increased safety, it can also lead to a false sense of security. The ability to call for help is not a substitute for proper prior planning and should not undermine the importance of self-reliance.

You alone have chosen to undertake these risks so the onus of responsibility must lie with you. That responsibility includes being prepared for problems that may arise and having a plan to deal with them. Calling for help is not a plan. It is a last resort when all else has failed.

First-aid training

In the 'Training' section of each chapter I have not mentioned first aid simply because I would recommend first-aid training for *all* expeditions. There are generic outdoor first-aid qualifications and many courses that can be adapted to deal with your specific environment: dealing with snake bites before going into the desert or cold injuries ahead of a mountaineering trip. For more serious expeditions, there are many advanced expedition and wilderness medicine courses available.

Toileting on expedition

Each chapter briefly answers the common question: 'Where do you go to the loo?'. I have not stressed the point in every chapter for fear of repetition but I will do so here: It it is important to deal with your waste in an environmentally-friendly manner.

You can read more about best practice for toileting in the great outdoors in:

How to Shit in the Woods by Kathleen Meyer;

'Leave No Trace', at: www.lnt.org.

Expedition planning seminar

Individual resources are recommended at the end of each chapter but one key resource applicable across the board is the Royal Geographical Society's 'Explore' conference which is held each year in November in London. The event has many great features in its itinerary but the workshops in particular are quite unique. A group of experts in a given field – mountaineering, polar, desert – gathered in one place and waiting to answer your questions. There are few better places to get information straight from the source.

You can read about the conference at: www.rgs.org/explore.

Common Equipment

Below is a short overview of some common equipment and its properties.

Shelters

There are many different shelters you can use on expedition and all manner of different tents but here a few common options:

	Description	Pros and Cons
Dome tent (geodesic)	Dome-shaped tent that looks like an igloo.	Strong design against wind from all directions but less room than tunnel tents. Good in tough conditions.
Tunnel tent	Shaped like a cylinder split down the middle and laid flat.	Roomier than a dome tent but weak against wind on their flanks. Good when wind is predictable or less of an issue.
Pyramid tent	Like a tipi. Single pole with triangle profile.	Used in the Arctic as they manage moisture well by funnelling it through vents at the top.
Tarpaulin (tarp)	A large, flat sheet of waterproof material that you string up to trees or walking poles to create a roof.	Light and spacious but little protection from the elements. Good for less harsh environments and if you like being closer to nature. Also useful as shade in hot climates.
Bivvy (bivi) bag	A large waterproof sack, big enough for your sleeping bag and some kit.	They provide limited shelter from the rain and are colder than tents but they are light, quick to set up and allow sleeping in very small spaces.

Dome tent

Tunnel tent

Pyramid tent

Tarpaulin with bivvy bag underneath

Fig. 1: Tents and shelters

Clothing properties

The following two terms are frequently used when describing outdoor garments:

- Breathability – This refers to the ease with which moisture passes through a garment. If you wear clothes that are not breathable then sweat will accumulate inside them making you wet and cold. Most ordinary clothes – like t-shirts and jeans – are highly breathable. However, because waterproof clothing is designed to keep water out, it will always suffer from reduced breathability.
- Wicking – This is a term which describes the action of removing moisture from your body. A 'wicking top' is designed to quickly get rid of sweat from your body.

Clothing materials

These are some common fabrics used in clothing worn next to the skin during outdoor pursuits:

- Cotton – Cheap and readily available, cotton retains a lot of moisture. This is bad for high-exertion activities where there is a risk of getting cold from dampness but works well at keeping you cool and minimising water loss in hot environments.
- Synthetic (e.g. polypropylene) – Cheap, durable and very good at removing moisture, synthetic tops are great for colder climates with more intense activity, like climbing a mountain. However, on longer trips they start to smell quickly and can be uncomfortable against the skin.
- Merino wool – Merino can be a very warm material that retains much less water than cotton. It is also renowned for absorbing odours allowing it to be worn for long periods. However, it doesn't handle moisture as well as synthetic tops and can be too warm for intense activity. It is also expensive and less durable than the alternatives. It works well in very cold climates (e.g. Poles) and for less intense activity over a long period (e.g. cycle touring).

- Bamboo – A less common material whose properties sit somewhere between synthetic and merino in terms of moisture retention, odour reduction and cost.

Sleeping bags

Most sleeping bags are filled with either down or synthetic materials. The properties of down sleeping bags include:

- good warmth for their weight and pack size;
- expensive;
- performance deteriorates in damp conditions;
- can be difficult to dry out properly.

The features of synthetic-filled bags include:

- larger and heavier for their warmth;
- cheaper;
- more resilient to damp conditions and more easily dried out.

If you are working in a dry environment and/or are willing to look after a down bag, then it will always be a smaller and lighter choice. In wet conditions or if you would prefer a cheaper bag that you don't have to worry about, go for synthetic.

Communications equipment

Some means of communicating with the outside world is useful on most expeditions. These are some common bits of kit:

- Mobile phones – Don't underestimate the coverage that mobile phones have these days. They won't work deep in valleys or out at sea but many other places will still have reception and they have the advantage of being cheap and easy to use.
- Satellite phones – Satphones look and feel a lot like mobile phones

from ten years ago. They can be big and clunky but use satellites rather than phone masts and can give coverage anywhere in the world where you have a clear line of sight to the sky. They can often be connected to a computer for a limited internet connection. New, they cost upwards of around £500. They can be hired for about £100 a month. Calls are charged by the minute and can be quite expensive. The three main network providers are Iridium, Inmarsat and Thuraya.

- VHF (Very High Frequency) radio – Like a walkie-talkie but with better range. These radios are common on boats but can also be used for communicating on land, on a mountain for example. They can travel up to 50 miles in ideal conditions but are largely limited by line of sight.

Emergency beacons

Emergency beacons are usually known by one of two acronyms:

- EPIRB (emergency position-indicating radio beacon); or
- PLB (personal locator beacon).

The former have an association with maritime usage but the function of each type is much the same:

1. send a distress signal;
2. relay your location by GPS.

The smallest ones are not much larger than a mobile phone. They cost from around £200 upwards and need to be registered before use.

The idea is that in a life-threatening situation where there is no means of resolving it yourself and when all other communications have failed, you can activate your EPIRB to call for help. The signals are monitored by various groups with search and rescue capabilities around the world and your nominated person will be contacted.

Here are some notes on their use:

- They should not be relied upon as a means of communicating. You should carry a satellite phone for that.
- They should not form part of a back-up plan. They are strictly for emergencies only.
- They should only ever be activated in a situation that is life-threatening.
- There can be significant fines for improper use.

Types of stoves
The two most common stove types used on expedition are:

- Gas stoves: Used for camping, these are generally small, simple burners that attach to a pressurised gas canister. They are cheap and quick and easy to use. Unfortunately, it is difficult to get canisters in less developed countries and you can't take them on planes which restricts their usage.
- Multi-fuel stoves: General term for a camping stove that burns a number of different liquid fuels. They are bigger, heavier, more fiddly and more prone to problems than most other, simpler stoves but they have two key advantages: First, they maintain efficiency in the cold. Second, they can burn many types of fuel including petrol which means you can refuel them almost anywhere in the world.

Other stove types include solid fuel stoves, spirit burners (like Trangias) and Kelly Kettles which can burn twigs and leaves. Open fires are an option in some places too.

Food and rations
There is a tendency to assume that 'extreme' expeditions require special food. In many situations, however, people on expedition eat very similar foods to that which you have at home. Pasta and sauce served from a rowing boat in the Pacific and a Mars bar munched on a Himalayan snow slope would be quite normal. In certain situations, however, 'rations' are preferable.

Dehydrated rations are dried foods that require water, usually hot, before eating. They typically come in a foil pouch into which you pour boiling water, wait for a few minutes and then eat – much the same process as if you were making a Pot Noodle.

They are popular on expedition due to the following features:

- high calorie-to-weight ratio;
- quick and easy to make;
- the individual packets make planning and rationing easy.

So called 'wet rations' also come in pouches like the dehydrated variety but are more like ready-meals. They can be boiled-in-the-bag or you can empty the contents into a pan and heat them that way. The advantages of these over dehydrated packs are that they:

- taste better;
- can be eaten cold if necessary;
- don't use any water (you can re-use the water in which they are boiled).

However, wet rations are heavy for the amount of calories they contain, compared to both dehydrated rations and other foods like pasta and chocolate.

The term ration, or ration pack, can also refer to an entire day's supply of food. Typically a package with several dehydrated or wet ration pouches along with enough snacks and drinks to give you a full day's calories.

Raising the Funds for an Expedition

Getting the money together is a barrier, or perceived barrier, to many people considering undertaking an expedition. The following notes may help.

Self-funding an expedition

My first piece of advice for anyone looking to fund an expedition is to work out whether you could pay for it yourself. In some instances, the cost may be prohibitive but given that expedition sponsorship can be elusive and make for many disheartening weeks, months and years trying to track it down, saving your own pennies can be a preferable alternative. In its favour:

• It stops the success or failure of your expedition being contingent upon other people.
• You are free to operate exactly as you want to rather than being beholden to others.
• You gain the satisfaction of knowing that you have paid your own way.

Travelling on a shoestring

I have tried to emphasise throughout this book the possibilities for completing expeditions cheaply. The idea of an all-expenses-paid trip to the Antarctic may be tempting but aside from such opportunities being rare, there is no reason to assume that this would necessarily be preferable. Surely part of the reason for pursuing these endeavours is for the challenge and the hardship? In sparing no expense and having the latest shiny equipment, you risk removing a hurdle before you have had the satisfaction of jumping it.

Applying for expedition grants

There are limits to how low the budget for certain expeditions can go and some people will simply prefer not to operate on a shoestring. The next place to look for funding is expedition grants.

There are a number of organisations that offer such grants and the The Royal Geographical Society (RGS) maintains a useful list at:

• www.rgs.org/grants.

If you are under about 25 years old then you will have a wider selection of grants available to you in the 'youth' bracket.

If you are applying for these grants then I would simply recommend that you:

- Carefully read the guidelines to check that you meet their criteria.
- Apply well in advance. Many organisations only give grants once or twice a year.
- Be realistic with your aims to avoid disappointing your sponsors. Under promise and over deliver.

Sourcing equipment cheaply

Equipment can be expensive if you buy it all brand new off the shelf. You can keep costs down by:

- buying second-hand, shopping on eBay, borrowing from friends, waiting for the sales and picking up last year's kit;
- joining a club or organisation affiliated with your sport or expedition environment and capitalising on the membership discounts most of them offer;
- approaching manufacturers for discounts if you think you can offer something genuine in return;
- remembering that you don't always need the latest and greatest equipment. Unless you are on a truly hard and ground-breaking expedition, you can often get by with slightly cheaper or customised kit.

Pitching to companies for sponsorship

There is no silver bullet for acquiring corporate sponsorship for an expedition. However, I would offer some of the following as advice when pitching for sponsorship:

1. Summarise your story in a single succinct and easily understandable sentence. Don't waffle on.
2. Make it personal, not generic, and explain why you are approaching that particular company.

3. Be honest. Exaggeration may bite you back further down the line and it is not a good foot to start on.

4. Explain what you can really offer them in return. Would you think it was a good investment if a similar pitch arrived in your inbox?

I am often asked about the best way to produce a sponsorship presentation. I do not think there is such a thing. Some people will be impressed by slick and polished graphical presentations, whilst others may prefer a handwritten and heartfelt letter. Just go with whatever feels right to you, based on the individual or organisation you are approaching.

For more information on expedition fundraising and sponsorship, visit: www.thenextchallenge.org/resources.

Final Notes

The writing process

I wrote this book over 18 months. It is a combination of experiences from my own expeditions and those that I have organised for other people; the books I have read and stories I have heard; the research I have conducted and the input of others more experienced than myself.

My job throughout has been to distil the information which I deemed pertinent. However, facts alone make for an unsatisfactory vehicle with which to deliver the many subtleties of expedition life. As such, I have included anecdotes about expeditions and people that illustrate points and which I think you will find interesting. There are accounts of a typical day on expedition from those who have been there and done it too.

Each chapter also contains advice from experienced expeditioners. I contacted various people that I knew about or came across during research and asked them each for one 'top tip' they would give someone considering their first expedition. I have written the briefest of backgrounds for each of these contributors but you could learn a lot more by Googling their names.

For two chapters, I took a slightly different approach. In Chapter 4 'How to Cycle Around the World' I posted the question publicly on Twitter and collected responses. For Chapter 5 'How to Sail the Seven Seas', I decided to go to the sailing community directly and ask my question in some online forums.

Finally, there is navigation advice for every environment courtesy of Tristan Gooley, whose excellent book *The Natural Navigator* teaches the art of finding your way without map or compass.

The language of expeditions

Expeditions have a lexicon of their own. Wherever possible I have explained new terms as they arise. In some instances I have opted to introduce the key terms at the start of a chapter but for every word that you see emboldened, a definition can be found in the Glossary at the back of the book.

Some last requests

This book is aimed to entertain and inform but, above all, its aim is to get people out there, doing stuff. If it plays any small part in getting you from armchair to adventure then it has done its job.

But this book has also been written in accordance with a set of beliefs and a certain ethos. I try to follow these rules in my own expeditions and would be greatly appreciative if you would consider the following requests which stem from those rules when conducting your own expeditions:

1. Don't exaggerate or make lofty claims. Better to do and be judged on merit than to deal in hyperbole.
2. Seek help from those more experienced but do so politely, thoughtfully and having first done your own research.
3. Document your adventure so that others may learn from it. A flashy website is nice but a simple report will suffice.
4. Let me know how you get on, email: tim@thenextchallenge.org.

Good luck.

How To
Cross a Desert

*'Always remember the bright side of life. The right
attitude is more important than the gear.'*

– Mikael Strandberg,
veteran of dozens of expeditions from Siberia to the Sahara

Setting the Scene

Deserts, for most of us, are on the one hand intriguing and exotic, and on the other hand, barren and forebidding. It is important to remember, however, that both animals and people have lived in these environments for thousands of years. They are still harsh places in which to exist but even if you don't capitalise on the modern proliferation of four-wheel-drive vehicles, it is quite possible to traverse even the largest of deserts on foot, with camel support or towing a cart loaded with water.

Statistics

USP:	Surviving sun and sand across a barren landscape.
Difficulty:	Moderate to difficult.
Cost:	£1,000–£5,000+.
Hurdles:	Lack of water, heat, sun.
Purest style:	Unsupported with camel or cart.
Who's done it?:	Thousands by car, dozens on foot.
Glory potential:	Moderate.

Background

People have lived in desert environments for thousands of years: the **Bedouin** in the Middle East, the **Tuareg** in North Africa, and the Australian Aborigines to name but a few. Records may not exist to document the journeys they undoubtedly made over the centuries but their ability to live and travel in these environments speaks volumes.

The deliberate exploration of deserts really kicked off in the 19th century with European explorers delving into the depths of North Africa in their droves and similar numbers trying to push their way through Central Australia.

In 1849, Scottish missionary David Livingstone – best known for his encounter with Henry Stanley: 'Dr. Livingstone, I presume?' – led the first crossing of the Kalahari by Europeans, albeit with much local assistance. Shortly afterwards, Heinrich Barth spent five years exploring North and West Africa. Barth crossed the Sahara in the process, spending much of his time travelling solo after his two team mates died.

In the 1860s, John McDouall Stuart rode the wave of Australia's expedition fever to complete the first north-south crossing of the continent with the aid of 70 horses. And 70 years later, Bertram Thomas became the first recorded Westerner to cross the Middle East's Empty Quarter with a group of Bedouin and their camels.

Not long afterwards, Wilfred Thesiger stubbornly clung to a bygone age with his traditional approach to travel in the Arabian Desert but, ultimately, his journeys marked the end of an era for desert exploration. Developments in vehicle-based exploration, pioneered by Ralph Bagnold and his Long Range Desert Group (of which Thesiger was a member) during the Second World War, would forever change access to deserts.

Deserts now make popular tourist destinations. They are easily accessible for short periods without much skill or preparation and can offer a fascinating, if brief, insight into an environment quite alien to most. However, this is where the experience ends for most people – a dip of the toe, click of the camera and back to civilisation. The idea of a longer journey is either anathema or implausible to most. As a result adventurous expeditions into the desert are rare and those of the independent, unsupported variety are rarer still.

But such journeys are surprisingly attainable. It is a small step from being a complete desert novice to gaining enough experience for an initial foray. And when at least the outskirts of so many deserts around the world are logistically easy to reach – compared to, say, the foot of a remote mountain – and travelling through them requires only the minimum of low-tech kit, the opportunity for a challenging desert expedition is never far away.

Introduction – What Defines a Desert?

The stereotype of a desert tends to include extreme heat and sand dunes but such features are not always present. The average temperature of the Patagonian Desert is only a little above zero, for example, and there is not a lot of sand there.

The most common definition is based upon rainfall, specifically that an area needs to receive less than 250mm a year to qualify. This simple measure does not always give satisfying results, however. One such example is that when evaporation and other factors are taken into account, some regions that do not make the cut are in fact notably drier than those that do.

Within this definition there are huge climatic variations. Yes, you get the scorching hot Arabian Desert averaging 40°C in the summer but you also have deserts like the Gobi which can drop to −30°C in the winter. Equally, other deserts can experience much milder temperatures if you time your trip right, the Atacama and Namib being two such examples.

Similarly, not all deserts are sandy. They can have all sorts of different surfaces from salt flats and boulder fields to gravel plains and scrub land.

But whilst heat and sand may not be the defining features of a desert in any scientific sense, they present the most novelty and practical implications for an expedition and thus will be the focus of this chapter.

Types of desert

There are many different ways to categorise and define deserts but here are three key types used throughout this chapter:

Subtropical desert – The stereotypical desert: hot in the winter and very hot in the summer. Includes the Sahara, Arabian and all of the Australian Deserts.

Cool coastal desert – West coast deserts kept dry by easterly winds, they tend to have more moderate temperatures year-round. Includes the Atacama and Namib Deserts.

Cold winter desert – Cool or cold in the winter, warm or hot in the summer. Outside the sub-tropical degrees of latitude. Includes the Gobi, Patagonian and Great Basin Deserts.

Options – Route and Style

On roads or tracks
Many deserts have roads running straight through the middle of them. If there is tarmac then a crossing is a fairly straightforward undertaking by car, bike or similar.

The Trans-Sahara and Cairo-Dakar Highways, many North American deserts and a soon to be completed road across the Empty Quarter between Oman and Saudi Arabia are all possibilities for this. A little more adventurous would be following tracks off-road which might take a bit more effort and equipment (e.g. four-wheel-drive or mountain bike) but are still notably easier than going entirely off the beaten track.

For the remaining areas of desert which do not have such routes already made for you, plenty of options remain.

Enter a race or rally
Racing through deserts on foot is becoming increasingly popular with many different organisations now offering desert ultra marathons all over the world. The formats vary but typically see you running long distances through various check points either in one big hit (e.g. 24 hours non-stop) or over a few days, sometimes carrying your own equipment and sleeping in tents.

It is rare that any such race would actually take you the width or length of an entire desert but they are a good way to get a taste of desert life and some physical hardship.

An alternative are motorised rallies. They are sometimes called **rally raids** and involve driving long distances over several days. Some are competitive with different classes for motorbikes, buggies, trucks and so forth, whilst others focus more on the fun and adventurous aspects with entries open for anything from cars that cost under £100 to fire engines and ambulances. Some will be primarily off-road and require appropriate vehicles, others will be entirely on paved roads. Of course, not all such rallies cross deserts but plenty of them do.

- The Marathon des Sables – The best known desert marathon. It covers 150 miles over six days. Costs £3,200+ including flights.
- Other desert marathons in e.g. the Atacama, Gobi and Namib – Varying distances and itineraries but typically cost around £2,000 including flights.
- Budapest-Bamako and Trans-Sahara – Popular, non-competitive rally raids. Registration typically a few hundred pounds but food, fuel and accommodation are extra.
- The Dakar Rally – The best known competitive rally raid. Originally from Paris to Dakar but now changing destinations each year. Registration from £12,000.

Crossing a big, a small, or part of a desert
Deserts come in all shapes and sizes. Many offer scope for epic voyages over several months and many more can be crossed in a matter of days or weeks.
Some larger deserts with potential for big expeditions include:

- The Sahara – Covers a dozen countries in North Africa. It stretches 1,000 miles high and 3,000 miles wide.
- The Gobi – Mongolia and China. 1,000 by 500 miles.
- The Arabian – Covers most of the Arabian Peninsula in the Middle East and contains the Rub' Al Khali Empty Quarter. 1,300 miles long and 700 miles wide.
- The Kalahari – Botswana, Namibi and South Africa. 1,000 miles by 600 at its greatest.
- The major deserts of Australia and North America.

Some smaller deserts which could be crossed more swiftly:

- Namib – Namibia and Angola. 1,000 miles long but less than 100 miles wide in many places.
- Atacama and Sechura – South America. Narrow strips like the Namib which are never wider than 100 miles.

- Sinai Peninsula – Egypt. Easily accessed and its wedge shape offers a variety of coast-to-coast distances from 50 miles upwards.

> **The great European deserts**
> Europe may not be known for its deserts but it does have a few areas which either meet the criteria or have enough sand to look as though they do:
> - Deliblato Sands – Long stretch of sand in Serbia.
> - Piscinas – Tiny sandy desert in Sardinia.
> - Oltenian Sahara – Nickname given to a desertified area of Romania following deforestation.
> - Tabernas – Arid region of Spain averaging 3,000 hours of annual sunshine.
> - Oleshky Sands – Sand expanse in Ukraine.

Hot deserts or cold ones
The colder deserts – which can go several degrees below zero – tend to be at the higher latitudes. Some examples are:

- The Asian Deserts above India and Iran.
- The Patagonian Desert in South America.
- The northern-most deserts in the United States.

Deserts closer to the equator – and that covers the majority of them – tend to be warm, if not hot, even in winter.

Sand, salt, gravel or rocks
Remember to check before packing your bucket and spade as many deserts do not have that much sand. In most situations you should be prepared to spend decent chunks of time on different terrain. Here are some common types:

- Salt flats – The Lut and Kavir in Iran do have big piles of sand, some of the biggest in the world in fact, but they also have huge areas of salt flats without a grain of sand in sight. The same goes for the Atacama.

- Gravel plains – Gravel is a common feature of many deserts including the Patagonian, Arabian, Gibson and Taklamakan to name a few.
- Rocky terrain – Vast expanses of barren, rocky terrain fill many deserts such as in much of the Gobi and Mojave, and parts of the Sinai Peninsula.
- Sand – Plenty of deserts, of course, do contain sand. The Empty Quarter, Sahara, Kalahari, Simpson, Karakum and Nebraska Sand Hills all have large concentrations.

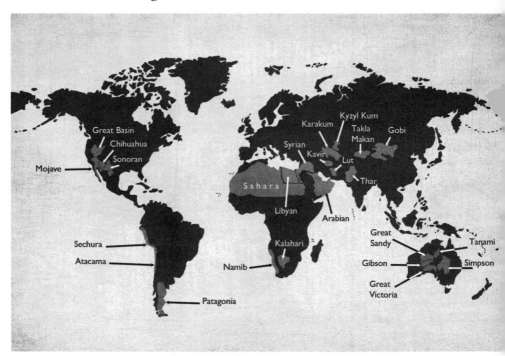

Map 1: World map of deserts

Deserts around the world

Below is a selection of deserts from around the world. Size and temperature are only meant as rough guides.

Africa and the Middle East

Name	Location	Length (miles)	Width (miles)	Type	Summer temperature	Winter temperature	Notes
Sahara	North Africa	3,000	1,000	Subtropical	Very hot	Warm to hot	Includes Algerian, Libyan, Nubian
Arabian	Most of peninsula	1,300	700	Subtropical	Very hot	Warm to hot	
Syrian	Syria, Jordan, Iraq	600	600	Subtropical	Very hot	Warm to hot	
Kalahari	Angola, Botswana, South Africa, Namibia	1,000	600	Subtropical	Very hot	Warm	
Namib	Namibia, Angola	600	60	Cool coastal	Hot	Warm	

Asia

Name	Location	Length (miles)	Width (miles)	Type	Summer temperature	Winter temperature	Notes
Gobi	Mongolia, China	1,000	500	Cold winter	Warm to hot	Cold to very cold	Extreme variations in temperature (+40°C to -40°C)
Karakum	Turkmenistan	300	500	Cold winter	Hot	Cold	
Kyzyl Kum	Kazakhstan, Uzbekistan, Turkmenistan	200	500	Cold winter	Hot	Cold	
Taklamakan	China	500	250	Cold winter	Very hot	Cold	
Thar	India, Pakistan	500	250	Subtropical	Very hot	Cool to warm	Also called 'The Great Indian Desert'
(Dasht-e) Kavir	Iran	350	200	Cold winter	Very hot	Cold to warm	Temperatures vary by up to 70°C
(Dasht-e) Lut	Iran	250	150	Cold winter	Very hot	Cold to warm	Recorded hottest land temperature on earth: 70.7°C

Australia

Name	Location	Length (miles)	Width (miles)	Type	Summer temperature	Winter temperature	Notes
Great Victoria	Australia	150	500	Subtropical	Very hot	Warm to hot	
Great Sandy	Australia	250	350	Subtropical	Very hot	Warm to hot	
Tanami	Australia	250	200	Subtropical	Very hot	Warm to hot	
Simpson	Australia	300	100	Subtropical	Very hot	Warm to hot	
Gibson	Australia	300	100	Subtropical	Very hot	Warm to hot	

North and Central America

Name	Location	Length (miles)	Width (miles)	Type	Summer temperature	Winter temperature	Notes
Chihuahuan	US, Mexico	800	300	Subtropical	Very hot	Cool to warm	
Sonoron	US	600	200	Subtropical	Very hot	Warm to hot	
Great Basin	US	900	600	Cold winter	Hot	Cold	
Mojave	US	200	200	Subtropical	Very hot	Cool to warm	

South America

Name	Location	Length (miles)	Width (miles)	Type	Summer temperature	Winter temperature	Notes
Patagonian	Argentina, Chile	1,000	250	Cold winter	Cold – warm	Cold	
Atacama	Peru, Chile	600	100	Cool coastal	Cold – hot	Cold – warm	
Sechura	Peru	1200	100	Subtropical	Warm – Hot	Cool – warm	

'Water is the most important factor. Always plan ahead to make sure you know where the water sources are located.'

– Helen Thayer,
who has walked across the Sahara, Death Valley,
and the Gobi Desert amongst others

How you source your water

A fundamental part of planning a desert expedition is where your water comes from. It will affect the style of the expedition and require some simple calculations involving the following elements:

1. how far you can travel each day;
2. how much water you need each day;
3. how much water you can carry.

Of course, each of these factors is linked to the other. For example, the amount you drink will depend on how far you travel and how much you are carrying. But juggling each of them will likely inform the decisions you make during planning.

Some broad options for your water supplies will be:

- travelling between water sources or settlements to refill;
- arranging caches to be dropped in advance or rendezvousing with re-supply vehicles;
- using a portable **de-salinator** if travelling in a coastal desert;
- carrying all the water you need for your journey.

Walking the Wahiba in a Weekend
by Tim Moss

'The Wahiba Sands of Oman is a tiny desert in Oman. It measures around 100 miles high and 50 miles wide, and is filled in its entirety by picture perfect sand dunes. Living in Muscat just a few hours' drive away, my wife and I decided we wanted to walk across it.

We considered all sorts of options for getting our water re-supplied – walking via a camp, arranging a jeep rendezvous, even hiking out to the road halfway through the trip – but eventually settled on just rationing our intake and carrying what we needed. We reckoned about ten litres each was enough.

We timed the trip to coincide with a full moon so we could walk at night and in the early mornings. It also happened to be on one of Oman's many national holidays which gave us a three day weekend and meant no time off work.

> *It was our first desert expedition and we spent two and a half days slogging uphill through steep sand, carrying heavy packs and praying that each dune would be the last. When we reached the end we made a bee line for the road, hitched back to our parked car and drove home again ready for work the next day. The trip cost around £20 for petrol and food.'*

Options – Transport

Travelling on foot

For journeys of a few days at a time, walking is the simplest approach. It does not require the skills of off-road driving or camel handling, nor the effort of dragging a cart. There is little specialist kit required and, logistically at least, it is as simple as packing a bag and putting one foot in front of another.

There is a stringent limit on how much water you can realistically carry, however. And the more of it you have, the harder each mile will be which means you will sweat more. As such, if you want to walk with a pack then you need to stick to short journeys.

You can do your own maths based on the water requirements discussed below – one litre = one kilogram – but three to five days' walking is about the limit that most people will manage.

Alone across the Namib

In 2006, Sam McConnell was dropped by helicopter on the Skeleton Coast of Namibia. In his backpack were 18 litres of water, two dehydrated meals, two apples and some chewing gum. The nearest water source was 100km away on the far side of the Namib Desert's dune sea.

It took Sam six days to reach his destination and the trip was made into a documentary for the National Geographic Channel. He said it nearly killed him.

Read more at: www.sam-mcconnell-expeditions.com.

Driving a 4x4

Travelling in a 4x4 is obviously not quite the same challenge as going on foot but there is nonetheless plenty of adventure to be had. Be aware, however, that whilst driving along flat, hard sand can be very easy, handling a heavy vehicle over steep dunes in a remote place is not something to be taken lightly.

Your primary constraint for a desert trip of any length by vehicle will probably be the amount of fuel you can carry. Off-road driving, and sand in particular, can guzzle many litres of fuel. Apart from that, you should have a large capacity for carrying equipment and supplies, a good range for travel and a decent ability to cover different types of terrain.

For any serious desert driving, a 4x4 is your best bet. Literature abounds on desert driving covering the pros and cons of everything from different vehicles to types of tyres and specific driving techniques. However, some general attributes to look for when selecting your vehicle might include:

- big wheels;
- high ground clearance;
- good power-to-weight ratio.

Driving in sand

Basic tips for driving in sand:

Go with at least two or three vehicles so you can help tow out any that get stuck or escape if need be.

Let air out of the tyres to get more surface area on the sand.

Keep gears low and revs high on tricky or steep sections.

Tackle slopes head-on rather than at a diagonal where there is a risk of tipping.

Always ease slowly to a halt rather than stopping dead in soft sand which can force the wheels in deeper.

If you get stuck in sand there are many different strategies you can take to aid extrication including:

rolling forward and backward to build momentum;

> rocking the vehicle sideways to allow sand to fill the gaps beneath the tyres;
>
> wedging things under the tyres to give better traction;
>
> wiggling the steering wheel to gain traction as you start moving.

Travelling by camel

Known as the ships of the desert, camels are embedded in desert exploration history and with good reason. Here are some facts about these beasts and what makes them such good team mates in the desert:

- A camel's hump does not store water. It is filled with fat. Storing it there rather than spread across their body helps keep them cool. Metabolising this fat produces water as well as energy.
- They have oval red blood cells which helps keep their blood flowing even when dehydrated.
- They don't start sweating until their body temperature is much higher than most animals – around 41°C – and they can lose significantly more body fluids before becoming dehydrated.
- Any sweat produced spends a long time in a camel's thick coat before evaporating so acts to cool the camel down.
- Their coat also reflects the heat of the sun and insulates them from the radiated heat of the sand.
- Their long legs help keep their body away from the hot sand and their tall, narrow profile means they can minimise the surface area of their body which is exposed to the sun by turning.
- Camels have three eyelids to help protect them from sand. One of them is translucent.

Walking with camels

Camels can tolerate high temperatures, go long periods without water and bear the weight of a human passenger and/or large volumes of kit so make excellent companions on an expedition. Travelling with them requires some practice and effort but, once mastered, opens up a world

40

of possibilities for desert travel.

However, modern camels – like modern man – are often not used to the rigours of expedition life. As such, you either need to choose carefully or toughen them up in advance; a process which can take weeks or months.

You could expect a typical fit-for-expedition camel to:

- carry between 100 and 250kg;
- cover in the region of 20 to 30 miles a day;
- go for a week or two without water in cooler conditions but only a couple of days if they are working hard in the heat;
- drink 20 litres of water a day if given free access to water;
- eat 2 or 3kg of food each day.

Food and water: It is not normally realistic to carry water for camels. Planning regular refills is more prudent. Where grass and shrubs are not available for grazing, grains are often used as food.

Walking and riding: It is common to both ride on and walk next to camels. There is not much difference in speed so in most circumstances it will probably be prudent to share the burden between you – walking on steep or difficult sections and when the camel is tired, and hopping on the back when the going is good and the camel is looking fitter than you feel.

Looking after your camel: If your expedition is reliant upon camels then it will pay to ensure that you know how to properly treat and handle them, and how to **hobble** them to contain the risk of their wandering off while you sleep. Enlisting the help of a handler or guide is an easy way of doing this although it could be a little more complicated if you are planning a lengthy trip. Alternatively it may be possible to get training from whoever is providing the camels.

How to Buy a Camel
by Jeremy Curl

How to find them ...

'Ask around. The livestock market is always the best place to start. This will be almost always on the outside of the town or village. Some are everyday, others are one day a week, so find out. You will be approached immediately, as you will undoubtedly look foreign, and expensive offers of a camel will follow. It's a good idea to bring someone local you trust with you to help you and if possible, who can act on your behalf with bartering: they will know if you are getting your money's worth and the price will almost certainly be lower for them.'

What to look for ...

'If you are using your camel for a desert journey, strength is key. It will have to carry loads and/or you and if your camel is not used to work or is weak then this could pose a serious danger. Ask to see it stand and sit down again. The knees are important, so check for any trembling in the legs, a sure sign of a weak camel. Their rising and sitting should be smooth, it should walk without a limp and the camel must be obedient. It goes almost without saying that a disobedient camel would spell trouble for you later. Check for any open sores and have a look at the pads on the underside of its feet, these should be without wounds. Also see that the camel can accept a rope through its nose or around its face and that it does not make too much of a fuss. Crucially this is to check whether it is a biter. Ask the camel's age. Four to eight is ideal, as it will be experienced enough but not too old.'

Costs ...

'The cost of a camel can vary dramatically depending on where it is bought, its size, its age and the conditions at the time (drought etc). A goodish camel at a time of plenty could go for £150, whereas a large camel in an area without many can be £1,000 or more. When planning your expedition, try not to buy your camel(s) in an area where camel is commonly eaten. This will push up the value. Lastly, remember there is no fixed price: barter like *mad. This could well take days to get the price you want.'*

What else will you need...?

'If you are riding, you'll need a saddle. A camel stick is useful too. You'll need rope to lead it with and to hobble it when you are letting it graze. You will also need some blankets to act as a cushion between its back and the saddle. If you are using it to carry loads you will need more rope and strong sacks. Ask the camel seller if he can throw in any rope as this will save you trying to find it later. If you are going across a desert that offers absolutely no grazing, then you must bring food for the camel, and the poor camel will have to carry this too. Camels will eat almost anything but hay is fine. Unlike their water situation, they must eat every day so be sure to bring enough.'

What to do when you're finished ...

'Try and sell it at an aforementioned livestock market. Again, barter hard as after a long desert journey they will try to take it off you cheaply. Make sure it has been well watered and well fed hours before selling: it will look noticeably larger. If you cannot find anyone to buy your camel(s), approach butchers. This may seem heartless, given that this animal has endured with you on your desert expedition, but they are expensive and to recoup some of your money a butcher's is always a safe bet.'

Jeremy Curl has crossed the Kaisuit and Koroli Deserts. In 2008, he traversed 2000km across the Sahara using camels with the Touareg tribes.

Read more and see his photographs at: www.jeremycurl.com.

Dragging a cart

If you do not like the idea of using a noisy car or a smelly camel, then you can shoulder the burden yourself with a cart: a two-wheeled contraption that you attach to your waist and drag behind you like a trailer. Think of an old-fashioned hand-pulled rickshaw and you are pretty much there.

Obviously, this is notably harder work than the other options but it does mean that, with mechanical failures aside, you are reliant only upon yourself and can carry enough supplies for many weeks at a time.

There is no commercial manufacturer of desert carts. Every desert traveller has made their own unique cart.

Typical design features include:

- a simple frame, usually made from aluminium;
- one or two wheels on either side. Motorcycle wheels are common, but tractor and strong mountain bike wheels have also been used;
- two parallel bars running from the trailer, either attached to a padded harness that straps around the waist or two handles to grip with hands.

The advantage of a cart over a rucksack is that the weight is not directly on your body. As such, you can carry a far higher pay load; 300kg is not unfeasible.

Of course, they do not come without their downsides. Dragging several times your bodyweight on wheels up a steep sand dune is no mean feat. Above all, however, the beauty of the cart is that they require very little skill or training but allow you to travel huge distances without having to worry about re-supplies.

The Pig and other notable desert carts

Paddy Wagon: Unlikely as it may sound, you may wish to consider some form of braking on your cart. Crossing the Simpson Desert in Australia, Lucas Trihey found his cart, the 'Paddy Wagon', would topple on steep descents and was only stopped by improvising some brakes. To stop punctures, he also ran a leather strap around the inside of each motorcycle tyre. See: www.escalade.com.au.

Molly Brown: Ripley Davenport – a veteran of many desert crossings – aborted his first attempt at walking solo across the Gobi when the ball bearings in his cart 'Molly Brown' got worn down after

---

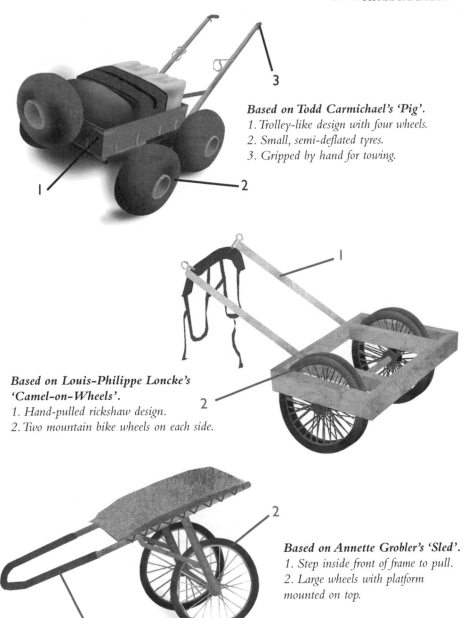

Based on Todd Carmichael's 'Pig'.
1. Trolley-like design with four wheels.
2. Small, semi-deflated tyres.
3. Gripped by hand for towing.

Based on Louis-Philippe Loncke's 'Camel-on-Wheels'.
1. Hand-pulled rickshaw design.
2. Two mountain bike wheels on each side.

Based on Annette Grobler's 'Sled'.
1. Step inside front of frame to pull.
2. Large wheels with platform mounted on top.

Fig. 2: Typical desert carts

just two days because dust was able to enter the chamber. The problem resolved, Ripley towed the cart 1,000 miles with an average weight of 220kg. Molly was last seen being dragged across China by adventurers Rob Lilwall and Leon McCarron (see: www.walkinghomefrommongolia.com).

Camel-on-Wheels: As with bikes, thinner tyres are faster but thicker tyres are better for difficult terrain. Belgian Louis-Philippe Loncke's 'Camel-on-Wheels' combined the best of both worlds. He used two pairs of thin bicycle wheels for speed on easier terrain but would wedge a strip of foam between them when going through deep sand to increase the surface area and stop it from sinking. See: www.simpson-desert-trek.blogspot.com.

Rag-and-Bone Man's Trolley: Singaporean mountaineer David Lim and his team spent six months designing carts only to have them impounded by customs upon arrival in Bolivia. Against a deadline, they were forced to improvise carts with the old steel rag-and-bone men's trolleys they found in the local township. The resulting makeshift trolleys carried 100 litres of water and six days' food all the way across the Salar de Uyuni salt flats. See: www.everest.org.sg/desertindex.html.

The Pig: Todd Carmichael has made two attempts to cross America's Death Valley towing all of his supplies in the cart he affectionately terms 'The Pig'. The second design of the cart runs low to the ground and has four small wheels with fat, half-inflated tyres. See: www.subzerosolo.com.

Paddleable Amphibious Carts (PAC): Chris Bray and Clark Carter added huge tractor inner tubes to two kayaks that they dragged across Victoria Island. In the Canadian Arctic they were up against mud, rocks and snow rather than sand. When not used for floating, they would let air out of the tyres – as you would with a jeep on sand – to give the wheels a greater surface area and not sink into mushy ground. See: www.1000hourday.com.

Practicalities

Where do you sleep?

In many desert situations, the mild night time temperatures and little fear of rain mean it is possible to sleep entirely outside and under the stars. In other situations, a tent is common for respite from the wind and curious creatures or if sleeping in a cold desert.

Pitching away from bushes and rocks reduces animal encounters and sleeping up high on sand dunes may also help avoid morning dews. Beyond that, however, you should be pretty much be free to sleep wherever has the best view.

What do you eat and drink?

In the desert it is water which will be your primary concern, more than food. The chances are that you will be carrying all of your water for several days at a time, if not weeks or months, and be limited in how much you can use.

For food, you could reasonably take anything that will last for a long time in hot conditions, survive being bashed around in a bag and can be prepared without too much effort. Although there is the usual weight penalty for carrying food containing liquids (e.g. tinned food or **wet rations**), it will all contribute to your daily fluid intake as long as you don't drain any of it away. Unless you take supplements, your food will need a high salt content to replace that which is lost through sweat.

You may find that heat and thirst reduce your appetite during the day. You can plan accordingly by focusing on smaller snack foods rather than anything too heavy, but make sure you compensate for any light eating with bigger breakfasts and dinners.

'Your ability to eat and make tea is vital when moving through the desert. It gives you energy to do the job. Light a fire whenever you stop and brew tea with plenty of sugar. As a result, be opportunistic when it comes to gathering firewood. If you see dead wood, break it up and bring it with you – you never know how much you'll find when you stop later.'

– Jeremy Curl,
who travelled 2,000km across the Sahara with camels

Solar stills and cacti

A commonly held belief for desert survival is that you can dig a pit, cover it with a plastic sheet and let the condensation drip into a container you place at the bottom. The theory is good but the practice less so. It requires certain conditions (e.g. no wind) and a degree of effort to construct. Some say, only half-jokingly, that you will expend more sweat digging the hole than you will gain in water. Regardless, it is not a practical solution for a regular water source on a desert expedition.

Similarly, cutting into a cactus and draining its liquid is largely the stuff of legend.

Where do you go to the loo?

Toileting away from any tracks would be courteous and certainly some distance from settlements but beyond that the desert is your toiletry oyster. Dry environments are not conducive to rapid decay so a shallow bury is advised or, better still, smearing over a rocky surface. The Tuareg have traditionally used rocks for wiping, as no doubt have many others, but the use of sand is rarely advisable. If burning paper, be careful not to ignite anything nearby given the dry environment.

How long do you actually spend walking?

Depending on the location and season, it is quite likely that the extreme ends of the day will be better for progress. Rising before the sun and pressing on after it sets are not uncommon as conditions can often be more pleasant at these times. An hour or two's rest is often taken during the heat of the day. An alternative in hotter deserts is to walk at night. It will be cooler still and there will be fewer flies. With a decent-sized moon you might not even need a torch. If you are in a cold desert then no doubt you will simply want to capitalise on the warmest parts of the day when the sun is up.

'Develop the native eye that Barry Lopez refers to in his book Arctic Dreams. Don't take a GPS, use the sun and stars as an opportunity to hone your skills in celestial navigation. Much more rewarding.'
– Mark Evans,
who runs Outward Bound Oman
and spent a month exploring the Empty Quarter

How do you know where to go?

Many desert areas are comparatively featureless and thus micro-navigation of the sort that might be required in other environments is less often necessary. Instead, a broad concept of where you are located and how you are progressing is probably more important than knowing exactly where you are in relation to specific terrain.

Some useful tools include:

- Compass – A simple method for maintaining direction. Be aware that iron content in some deserts, such as the Namib, can distort your compass reading.
- GPS – The easiest means of locating yourself in a vast, featureless environment. Particularly useful if you are using caches of food and water dropped in advance.

- Celestial navigation – Deserts are frequently blessed with clear skies which makes navigation by sun and stars quite feasible, particularly when the emphasis is on general direction rather than pinpointing.
- Sun compass – Another alternative, this calculates direction using the time and your latitude – or any one piece of information from the other two.

'1. The best tip for anyone heading into a desert is to try to do a little homework on the stars before you get there. The vast majority of desert travellers learn interesting things about the stars they have seen in the clear nights of a desert trip after getting back. And then kick themselves gently.

2. Look for what I call desert "tell tails". These are the little tails of sand left in the lee of scrub bushes, rocks and other small obstructions. They will mark direction very clearly and help orientate you in an otherwise homogeneous stretch of dunes or plain, especially when the sun is too high to be helpful. These tails will remain consistent until the next strong winds or sandstorm blows through.

3. Try to relate the difference between the slip faces of dunes to the prevailing wind direction. The slip face is the steeper downwind side. This will help you make sense of the dune shapes around you and even help you plan the best routes for approaching systems that lie further ahead.'

– Tristan Gooley, author of *The Natural Navigator*

When to go
It is temperature that will have most control over when you attempt your crossing.

- Subtropical – You will almost certainly want to opt for the cooler winter months as the summers can be very hot.
- Cold winter – These vary somewhat in their conditions. The Gobi has very cold winters but moderate summers, for example, whilst the Lut's winter is mild but its summers are some of the hottest on earth.
- Cool coastal – More moderate in their range than the other two, some will be feasible at any time of year and the others have shorter prohibitive hot periods.

What happens if things go wrong?
Some desert areas will be reachable by helicopter but many will be too far away meaning that rescue by vehicle is most likely. In difficult terrain this may mean a long wait or require you to travel to a more accessible spot. If you do have a long wait then do so in whatever shade you can muster. An alternative in a life-threatening situation is to bury yourself in sand with only your head poking out. A few inches below the surface the sand will be cooler and a good way of keeping your temperature and fluid loss to a minimum.

'A clearly set out emergency plan for your back up crew is essential. You need to think about unforeseen problems: What if your sat-phone gets a dunking and doesn't work? Will your back up crew call a premature rescue (costly and embarrassing) just because you missed a sked [scheduled call]? Have back up plans in place and advice written down that will cover all possibilities.'
– Lucas Trihey, who crossed the Simpson Desert with a cart

Difficulties

Working out how much water you need

Travelling through a desert, you will need to take enough water to replace that which your body loses in the hot, dry environment but you will almost certainly have constraints on the amount you can carry. Working out how much you need is both complicated and critical.

Some factors influencing water requirements include:

- the temperature;
- how hard you are working – riding a camel on the flat will be easier than dragging a cart uphill;
- how long you are moving for each day;
- how well adapted you are – you should adapt to the heat over a few days or weeks so you might consider extra water rations at the start;
- your own physiology – some people just need more than others.

Thirst alone is not a reliable indicator. Just as your body will want to stop running halfway through a marathon even though you know that finishing is well within its ability, your body will crave water when it is actually capable of continuing without it. You need to learn to read your body better than it can read itself.

A better method for keeping track of your hydration levels is to check the colour of your urine – dark yellow means you are not drinking enough, and transparent, on a desert expedition, probably means too much.

Limiting water intake whilst exerting yourself in hot conditions is a potentially very dangerous game. There is no definitive way to determine how much water you will need each day and there is no substitute for testing your body in advance.

Finally, when calculating your requirements, do not forget to factor in water for cooking and washing if you plan to do either.

How much did they drink?

It may be surprising to learn that desert travellers often live for many weeks and months at a time, working hard in hot conditions, with only a few litres of water each day. Conventional wisdom may dictate drinking many times more (up to ten litres in some instances) for that level of exertion in those temperatures but evidence from desert expeditions indicates that, if properly managed, you can safely operate for long periods on considerably less.

Here are the daily water rations of some different desert travellers:

Name	Expedition	Consumption	Used for	Information source
Regis Belleville	Across the Sahara with camels	4 litres	Drinking and cooking	www.regisbelleville.com
Louis-Philippe Loncke	Across Simpson with cart	4 litres (average of 2.5 to 5 litres)	Drinking	Louis-Philippe Loncke
Tim Moss	Across Wahiba Sands on foot with pack	3.5 litres	Drinking	
Michael Asher	Eastern Sahara with camels	1.5 (cool season) to 3 litres (hot season)	Drinking	Michael Asher
Pierre Schmitt	Across the Ténéré with cart	4 litres	2.5 lites drinking, 1.5 litres cooking	www.pierreschmitt.com
Sam McConnell	Across Namib with pack	3 litres	Drinking	Sam McConnell
Regis Belleville	Static in the Sahara	1 litre	Drinking and cooking	www.regisbelleville.com
Wilfred Thesiger	Across the Empty Quarter with camels	1 pint (568ml)	Drinking	*Arabian Sands* by Wilfred Thesiger

'In the desert water is life: never underestimate the amount of water you need. Most adults, travelling on foot, need up to 5 litres a day in the cool season, and 10 litres in the hot, just to maintain equilibrium. You only have to lose 5% of your body weight through

water loss to get into a dehydration cycle that can be fatal. Keep drinking: desert nomads travel between water sources and never miss a chance of filling up.'
– Michael Asher,
who has travelled some 30,000 miles through deserts with camels including a nine month west-east crossing of the Sahara

Replacing minerals to avoid dehydration

In loose terms, dehydration is a loss of water and/or a loss of **electrolytes** – a group of minerals that your body needs to function properly – both of which happen when you sweat.

The main minerals lost through perspiration are:

- potassium;
- magnesium;
- calcium;
- sodium.

There are many ways to replace these minerals, of which sodium you will need most. Eating a decent spread of food should cover most of it – check the labels – and you can supplement your intake with:

- Powdered sports drinks – check that they actually contain the useful minerals rather than just sugar.
- Electrolyte replacement tablets – like sports drinks but without the sugar.
- Rehydration salts from a pharmacy – they may not taste as nice as sports drinks but they are a lot cheaper.
- Unrefined salt – processed table salt may only give you the sodium but the unrefined stuff will cover all four of the basic minerals and more.

Managing water loss

With the lack of humidity, it can feel like you are producing very little sweat but that is usually misleading; it is just that the dry air instantly wicks it away without you noticing.

A degree of additional fluid loss is inevitable given where you are and what you are doing but there are a number of ways in which you can help minimise the amount:

• Manage your exertion and move slowly to avoid unnecessary perspiration.
• Seek shade wherever possible and stay in it whilst resting.
• Avoid activity during the heat of the day. Use mornings, evenings and the night instead.
• Wear appropriate clothing (discussed below).

Avoiding hyper-hydration by drinking too much
Hyper-hydration is potentially fatal and thus just as dangerous as dehydration. It occurs through drinking excessive amounts of fluid and not replacing the minerals discussed above.

You can avoid it by:

• staggering your water intake over the course of the day rather than glugging several litres at a time;
• maintaining a regular supply of electrolytes;
• checking that your urine is not regularly transparent.

Protecting yourself from the sun
Sunburn should be easily avoided. Ninety nine per cent of your skin should be covered and anything left exposed can get a dollop of sun cream. Just as it is prudent to wear sunglasses to prevent damaging your eyes when skiing on white snow in bright sunshine, the same goes for sunny deserts.

Heat exhaustion and heat stroke
Although you will spend much of your time in the desert feeling hot, your internal body temperature is supposed to stay fairly constant. If it rises by more than a degree or so then you will start experiencing some side effects.

Heat exhaustion is a term used for the milder end of the spectrum. Symptoms include:

- cramp;
- lethargy;
- headaches;
- vomiting;

If your core temperature is even higher or symptoms persist then you run the risk of heat stroke which can be fatal. Warning signs for this include:

- rapid breathing;
- rapid pulse;
- confusion;
- difficulty breathing.

Sand storms

When winds pick up in desert environments they will carry dust and sand with them. This can have all manner of negative impacts on your expedition:

- reducing visibility;
- getting in your eyes, nose and mouth;
- filling your bags with grit;
- trashing your kit;
- scaring your camels.

If you are on the move and it is not too severe, it may just be a case of wrapping yourself up and toughing it out. When stopped it can be difficult to get much done outside of a tent so your options may be limited to just waiting for it to finish. Sandstorms can sometimes last for hours, even days.

'From the heat of the midday sun to the dark chill of the night, temperature variations can zap you quicker than it takes me to type these few lines on paper. Cover your body from head to toe with layers of clothing, not just to protect you from the damage that can be inflicted by the hot and the cold but protection from the havoc on your skin caused by the potential of millions of particles of sand constantly blowing your way.'
– Julian Monroe Fisher,
who has run vehicle expeditions to the Atacama, Kalahari,
Patagonian, Syrian and many other deserts

Spiders, snakes and scorpions

Most deserts are home to some poisonous beasties: rattlesnakes in the Gobi, death stalker scorpions in the Sahara, black widows in the Great Basin desert. The names alone are enough to give you nightmares but it is worth remembering that most venomous creatures prefer avoiding big things like humans. They also tend to save delivery of their biggest doses of poison for prey rather than in self defence. Seeing such critters on desert travels is not rare but getting a bite or sting should be.

Good practice for avoiding the need to test those ideas, however, is:

- Don't leave unattended bags and tent doors open.
- Sleep away from bushes and rocky areas.
- Check your boots before you put them on in the morning.
- Avoid walking around barefoot at night when they tend to be most active. Indeed, some would advise against going barefoot at any time.

If you do get bitten then advice varies but typically includes:

- Keep the body part below your heart to help stop the venom reaching it.
- Keep the body part as immobiled as possible to delay the venom's spread.
- Stay calm. Easier said than done but the faster your heart beats, the faster the venom will spread.
- Take a photo for later identification purposes if it is easy and safe to do.
- Some also recommend wrapping a bandage above the bite.

Getting through the cold nights
With little humidity and cloud cover a rarity, as soon as the sun goes down, the day's heat escapes the desert rapidly. However, unless you are in a particularly cold winter desert, most night time temperatures are not actually that low, they are just cold by comparison to the hot days.

'Keep mentally focused and don't let a shred of doubt plague your thoughts. Keep moving forward and take each day as it comes.'
– Ripley Davenport,
who was walked in and across the Namib, Kara-Kum,
Thar and Gobi Deserts

Kit

Shelter at night and from the sun
Depending on the temperatures of your chosen desert, your priorities for shelter will probably be protection from the sun at midday and the cold at night.

In a hot desert, the latter may not be an issue and you could make do with sleeping outside. Options include:

- **Bivvy bag** – Large waterproof cover that goes over your sleeping bag. Gives you some respite from the outside world, keeps you dry in a dew and protects from bugs.
- **Swag bag** – The traditional Aussie version of a bivvy bag. Made from a cotton canvas, they are heavier than bivvy bags but much tougher and less sweaty.
- **Tarpaulin** –Thin, nylon sheet that you can tie to trees, walking poles or off your cart to give shelter from the sun (or rain). If the ground is not suitable for pegs then weigh down the guy lines with rocks or by filling plastic bags with sand.

If you are going somewhere that gets cold at night or just prefer some respite from the elements then you can take a tent. There are not too many special requirements for tents in a desert environment, just consider whether:

- it is sufficiently sturdy if you expect high winds;
- it is light enough to carry;
- you can pitch the inner tent separately without the flysheet over the top as it will be a lot cooler in hot weather.

Finally, if you are travelling with the luxury of a vehicle or large caravan then a big tent with removable side walls will provide shade with a breeze. You could also take camp beds that lift you off the floor to help avoid unwanted interactions with animals.

Something to put on your feet

Footwear choices for deserts vary greatly, partly depending on the terrain and partly depending on personal preference. Here are some options:

Boots: You could use ordinary hiking boots or specific desert boots which have more emphasis on breathability and keeping cool rather than waterproofing. Army surplus is a cheap source of desert boots. The pros and cons of boots are:

- high ankle gives support and limits sand getting in;
- good grip on rocky ground;
- protection from thorns and sharp rocks;
- protection from snakes and scorpions;
- can be heavy and very hot;
- stiff material, rubbing sand and soft feet from sweat can be a disastrous recipe for blisters.

Running shoes: Typical running or trail shoes may do the job. Alternatively, myriad specially designed and converted trainers are used for the Marathon des Sables and other races. The focus for these custom shoes tends to be keeping out sand. However, the broad advantages and disadvantages for wearing running shoes remain the same:

- lightweight;
- comfortable to wear;
- less grip and protection on rocky terrain.

Sandals: An obvious choice on the beach but sandals can also be used for long desert trips or as a second set of footwear alongside one of the above. Their pros and cons are:

- easy to get rid of sand and thus avoid blisters;
- keep your feet cool;
- poor support for feet and ankles;
- very little protection from sun, thorns or bites.

Socks or barefoot: Finally, it is possible to travel through sandy deserts barefoot. Alternatively, the Bedouin use special thick woollen socks (**Bedu socks**) covered in tiny hairs which help keep scorpions away. You could get a degree of protection from ordinary hiking socks. The advantages and disadvantages are:

- easy and comfortable;
- no added weight on your feet;
- no protection from sun, thorns or bites if barefoot.

Whatever footwear you choose, bear in mind that your feet will swell with the heat so factor this into your sizing.

Barefoot through the Empty Quarter

Bertram Thomas and St John Philby may both have crossed the Rub' Al Khali Empty Quarter Desert first, but the journeys of Wilfred Thesiger will always be the most memorable.

Despite travelling in a time of vehicles and radios, Thesiger shunned modern trappings, preferring instead to undertake his journeys as traditionally as possible. He travelled with Bedouin – to whom he gives all credit for his successes – and camel, and walked barefoot. His group lived off minute amounts of dried dates and flour. And he would walk all day through the scorching heat of the Arabian Desert without so much as a sip of water until nightfall when he would ration a single pint.

As well as having to contend with all the hardships of the desert, Thesiger was also up against religion. Travelling in the Middle East in the 1940s meant his Muslim team mates were constantly having to conceal his presence as a Christian for fear of violent repercussions.

Thesiger wrote several books about his travels. The best known of which are *Arabian Sands* and *The Marsh Arabs*.

Loose, long and light clothing

The basic principles for selecting clothing are:

- Cover as much of your skin as possible to protect from the sun and slow the rate at which it wicks away sweat so you lose less water.
- Wear loose clothing to help trap a layer of moist air to keep you cooler.

Such clothes are often more appropriate in culturally sensitive regions of the world anyway, particularly for women.

- Choose light colours which reflect more radiated heat.

Light walking trousers and a long-sleeve shirt work well. Traditional garments such as the light kaftan, thobe and jellabiya robes worn throughout the Middle East are also good.

Synthetic materials tend to remove moisture quickly which is counterproductive. Natural fibres like cotton retain more moisture and work well in hot conditions.

For headwear, turbans and similar headdresses work on the same principle of retaining moisture and often give you some flexibility to cover other parts of your face if the wind picks up. Otherwise, any hat that covers the majority of your head, neck and face should suffice.

'Protect from the sun in any situation and ask people who've been before. If Touaregs are wearing what they wear, it is the way to do it.'
– Louis-Philippe Loncke,
who dragged a cart solo across the Simpson Desert

Extras for your car
Travel by four-wheel-drive is a well-documented sport for which plenty of information exists on what you should pack for heading off-road.

However, a few notable items for desert travel include:

- plank for supporting a jack on soft sand;
- tow-rope and shackles because you are hopefully not travelling alone;
- fire extinguisher since the engine is likely to get even hotter than normal;
- a pressure gauge and a pump or compressor to adjust tyre pressure between sand and solid ground;
- sand tracks to wedge under the wheels when you get stuck.

And don't forget to bring ...

Don't forget to pack:

- warm clothes for nights;
- tight wrapped sun glasses and perhaps some anti–UV swimming goggles or similar if you anticipate sand storms;
- sun screen for any skin that gets exposed;
- walking poles to help you up steep sand dunes or for extra strength when dragging a cart;
- navigational aids and some notes on celestial navigation;
- waterproof cases to protect electronic gadgets from sand;
- a camping stove that won't get blocked with sand if you want to cook or something with which to start a fire;
- tough, durable water bladders;
- solar panels if you want to make use of the daylight to charge electronics.

A Day in the Life of a Desert Explorer
by Charles Foster

Charles Foster is a traveller, author, barrister, and a Fellow of Green Templeton College, University of Oxford. Much of his life is spent in deserts. His desert experience includes expeditions in the Sahara, the Sinai and the Danakil Depression. He has also run the Marathon des Sables and skied to the North Pole.

'My sleep was thin, and broken by grunts, howls, and itches. But towards dawn I slipped into a troubled dream of writhing green. You dream about what you can't have. I wake because the sun bores into my head. There's nothing green here. I lie on a patch of grey sand away from the main camp, in the hope that the ticks that scurried to meet the camels last night won't find me. But they have. A couple hang from my groin. I pull them carefully off with tweezers and stamp on them. A Tristram's Grackle flutters to a nearby rock, cocks its head to one side, and swoops down to peck at the blood.

Smoke from an acacia-wood fire trickles up. The Bedouins I'm travelling with have been up for hours. The morning smells of rock, the sour belches of camels, and tinned tuna. The Bedouins of Sinai love tuna.

I shave with some of our precious water. T.E. Lawrence always shaved too, thinking that the expensive gesture would stop him degenerating morally. I agree. The sand, the grit and the wind are out to get you. You've always got to do things to remind them that there are parts of you they can't reach.

I greet the Bedouin elaborately. They're father and son. I have known them for years, but they are strangers. It's not just the language, but that doesn't help. I can get by in the rough Arabic of the Levantine gutter, but their dialect is impenetrable. I know their names, that they support Aston Villa, and that they think toilet paper is disgusting. But that's it. It's a slender basis for a relationship that has to last weeks at a time and deal with sandstorms, scorpions, dry wells full of camel bones, snakes (I stepped on one last trip: it chewed on my boot, and the venom ran into the lace-holes), and the aching, echoing loneliness of the afternoons. I don't romanticise them. I know that they'd rather travel by Land Cruiser than camel, cook on gas rather than sticks, and I suspect they're saving up for a flat-screen TV. I don't know what they think of me, and I don't much care.

They've baked flat bread by pouring a flour and water mix over the bottom of a bowl, upturned on the fire. We eat it in silence, watching the flames. There's tea too, with mint brought from Nuweiba.

I'm always desperate to be off. The place where we've camped always disgusts me. We've scorched the rock and pissed on the sand. I want to walk away from part of me that arrived last night. So I'm first to the saddles.

The boy leans against one of them. I push him away, pick up the saddle, and swear. One of the camels, despite his hobble, has wandered a fair way down the wadi. I go to get him. He spits and farts. Back at the camp, I pull on his head-rope to get him down. If they were my own, and we understood each other, I wouldn't need to pull. His neck is like a hairy anaconda.

We load up. There are few rules. You should try to put the load over the forequarters rather than the hindquarters: camels have pretty pathetic back legs. And you should load symmetrically, or you'll have a lame and saddle-sore beast.

The boy points out a cut on another camel's penis. The flies have got there first. The wound writhes. It can't be left. I've been kicked by too many camels to try a quick job. We cast the wretched animal, truss him up, and I scrape the maggots out with the margarine knife and wash the wound with iodine. The whole episode loses us nearly an hour.

It's getting hot by the time we amble out. We walk, leading a camel each. I would like to ride, for a change, but the others aren't riding, and I don't feel I can.

There's a sort of joy on the road, and all the more so if the road is not a road at all. It's not just the joy of leaving old things behind. It is the joy of the high blue and white; of sweat and the knowledge that your legs work when you ask them; of the knowledge that it will end; of the knowledge that I will end, but that it doesn't matter much. And that's a relief.

We leave it too long. The sun gets too high too fast. We come to a place between high walls. It's a really stupid place to stay: remember flash floods. But there are some spikes for the camels to eat. We do tea, tuna and beans, and then the Bedouins go to sleep, leaving me alone. Although I have nothing to say to them, I hate them for it. The afternoons are when the demons come. And come they do. Deserts are haunted in the hot sun between two and four. The nights are clean.

When the sun drops I drop out of the stone eye-socket of the rock-skull where I'd been, shouting and whistling. I catch and load the camels again. I couldn't be happier. The well-water in my bottle might be ancient Burgundy. The land, flattened by the noon-sun, now ripples. It has depth and substance, and therefore so do I. You become the place, for better or worse. Colour springs from the sand. I run this time.

It's obvious where we should spend the night. It always is. No one in a desert really believes he has choices. That too is a relief. Choices are burdensome things, as is the illusion of significance.

I hobble the camels, throw down some of the hay we'd brought along (never assume that camels don't need to eat, or will find enough of their *own), and sit down to gaze into the fire. Tonight, I think, I'm going to sleep in the stockade of saddles, and watch the father and son until I know what they're about. I read the Odyssey, and think about gulls and surf over Ithaca, and about steak and women.*

I sleep, of course, on a rock edge three hundred yards from the fire. Yes, the stars are wonderful; yes the night is as high and holy as it always is in desert literature. But still the ticks have found my groin by the time the sun comes up.'

Read more at: www.charlesfoster.co.uk.

Costs

- Transport – £300–£2,000. This is entirely dependent on where you want to go but the edge of most deserts are not normally excessively difficult to reach. A drop off or collection from a remote spot would push costs up.
- Equipment – £100–£1,000+. There is not much specialist equipment required for desert travel and you can often get away with very little and/or using second-hand kit.
- Supplies – £4–£10/day. This will be cheapest with supermarket food, tap water and no fuel. It will cost more with **ration packs**, bottled water and a cooker you intend to use every day.
- Communications – £0–£800. From nothing to a regularly used **satellite phone** and a few other gadgets.
- Camel – £150–£1,000+ each. Price depends on availability and where in the world you are. You may also need to pay for training or even a handler. See the 'How to buy a camel' box above.
- Cart – £250–£1,500+. Since you will be building from scratch it will be up to you how much you spend on your cart and will depend on whether you have the skill to build it yourself or the offer of free labour.

Lowest total cost – £1,000
A budget flight, borrowed kit and a bargain cart or camel for a few weeks' desert travel.

More typical total cost – £5,000
Long-haul flight and remote transfer, some new equipment, a good cart or couple of camels, and a satellite phone for a month or two in the desert.

Training

Acclimatise to and familiarise yourself with the heat
Of critical importance ahead of a desert trip is to get used to the heat and learn how to deal with it.

- Find opportunities to exert yourself in a hot environment. If it's not hot outside, put the heating on or wear extra clothes.
- Work out how much you need to drink and what it feels like to ration your intake.
- Develop a walking pace that will balance steady progress with the need to avoid over exertion.

Learn your craft

- Cars – Practise off-road driving and particularly on sand.
- Camels – Learn the basics of looking after and handling a camel. If you can't get access to camels before your trip then read about it instead and learn how to look after horses.
- Carts – If you build your cart in advance then take it out for practice to get used to how it handles, what it feels like and what your limits are. For fitness, you can drag tyres around like the polar explorers do.

'If taking a camel train across a desert, ensure that the lead camel carries the all-important water supply – that way you'll stand a chance of re-establishing control of your most precious resource if the camels at the rear get spooked by a snake or loosened baggage and kick out or run.

Also, as you journey along, keep a careful eye on animal tracks that you pass; you'll get a sense of them heading this way and that to various sources of water – often clearly radiating out from permanent springs or wells like the spokes of a wheel for many dozens of miles.'

Benedict Allen,
who has spent many months travelling through the Namib
and Gobi Deserts with camels

First Steps

1. Find somewhere hot and go for a long walk without drinking a lot of water. Don't go crazy – do it somewhere safe carrying spare water and a mobile phone – but do give yourself a sense of what it is like to work hard in the heat without water on tap. If you enjoy it, go to step two.
2. Find a desert that suits you: the right size, the right level of remoteness, and the right temperature at the right time of year.
3. Pick your approach: walking or driving, with a camel, a cart or a rucksack.

4. Do some calculations: How far is it? How long will it take? How much will I have to carry? Will I need re-supplies and, if so, how and from where? Start planning accordingly.

5. Meanwhile, condition your body to working hard in the heat and work out how much water you think you will need.

6. Do some test runs, either at home with as close an environment as you can replicate or by incorporating time into your schedule for a short trial trip at the start.

'Speed kills, a slow steady pace is what you need.'
– Sam McConnell,
who has led teams on over a hundred desert trips

Excuse me, do you know where I can buy a camel?
Patrick Hutton and Richard Johnson flew to Mongolia, took a 33-hour bus to the town of Altai and enquired at their hotel where they might be able to buy three camels.

Once the staff had finished laughing at the two young Westerners, they put the pair in touch with someone who could help. A few days later, they were the proud owners of three camels at a cost of £400 each and had found a herdsman to join them.

They set off on their camels into the Gobi Desert and quickly reverted to walking after suffering severe saddle soreness on their first day. The camels had several aggressive moments – on one occasion throwing the herdsman from his saddle – and the team had to disinfect one camel's foreskin after a maggot infection. But Patrick and Richard made it 1000km across the Gobi and donated the camels to their herdsman in exchange for a bottle of vodka. See: www.wix.com/patrick_hutton/adventure.

Easier, Harder, Different

- Cross a cold desert in winter where frostbite may be of more concern than heat stroke.
- Cross a **semi-desert** that has more rainfall but other desert-like properties. Examples include the Highlands of Iceland, the Karoo in South Africa, areas of Western Canada, and many of Europe's small offerings.
- Cross a high altitude **Montane desert** as found in Ladakh and on the Tibetan Plateau, for example.
- Cycle across a desert on a bike specifically designed for travelling on sand.
- Cross Antarctica, technically the biggest desert in the world.
- Cross a desert on every continent (Antarctica optional), perhaps the biggest on each.
- Do it the old-fashioned way without vehicles, GPS or footwear.
- Do a mini crossing. Many deserts can be crossed in anything from a day upwards.
- Walk across the Sahara and Arabian Deserts from the west coast of north Africa to the east coast of the Arabian peninsula. It is probably the longest desert crossing available.

Resources

- *Camel Expedition Handbook* by Michael Asher – see: www.rgs.org.
- *Desert Expeditions Handbook* by Tom Sheppard – see: www.rgs.org.
- Louis-Phillipe Loncke's 'Simpson Desert Trek' – Blog with fantastic detail on preparations and equipment used – see: www.simpson-desert-trek.blogspot.com.
- Piere Schmitt's Ténéré Solo Expedition – In French but has useful details from Schimitt's travels – see: www.pierreschmitt.com.

Contributors

Sam McConnell

Sam has led over 100 trips into the desert. After six years living in Namibia, training and working as a desert guide, he walked solo and unsupported across the dune sea of the Namib Desert in 2002. He has since led an unsupported expedition up the Skeleton Coast to Angola.
See: www.sam-mcconnell-expeditions.com.

Louis-Philippe Loncke

Louis-Philippe is a Belgian adventurer who has completed several world first, solo, unsupported treks in remote regions of the world including walking across Iceland. In 2008, he completed a north-south traverse of the Simpson Desert in Australia carrying all his supplies in a cart.
See: www.louis-philippe-loncke.com.

How to Get to the North Pole

'Consider deeply what you think will be achieved by reaching the Pole, and let this inform how you go about reaching it.'
– Pen Hadow,
the first Briton to reach the North Pole solo
and unassisted from Canada

Setting the Scene

Sitting at the top of the globe, ever moving on a platform of frozen ocean, the North Pole is one of earth's great adventure destinations. Originally reached by dog sleds from the coast and now attainable by mere pleasure flight, opportunities still remain for traditional and tough expeditions pulling sleds over snow and ice and snapping icicles from your nostrils.

Statistics

USP:	Reaching the top of the world.
Difficulty:	Easy to very difficult.
Cost:	£20,000–£250,000+.
Hurdles:	Open water, mounds of ice, extreme cold.
Purest style:	Skiing unsupported, full-distance from land.
Who's done it?:	Thousands visited, 100+ skied from land.
Glory potential:	High.

Background

The history of Arctic exploration is one dogged with mystery and controversy. The first claims of having reached the North Pole come from Frederick Cook and Robert Peary in 1908 and 1909 respectively. Both claims are widely disputed, but, if true, these early polar explorers would have been several decades ahead of the next successful surface journey.

Renowned Norwegian explorer Roald Amundsen made the first undisputed sighting of the Pole from his airship in 1926 but it was not until 1948 that a Russian team landed planes nearby and walked to it. It was another 20 years before an expedition made a successful surface crossing using skidoos and the year after this, 1969, Sir Wally Herbert made it there with the help of dog-sleds.

Since then a number of variations of the journey have been completed. The first to complete the trip by human power alone – that is, without vehicles, animals or the wind to help – was a Russian team in 1979; the first to do so without outside support was Borge Ousland in 1994, who also happened to complete the trip solo; and the first return journey under the same criteria was completed by Richard Weber and Mikhail Malakov in 1995.

Now, in the 21st century, there are many ways of gaining the Pole, some of which do not even require breaking a sweat. So whilst the traditional method of setting off from the coast is still largely regarded as the purest and toughest route, other options exist including organised races to the Magnetic North Pole and **Last Degree** expeditions skiing the final 70 miles to the Geographic North Pole. Add to that pleasure flights, the North Pole Marathon and mini-expeditions of a few days and your options are myriad.

The language of polar expeditions

Polar expeditions almost have a language of their own. Here are a few key terms that will help you understand what is involved:

Pulk – The sled full of equipment and supplies that you drag behind you.

Last Degree – The distance between the 89th degree of latitude and the 90th where the Geographic North Pole is located.

Full distance – Expeditions that start from land and finish at the Geographic North Pole.

Barneo – A temporary Russian base that is set up every year on the sea ice about 60 nautical miles from the Geographic North Pole. It has an ice runway and helicopters at its disposal and is thus used as a stepping stone for many expeditions. Sometimes spelled 'Borneo'.

Cape Arktichevsky, Ward Hunt Island and Cape Discovery – Locations on the coast of Russia and Canada commonly used as start points for full distance expeditions.

Sea ice – The frozen ocean which you will be walking on for the majority of your trip.

Leads – The stretches of open water that appear amidst sea ice on the Arctic Ocean.

Pressure ridges – Large blocks of ice that rise up from the pressure of the moving sea ice.

Nautical miles – The standard measurement for travel at sea is also used in the polar world. It is equal to 1.15 miles.

Unsupported – An expedition can be called this if it works under its own steam (e.g. walking or skiing) and does not use any aids like dogs, kites for wind support or motors.

Unassisted – An expedition can be called this if it is entirely self-sufficient and does not use external help such as having a plane drop off supplies. The term 'without re-supply' is often used too.

Introduction – Where is the North Pole?

First, it is worth noting that unlike its southern counterpart, the North Pole does not lie on a land mass but in the middle of the Arctic Ocean. For the most part, it is frozen over and hence, at the right time of year, it is possible to travel there on foot, ski, dog sled or similar.

The question of its location is slightly more complicated than you might assume as there are a total of four different North Poles. Their varying locations and the different means by which you reach them will have a significant impact on the difficulty of your undertaking. TV presenter Jeremy Clarkson may have been to one of the North Poles in a converted 4x4 but he actually finished further south than many North Pole expeditions begin. The following explanations should help clear things up:

1. Geographic North Pole
Put your finger on top of the globe and you will be pointing at the

Geographic North Pole. This is the goal that early explorers sought after and is often aptly known as 'True North'. The Geographic North Pole is most often what people are referring to when they talk about the North Pole and is the most commonly visited.

Who got there first?

There is some controversy around who reached the North Pole first. In 1909, emerging after two years in the Arctic without contact, Frederick Cook claimed to have reached the Pole with two Inuit men the previous year and then became stuck in the Arctic for a season. His account soon came under heavy criticism from Robert Peary, however, who also claimed to have reached the Pole the following year. Specifically, Peary pointed towards a lack of records for Cook's journey and similarities between Cook's account and a Jules Verne novel. Peary's claims, however, proved to be even more controversial.

Peary attempted the trip in 1909 using dogs and claims to have reached his goal after most of his expedition turned back with 130 nautical miles remaining. According to Peary's account, the remaining team covered those final miles in five days. Aside from the fact that this represented double their usual progress, there was also no one else left on the team apart from Peary who could calculate their position on the ice and thus no way of corroborating the claims.

In 2005, a team set out to provide evidence in support of Peary's claim by completing the same journey using dogs to demonstrate that it was possible to cover the distance in the time frame. They completed the journey five hours faster than Peary (and set a record – see box 'The Fastest') but never managed to cover as much ground as Peary claims to have done in his controversial final five days. Indeed, no one ever has.

The first undisputed expedition to the North Pole was not until 1969. It was led by Wally Herbert using dogs and went all the way over the Arctic Ocean from Alaska to Svalbard (the islands half way between the top of Norway and the North Pole).

2. Magnetic North Pole

This is where your compass points which is not, in fact, the top of the world as you may have been led to believe. Keen navigators amongst you will understand that this is why you have to adjust your compass readings depending on where in the world you are standing.

To make things even more complicated, the Magnetic North Pole is continually moving and was last seen some way west of north Greenland. However, its position in 1996 is often used as the standard for organised races, partly following an expedition that used various methods to pinpoint it that year and, one suspects, because it is at a relatively convenient location. Both the 1996 location and its present position are several hundred miles from the Geographic North Pole. The Magnetic Pole is sometimes located on land rather than frozen ocean and is typically a lot easier and cheaper to reach than the true Pole.

The Magnetic North Pole was first reached by James Clark Ross in 1831. In 1903, the Norwegian Roald Amundsen – later famed for beating Captain Scott to the South Pole – returned to the location of Ross' expedition, discovered that the Pole was no longer there and thus established that it must be moving over time.

Driving to the (1996 Magnetic) North Pole

In a special episode of the popular British TV show 'Top Gear', presenters Jeremy Clarkson and James May drove to the 1996 position of the Magnetic North Pole. They used two modified Toyota Hilux and a Land Cruiser and were the first to do so by vehicle. They won their race against co-presenter Richard Hammond, who travelled on a dog sled guided by Baffin Island-based polar explorer Matty McNair.

3. Geo-Magnetic North Pole

This one is a little more complicated than the others: imagine the earth as surrounded by a magnetic field. Like any magnet, this field has a positive and a negative which, in the case of the Earth, sit in the sky some way above the Geographic North and South Poles. There is a line that connects these two points known as a dipole. This line is not a straight one and where it touches the earth's surface at the northern end is what we call the Geo-Magnetic North Pole.

There are far fewer expeditions to the Geo-Magnetic North Pole than there are to the Geographic or Magnetic (perhaps because it's so confusing?).

4. Northern Pole of Inaccessibility

This is the point in the Arctic Ocean which is furthest from land. There are different methods with which to calculate its exact location but wherever you aim for, it will always make for the longest North Pole journey from the coast, probably around 800 miles. This point is also called the Arctic Pole.

An Inaccessible Pole
by Jim McNeill

Where is the Northern Pole of Inaccessibility?
'I worked with NASA-backed NSIDC scientists in 2005 to verify the actual position of the Northern Pole of Inaccessibility.

Using GPS and satellite technology, and a technique originally established by Sir Hubert Wilkins when he wanted to traverse the Arctic Ocean for the first time in an aircraft in 1927–28, we calculated a new location.

This position is some 200km different from the original one and has recently been ratified by scientists at the Scott Polar Research Institute. I will announce it officially soon.'

Has anyone been there?
'I have done extensive research about whether anyone has visited the Northern Pole of Inaccessibility and these are my findings:
1. Rumours of a Russian ice breaker in the late fifties – but I cannot get any verification of this.

2. Russian scientists walking through the Pole from one station to another – but, again, I cannot verify this despite talking to one of the participants.

3. Wally Herbert reaching it in 1968 – by his own account he didn't make it due to ice flowing away from the Pole (so whoever wrote the Wikipedia article is wrong!)

Therefore I cannot find anyone who has reached the original position of the Northern Pole of Inaccessibility.

In conclusion, we have a genuine North Pole which has not been reached and therefore arguably constitutes the last significant world first in the polar regions.'

Jim is a polar explorer with 26 years' experience of Arctic travel. Read more at: www.ice-warrior.com.

(Geo-Magnetic) Pole to Pole

In 2007, two young British adventurers, Rob Gauntlett and James Hooper, set out on a journey from the Geo-Magnetic North Pole to the Magnetic South Pole under natural power alone. Despite early drama when Gauntlett fell through sea ice off the coast of Greenland, the pair skied, cycled and sailed all the way to complete their journey, landing in Australia six months later.

So, how do you know which is which?

Unless otherwise stated, references to the North Pole in this chapter are references to the Geographic North Pole. In both geographical and adventure terms, this is the worthiest claimant for the title. The chapter, however, will explain how to get to any of the four, each of which can be reached in a number of different ways.

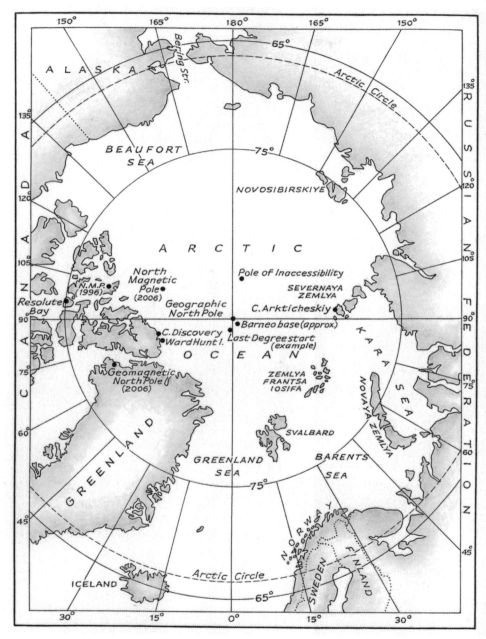

Map 2: Map of the Arctic Ocean

Options

'Be creative. Don't follow the crowd when getting involved in expeditions – it's the only way things move forward. Learn the skills, learn the art, report your achievements honestly and enjoy the privilege of seeing the best places on Earth.'
– Alex Hibbert,
who holds the record for the longest ever polar journey

Fly to the North Pole

You can fly direct to the North Pole. The most common method is flying first to the Svalbard archipelago and then on to **Barneo** ice station. From there you can take a helicopter for the final 60 nautical miles to the Pole. This costs upwards of about £10,000. For less money, you could take a pleasure flight that passes over the North Pole without actually landing there.

Enter the North Pole Marathon

For about £10,000 you can enter 'The World's Coolest Marathon'. The race actually occurs at the Barneo station which is a short flight away from the Geographic North Pole but is thrown in with the bundle after you finish running.

Running 26 miles in the Arctic might sound a little extreme but will require far less expertise than the other options. Support will be on hand the whole time and you will be on the ice for only a few hours.

You will want to be fit enough to run a normal marathon first and have some experience running in the cold. Any other preparations can be guided by the event organisers, Polar Running Adventures.

Race to the Magnetic North Pole

There are currently two organised races to the Magnetic North Pole:

- The Polar Challenge – see: www.extremeworldraces.com.
- The Polar Race – see: www.polarrace.com.

They both start from Resolute Bay in the northern Canadian region of Nunavut and take you 300 miles or so over frozen ocean and a few islands on the way.

This is a great way to get a taste of a real polar expedition without the high levels of expertise and even higher levels of money required for a full distance expedition.

It is still expensive (around £20,000 plus equipment) and you still spend several weeks hauling a pulk in sub-zero temperatures, but you gain confidence from going through a training programme and having some degree of support on the ice.

It is also quite possible to organise your own expedition to the Magnetic North Pole, or indeed the Geo-Magnetic North Pole. To plan for this you might follow a similar itinerary to the above races but apply some of the logistics of a full distance expedition.

Ski the Last Degree

It is possible to be dropped off almost anywhere on the Arctic Ocean, by plane or helicopter. So, in theory, you can start skiing to the North Pole from as close or far away as you like.

There are itineraries offered by various companies to walk the final few yards or ski for just a couple of days but the most common routine is to get a lift to the 89th degree and travel from there. This journey is known as 'The Last Degree'. It will leave you with about 60 nautical miles to ski as the crow flies, though in practical terms with pressure ridges, open leads and shifting ice, it tends to be much further.

As with any of these trips, it is possible to organise it yourself but for Last Degree itineraries in particular there are many companies that will arrange the logistics for you, have groups that you can join or provide a guide. Organised packages tend to start from around the £17,000 mark.

As with the organised races above, a Last Degree trip can give you experience of genuine polar travel whilst avoiding some of the extremes of a full distance expedition.

'The key rules for an expedition are: 1. No whining 2. Treat yourself and others with respect 3. Have fun.'
– Matty McNair,
who runs North Winds polar expeditions and training company on Baffin Island and has been to both Poles

Options – Full Distance Expeditions

Broadly defined, a full distance expedition is any surface trip to the Geographic North Pole that starts from land. This is the assumed approach for the remainder of the chapter.

Such trips are generally considered to be magnitudes harder than Last Degree or Magnetic Pole trips, as evidenced by the low numbers of people who have completed the journey: only around 100 or so people have ever walked the whole way but a few thousand have completed the shorter itineraries.

N.B. An expedition to the Northern Pole of Inaccessibility would be similar although with further to travel.

Start positions on the coast
For this itinerary, a charter plane is used to deliver people to as northerly a section of land as possible. This is typically either:

- **Ward Hunt Island** and **Cape Discovery** on the Canadian coast;
- **Cape Artichevsky** on the Russian coast.

In recent years, however, trips from the Russian side have become increasingly rare due to difficulties obtaining permits and unfavourable currents creating stretches of open water near the start.

From wherever you start, you travel overland (or rather over frozen sea) all the way to the North Pole, somewhere in the region of 500 miles away. Starting early in the season is the most common practice as it maximises your chances of good ice conditions under foot, but this also means that you get colder conditions and long hours of darkness.

Charter flights on the Arctic Ocean

Canadian airline Kenn Borek offers charter flights to most locations across the Arctic Ocean including the North Pole. In contrast to the comparatively regular short hops to and from Barneo, these flights can take up to 24 hours' return and involve using a second plane to refuel the first plane halfway.

As such, they do not come cheap. Expect to pay in the region of £100,000 for a pick up at the Geographic North Pole from Canada.

Most full distance expeditions tend to finish after Barneo has closed for the season so it is not possible to rely on a cheaper helicopter collection when you reach the Pole. Even if your itinerary did mean you arrived in time for a helicopter pick-up, it is against the airline's policy to drop people off at the coast unless they have enough money in the bank to cover an emergency pick up.

Transport methods over the ocean

Some options for travelling on these expeditions include:

- walking and skiing;
- dog sleds;
- skiddoos;
- kite skiing (also known as a **parasail**).

Of these, walking and skiing are the most common, whilst the use of kites can be difficult and dangerous so has been very limited.

To re-supply or not re-supply?

You can expect to be on the ice for between 36 days (the current record) and upwards of double that. That means you either need to take a very large pulk filled with supplies or arrange a re-supply by chartering another plane.

Re-supplies save you carrying large volumes of supplies but they also:

- cost a lot of money as you need to charter at least one more plane;
- add another logistical element to balance;
- lose you the 'without re-supply' badge of honour.

As if that wasn't hard enough

Reaching the Geographic North Pole from land is tough no matter how you approach it and many people have tried many different methods but one man stands out from the rest. In 1990, Norwegian explorer Børge Ousland became the first person, along with team mate Erling Kagge, to reach the North Pole on foot. Four years later, Ousland repeated the journey solo and without re-supply. In 2001, he completed a traverse of the Arctic Ocean – via the North Pole – with the aid of a kite to harness the winds. Then, in 2006, with American explorer Mike Horn, he attempted to reach the Pole again, this time in winter. They arrived just days after first light.

Practicalities

Where do you sleep?

On a North Pole expedition you will sleep in a tent pitched on frozen sea. This has two significant implications:

1. It will be cold. Managing the cold in your morning and evening tent routines is a tricky game. You will want to pitch your tent as quickly as possible. The longer you spend between the end of the day's skiing and getting into your sleeping bag, the colder you will get.

2. All that separates you from the Arctic Ocean is a layer of ice. You need to be as sure as you can that the ice on which you are pitching your tent is going to hold firm all night and not give way for an early morning ice bath.

What do you eat and drink?
You will want food that packs a lot of calories per kilo and can survive the low temperatures. You generally have to carry all of your food too, sometimes for weeks at a time, so keeping weight down is important. In fact, it is not uncommon to spend a lot of the time hungry as a result of this.

Typical food includes:

- Meals: almost always dehydrated ration packs as they are light and easily prepared by just adding boiling water.
- Snacks: foods like chocolate, nuts and cheese are normal but bear in mind that most things will need thawing before eating.

Many foods lose their flavour at such low temperatures and will need defrosting. Common techniques for dealing with this include:

- cutting them into smaller pieces in advance to avoid losing teeth to a rock solid Mars bar;
- carrying your day's snacks in a pocket close to your skin to keep them warm.

Water comes from melting snow and ice on a stove. A laborious process, this will likely see your stove burning for several hours each day in an effort to melt enough water to rehydrate your dinner and yourself.

'As the cold can hide your personal hydration levels, make sure you drink plenty throughout the day, even if you don't feel thirsty, otherwise this will have a knock on effect further down the line.'
– Charlie Paton,
the first Scotsman to walk unsupported to the North Pole

Where do you go to the loo?
Toileting happens outside in the cold, as swiftly as possible to avoid the very real risk of frostbite where no frostbite should be.

The Arctic Ocean is a big place that is forever changing and has comparatively few visitors. As such, al fresco toileting is generally considered acceptable from an environmental perspective. Some advocate removing waste and toilet paper but most leave it to be consumed by the sea.

A basic wash can also be achieved by defrosting wet wipes or with a roll and a rub in the snow. Needless to say, the latter option should be done with a degree of swiftness.

How long do you actually spend skiing?
Skiing days will be as long as required and you can manage.

You may experience both long hours of darkness and 24-hour daylight within a single trip. As such, it will be down to your body clock, your strength, and your itinerary to dictate the length of your days.

The two conflicting elements are:

1. Urging more time in the tent are the facts that melting snow can take a long time and you will want to get a reasonable amount of rest each night.
2. On the other hand, time on sea ice is often at a premium so you will want to keep making progress. Equally, lower temperatures at the start of an expedition can mean moving is the only way to stay warm.

Somewhere between five and ten hours outside your tent is typical although this can certainly creep up if you are in a hurry.

'How quick you get to the Pole depends on how much you are willing to suffer.'
– Conrad Dickinson,
who has walked unsupported to the North Pole, South Pole and across the Greenland icecap

How do you know where to go?
Despite heading for the North Pole, you cannot rely solely on the needle of your compass to the point the way.

- Compass: This points at the Magnetic North Pole but can still be used by accounting for the significant variation. The needle also tends to jump around when you are that far north.
- GPS: This is the standard means of pinpointing oneself. Indeed, it is the only realistic way you will know when you have reached the pole. The problem is that they tend to require batteries which drain rapidly in the cold and can be fiddly to use with big gloves on.
- Wind direction: Prevailing winds tend to be fairly consistent and can provide a more practical cue for maintaining direction than relying on compass and GPS. Attaching ribbon to a ski pole is an easy way to monitor this.
- Your shadow: During the day, another simple method for working out direction is to use your shadow as a sun dial.

'The northern experts, like the Inuit, have learned to find their way using the sastrugi, the ice ridges that have been sculpted by the wind. Each wind chisels the ice and gives it recognisable character in the

shape of the ridges it forms. The Inuit remember this by giving each wind a character. They can then recognise the shapes in the ice and the "character" that formed them, and therefore what direction the sastrugi lie in.'

– Tristan Gooley, author of the *Natural Navigator*

When to go

North Pole season is between February and early April or May. The key factor is temperature.

- Go in winter and it is going to be even colder than usual, as well as pitch black as the sun will not rise that far north at that time of year.
- But go in summer and the ice will be riddled with leads of open water and dangerous stretches of thin ice, if any at all.

Although rare, people have reached the North Pole on skis during winter and by boat in summer.

It is not uncommon for all of the full distance expedition teams in a given year (there are rarely more than a handful) to start within a week or so of each other, often sharing flights to save costs.

What if things go wrong ...?

The main dangers with a risk of instant impact on a North Pole expedition include:

- falling through the ice into the water;
- a polar bear attack.

The latter is fairly unlikely and the former can be managed to an extent using shrewd judgement and careful planning.

Other possible incidents include:

- falling from a pressure ridge;
- having a heavy pulk hit you at speed;
- your tent catching fire.

Unless you are close enough to the Barneo ice base for a pick up by helicopter, the chances are that your only route out is by plane. This is contingent upon the weather and the ice conditions accommodating a landing. If they don't then you may have to wait or move. You can call for help by satellite phone or, if for some reason it doesn't work and your life is in danger, you can activate your **EPIRB** or **PLB** emergency beacon.

'If you say it is impossible for you to walk to the North Pole, and I say you can, we're probably both right.'
– Erling Kagge,
half of the first team to walk unsupported to the North Pole

Difficulties

Long and short daylight hours
The extreme ends of latitude experience extreme hours of daylight.

At the time most people leave from the coast, it is dark for most of the day. This gradually gives way to 24-hour daylight by the time you reach the Pole.

Falling through the ice
Remember that there is no land mass beneath the North Pole and a journey to any of the four northerly Poles will be conducted largely on frozen ocean. That means there is an almost omnipresent risk of falling through into icy waters.

Learning to 'read' the ice is arguably the most important skill for a North Pole trip and one for which there is little substitute for experience. You will need to learn which patch of ice will take the weight of a tent overnight and which patch is an accident waiting to happen.

Should you fall, you will need to act quickly to haul yourself out while your body and brain fight the cold. You will probably be attached to a heavy pulk too which could help or hinder depending on whether or not it falls in too.

Open water blocking progress

As well as the risk of unexpected falls through the ice, there are many large stretches of water with only a thin or mushy crust of ice that will undoubtedly block your path at some point. These have got worse in recent years which is taken as a sign of global warming.

Options for getting past them are:

- walk around, which can sometimes be very lengthy and thus impractical;
- swim or crawl in a specially made dry-suit, breaking the surface with your clbows as you go;
- use a floating pulk or inflatable raft to paddle across.

Ice drifting beneath you

The fact that you are walking on the frozen sea also means that the surface beneath you is moving, whether you can feel it or not. If you are really unlucky then you might ski for a whole day only to find yourself further south than you started. Equally, it has been known for expeditions to set up camp a few miles from the Pole only to drift over it in their sleep. Even if the effects are not so drastic, they will invariably need to be accounted for when it comes to navigating and monitoring progress.

Dealing with the cold

Needless to say, any polar expedition is going to be pretty chilly – anything from −50°C or below in the wind if you start in the February darkness for a full distance trip, to closer to a balmy −20°C or warmer nearer the Pole in May. This can make even the most basic of tasks difficult and time-consuming and you may spend much of your time praying for higher temperatures. However, as the season wears on and temperatures rise, the ice beneath your feet will become less stable so, in some ways, the cold is an ally.

Climbing over blocks of ice

As a result of the constantly moving sea ice and repeated heating and cooling the Arctic Ocean experiences, large ridges and blocks of jumbled ice are strewn erratically across most of its surface. Sometimes these pressure ridges are many miles long and up to the height of two-storey buildings. And whilst such obstacles might provide an entertaining distraction in another setting, when it's −40°C and you are wearing 4ft skis with a heavy pulk attached to your waist, they can require no small amount of effort to pass.

'Learn to love the challenges and the pain you are guaranteed to experience on the sea ice. These are what make the journey more rewarding in the end. When the going gets tough, don't forget you chose to be there.'

− Ann Daniels,
joint first woman to reach the North and South Poles
as part of all women teams

Protection from polar bears

Penguins are in Antarctica, polar bears are in the Arctic. Encounters with bears tend to be reasonably rare, especially as you get further away from land. Defences include carrying a gun and flares, and generally keeping your eyes peeled to avoid close encounters. Trip wires around the tent are often used in other Arctic settings but less so further north where the continually moving ice makes this a little trickier. Polar bears are protected in many countries. Killing one is not something to be done lightly so it pays to be prudent.

Managing moisture

You might normally associate high humidity with warm environments but you get the same thing on the Arctic Ocean. This can impact on your choice of equipment – you may think twice before using sleeping bags and jackets filled with down for example – and how you store it – electrical kit is best kept in zip-lock or dry bags. It also affects your tent routine as you will soon find any moisture escaping from your body or the pan of snow you are melting will re-freeze on the inside of your tent. Brush against it and get showered with frost, heat it up and you will get dripped upon.

As counter-intuitive as it may seem as you shiver inside your sleeping bag, opening a zip or using a specially designed chimney is often advisable to manage the moisture. It also reduces the risk of carbon monoxide poisoning from your stove.

The lack of pole

In the interests of managing expectations, please note that unlike the Antarctic equivalent, there is no barber's pole up north. Instead, you will need a GPS to confirm that you've reached your destination. Because of the drifting sea ice, if you plant a pole or flag at the location your GPS tells you is the North Pole (any of them) and sit down for some lunch then you will discover that by the time you have finished, your GPS reading will reveal a different location. That means no welcoming party but does guarantee an entirely unique North Pole of your own.

Solo women at the North Pole

The North Pole has never been reached from land by a solo, unsupported woman. Hannah McKeand, who set a speed record at the South Pole in 2006, was airlifted two weeks into her attempt after injuring herself falling from an ice block. In 2009, Christina Franco aborted after two days with stove failure. She managed 30 days the following year but ended her trip after reaching a large

> stretch of open water.
>
> The closest attempt yet comes from Rosie Stancer in 2007. Rosie, who had previously skied solo and unsupported to the South Pole, was airlifted after 84 days on the ice having covered 326 nautical miles, when deteriorating ice conditions threatened her chance of a pick up. She was 89 nautical miles from the Pole. The race continues.

Kit

'Think ahead, travel light and leave your fears behind.'
– Børge Ousland,
who has skied to the North Pole four times including solo, winter and traverse expeditions

Pulk for carrying your equipment
Your best friend and worst enemy on the ice, the pulk is the sled you will likely be towing the whole way to the Pole – friend because it is filled with food and warm clothes, and enemy because it might weigh more than you do and be constantly jerking at your waist.

They can be made from a few different materials:

- Plastic: Light and very cheap but flimsy thus usually only suitable for short journeys.
- Kevlar: The strongest and most expensive option. Good for long and hard expeditions.
- Fibreglass: The most common material, sits somewhere between kevlar and plastic in terms of strength and cost.

Pulks made for the North Pole tend to be attached with a rope to a

1. *Thick jacket with furry hood which traps warm air around your face.*
2. *Extra large mittens which pool the heat of your fingers to keep them warmer than gloves.*
3. *Rope trace rather than solid so you can drag your pulk over ice blocks.*
4. *Pulk in which to carry your supplies.*
5. *Ski poles, useful for climbing over pressure ridges.*
6. *Skis for speed and to spread your weight over a greater surface area.*

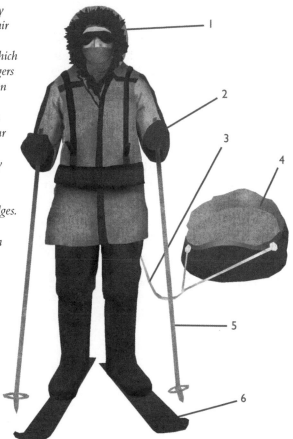

Fig. 3: Typical polar explorer

harness around your waist. This allows you to haul them over blocks of ice and ridges.

It is advantageous if your pulk floats too. Even if you are not planning on swimming across leads, it pays to be prepared. Sir Ranulph Fiennes lost the ends of several fingers after dragging a sinking pulk from the water.

The size of your pulk will depend on the itinerary you follow:

- Pulks for long or unassisted expedition: Expect to carry anywhere upwards of 100kg in a pulk that is bigger than you. Some people opt to take two or more pulks tied end-to-end instead. This gives the advantage of being able to split the weight when lugging it over objects.
- Pulks on a Last Degree trip or similar: You typically only need a week or two's supplies so your pulk may only weigh 30 or 40kg.

Skis for speed and spreading weight

The terms 'skiing' and 'walking' are often interchangeable in polar expeditions because you so frequently switch between the two. When skiing is possible, it is very much of the cross-country variety rather than anything more glamorous and comes with the obvious restriction of a hefty pulk attached to your waist.

Despite this, skiing is usually faster than walking, and adds the benefit of spreading your weight across a larger area and thus reducing your chances of falling through the ice. However, having big planks attached to your feet will often be a hindrance when negotiating pressure ridges and the like. As such, you will spend a lot of time with them off too. Some people opt to use snowshoes either instead of or in addition to skis. They tend to be slower overall but make clambering over ice rubble easier than skis.

Skis need to be modified so that they allow easy gliding forward but dig in when downward pressure is applied so you don't slip backwards. This is achieved with a variety of different methods. Some skis have patterns cut into their base, other people will apply wax or alternatively you can attach a synthetic skin.

Dry suit for getting in the water

An unfortunate reality about North Pole expeditions in the 21st century is the very real risk or requirement to get in the water. If you need to swim across an open lead then you want to come out the other side dry and that means taking a dry suit. You wear it over the top of your clothes and it seals you in up to your face which you try to keep above water. You may also choose to wear it when crossing dubious stretches of weak-looking ice.

Sleeping system to keep you alive at night
With temperatures as low as −50°C for a full distance trip, staying warm (or at least alive) at night requires the right kit. Despite being heavier, synthetic sleeping bags are often used as well as down bags because of the high humidity.

They are sometimes combined with a **vapour barrier liner** – a thin waterproof liner that goes next to your body inside the sleeping bag to stop the moisture (i.e. sweat) from your body seeping into the sleeping bag and making it wet and/or frozen. The experience can be a little unpleasant but better than a wet and frozen sleeping bag. It is common to use at least two sleeping mats.

Clothes to keep you warm
It is cold up there and you will want to do your best to stay warm. Many layers tend to be the answer. Typically:

- a couple of pairs of thermal base layers that are warm but don't absorb sweat. Merino wool is good for this;
- a few layers of fleece and other insulating fabrics;
- a waterproof and/or windproof jacket over the top is normal when on the move. It won't rain but waterproof clothing also gives good protection from wind;
- large down jackets and synthetic equivalents are often used as extra layers to throw over the top of your other clothes whenever you stop.

Other clothing includes:

- Gloves: Thin gloves are often worn almost all of the time with a big pair or two of mittens over the top and often some fleece specifically covering your wrists which lose a lot of heat.

- Face protection: At times it may be necessary to cover all exposed flesh so a pair of goggles with a neoprene face mask beneath or attached can be used.
- Shoes: Footwear generally needs to be compatible with your skis and a common choice are the boots often referred to as *mukluks*. These are soft, fleece or fur-lined boots, some of which, like the Alfa Moerdre Extrem boots from Norway, look wonderfully old-fashioned. A few pairs of decent socks are a good idea, making sure you still have plenty of room to wiggle your toes and keep the blood flowing.

Stove for melting snow and heating meals

The stove is your lifeline on the ice. It is your only route to water and vital for warming you up through hot drinks and meals. Multi-fuel stoves are the cookers of choice on the Arctic Ocean as, unlike gas stoves, their performance does not deteriorate as the temperature drops. However, it will always take longer to melt snow and heat water in lower temperatures and thus use more fuel.

Mounting stoves on a plywood or plastic board is a common technique to avoid them melting the ground on which they rest. It also means that you can keep the stove ready-assembled in your pulk.

As well as gaining a good working knowledge of your stove before setting foot on the ice, it would be wise to take tools and spares to repair and maintain it.

Tent

Tents at the North Pole tend to be one of the following types:

- Geodesic dome tents: These are shaped vaguely like an igloo and strong against winds from any direction.
- Tunnel tents: These are usually roomier but do not take so kindly to wind against their flank.
- Pyramid tents: They look old-fashioned but are easily erected and manage moisture well.

It is possible to make use of having a large pulk in which to carry kit rather than a rucksack by storing your tent part-assembled to make pitching and striking quicker. You need to be careful with this, however, as your pulk and its contents will likely take a routine beating as you drag them across all the frozen rubble.

And don't forget to pack ...
Make sure you pack the following:

- large loops of cord on all zips so you can operate them easily whilst wearing mittens;
- a fur-lined hood to trap warm air around your face and make you look like a real polar explorer;
- tent booties as a treat for your feet at the end of the day;
- a **pee bottle** so you don't have to leave your tent or even your sleeping bag;
- a brush to clear your tent of snow;
- a GPS so you know when you've arrived;
- a thermometer to record just how cold it is;
- an eye mask to help you sleep in sunlight;
- at least one portion of pemmican for old times' sake (flavoured animal fat and protein, a staple in earlier polar diets).

'Ladies, whatever the blokes say, pack twice the amount of toilet paper they decide is adequate. Running out of paper is no laughing matter when snow is the only alternative!'
– Helen Turton,
who has skied the Last Degree as both participant and assistant

A Day in the Life of a North Pole Explorer
by Sarah McNair

Sarah McNair-Landry comes from an adventurous background: both her parents, Matty McNair and Paul Landry, have skied to both the North and South Poles, and so has Sarah.

She has completed full distance North Pole expeditions from Canada on skis and from Russia using dogs and has skied to the South Pole using kites for the return journey. In 2005, she also set a speed record with her brother, Eric, crossing the Greenland icecap with kites in seven days and more recently they skied 2,000 miles through the northwest passage.

'A typical day on the Arctic Ocean does not exist; it's unpredictable, and at times indescribable. I've spent 160 days on the Arctic Ocean; I will retell one day early on during a 100-day dog sledding expedition to the North Pole. It goes like this …

The winds were gusting outside, whipping the snow into the air, obscuring our visibility. Our 16 dogs tethered outside the tent were curled into tight balls of fur, as snow drifts formed around them. We couldn't fight the weather; we could only wait for the storm to decrease.

By mid morning the winds started to let up, and we quickly stuffed sleeping bags, laced up our boots, dropped the tent, packed the sled and harnessed the dogs. The North Pole was still a long way away. Paul strapped on his skis and left camp first, scouting a route ahead. I called "ready hike", as the first team eagerly took off, followed close behind by David driving the second team.

The winds blowing from the north combined with a full moon was bad news. Not only did the headwinds force us to keep our faces completely covered and sheltered by our hoods, but the strong breeze also set the entire ice pack into movement. The full moon brought higher tides, causing the ocean to pulsate as if its heart was beating. The ice was being ripped apart leaving the black water of the Arctic Ocean exposed; then enormous pans of ice came back together colliding with other pans, heaving them up into walls of ice blocks. An eerie creaking noise resonated as the ice crashed and broke apart. The ocean was alive.

By the afternoon the winds had only settled slightly. Ahead lay a series of big leads covered in a layer of thin ice. An expedition to the North Pole is a race against ice and time; very minute critical decisions had to be made. Is it better to go left or right around a pressure ridge? Is the ice thick enough to support our weight? How will we cross this lead of open water? There are no right answers, just good and bad results. The ice that lay ahead of us was thin, but we ventured out onto it. The dogs, nervous on thin ice, increased their speed to a gallop to get to solid ice as fast as possible. I was skiing beside the sled, holding onto the handle bars. Just as the dogs leaped onto the thick ice, I felt a sinking feeling. The back of the sled was slowly being sucked down into the Arctic Ocean, along with myself. Adrenaline took full control, as I grabbed the sled and pulled myself out of the water. Paul was ahead and ran back to help the dogs haul the sled out of the water onto thicker ice. Wet up to my chest, I quickly rubbed myself with snow.

The second team of dogs with David was close behind. When his team spotted the broken ice they swung hard right. It was deja vu: just as the dogs reached the thick ice, the sled and David broke through. As the water soaked through his clothes up to his knees, he quickly jumped onto the sled, while together, the dogs, Paul and I hauled the sled to the safety.

The ice was in movement all around us, a less than ideal place to camp. David and I added extra layers of clothes over our wet layers, and with Paul scouting ahead, we continued to navigate our way through the maze of ice blocks and open water.

As the sun hung low in the sky, we found a thicker pan of multi-year ice to set up camp for the night. The wind had settled down outside; the smell of dinner cooking filled our warm tent, as we sipped on a well-deserved warm hot chocolate. David and I dried our soaked gear over our MSR stoves, Paul checked the GPS. He announced our total distance, after eight hours of travel northwards through ice hell we had travelled a total of: "negative one nautical mile!". The headwinds had caused the ice to drift south; despite our arduous efforts we were further from the North Pole that we had been the night before. Each with a heaping bowl of re-hydrated spaghetti bolognese in hand, we couldn't help but laugh at our situation.'
Read more at: www.pittarak.com and www.northwinds-arctic.com.

Costs

Costs for North Pole expeditions can increase quite significantly each year. These guidelines are based on the 2011 season.

Organised events

- Flights: £10,000 and upwards.
- Marathon: £10,000.
- Last Degree expedition: £17,000 and upwards.
- Magnetic North Pole races: £20,000 plus equipment.

Independently organised expeditions

- Flights: £150,000–£400,000. Expensive charter flights are unavoidable. Re-supplies and more remote locations will push the costs up further. The expense can be shared between team members. It is not charged per person.
- Equipment: £5,000–£15,000. The Arctic Ocean is not a place to cut corners on kit and much of it can be expensive. Smaller, fibreglass pulks may be cheaper but large kevlar pulks can cost several thousand pounds alone.
- Food and fuel: £500–£2,000.
- Communications and insurance: £1,000–£4,000.

Lowest total cost – £20,000
Join an organised Last Degree expedition, using as much hired equipment as possible.

More typical total cost – £250,000 (£125,000 each)
Two people on a full distance expedition dragging pulks without re-supplies and splitting the expensive flight cost.

The fastest

The current record for reaching the North Pole from land is 36 days and 22 hours. It was set in 2005 by a team of five people including Matty McNair and Tom Avery. They used dog sleds and air-dropped supplies.

British polar explorer Ben Saunders – the youngest person and one of only three to have skied solo and unsupported to the North Pole – believes he can not only beat this record but do so solo, on foot and without re-supply. He has honed his kit requirements to a bare minimum to aid swift progress but his first three attempts have been thwarted by a broken ski binding, leaking fuel container and weather conditions not allowing him to reach the start line. His quest continues.

Training

Adapting to operating in a cold environment

To prepare, you need to spend time doing physical activity in a cold environment. This is partly to get your body and mind to the rigours but also so that your routines are swift and efficient. You want your rest stops on the ocean to be as quick as possible and you want to minimise the time between stopping for the night and getting inside your sleeping bag with the stove on.

Scotland and Scandinavia are good places to start with this but Arctic Canada is a popular choice for the more extreme temperatures.

Getting fit and strong

A good all-round level of fitness is important but your priorities should include:

- endurance for repeated days of long, slow exertion;
- strength for dragging a dead-weight behind you on uneven ground and over large obstacles.

As well as tying a rope around your waist, attaching it to some tyres and dragging them through a field for several hours – surely as much a part of a polar experience as the time on the ice – dedicate some time to the lumpier stuff too like hauling your tyres up stairs and over walls.

(A more detailed description of tyre dragging can be found in Chapter 6 'How to Get to the South Pole'.)

Learning to 'read the ice'
Sea ice experience is a little trickier to obtain outside of polar waters but there is no safe way to plan an expedition without it. Arctic islands tend to be the best places for testing the ice. For example:

• Greenland;
• Svalbard;
• Baffin Island and surrounding area.

This is not the kind of thing that lends itself well to trial and error, even in training, so it would be prudent to seek guidance. Options include:

• attending a course organised through a polar training company based at one of the Arctic locations listed above;
• North Pole expedition companies and guides may not advertise specific courses but might be able to help with some bespoke training;
• joining a Last Degree expedition or organised race will give you some experience in a comparatively safe environment, particularly if you make the most of having experienced people around you.

Practising cold water drills
It is likely that you will have to get in the water at some point on your expedition. Hopefully this will only be to swim across short leads but you also need to be prepared for an unexpected fall.

Practising routines for cold water is useful for:

- learning to swim dragging a pulk whilst breaking through mushy ice with your elbows;
- experiencing the cold shock;
- practising the removal of skis under water;
- working on a technique for extricating yourself on the other side.

'Push your boundaries accumulating the knowledge, skills and experience; don't leap over them, fail unnecessarily and get into trouble.
All the best explorers took time to learn their "trade", frequently living with indigenous populations.
(Principally why I have accumulated 28 years, now.)'
– Jim McNeill,
experienced polar explorer who has made two attempts on the Northern Pole of Inaccessibility

First Steps

1. Go ski-touring. Attend a course or hire a guide in Scandinavia, or rent some skis in Scotland.
2. Build up to multi-day ski-touring trips, ideally towing a pulk and camping outside to get used to exertion and living in a cold environment.
3. Plan a trip to somewhere really cold (e.g. −20°C and below), that has sea ice, Baffin Island perhaps. You may want to attend a course and then undertake a small expedition from there.
4. Enter a race or join a Last Degree expedition. It may seem daft to go to the North Pole as training for a North Pole expedition but there are few better ways to get experience.

5. The gap between Last Degree and full distance expeditions is big but there are not many stepping stones in between. As such, your best bet is to simply accumulate more experience by repeating steps three and four until you feel you are ready.

'Determination and experience go in partnership on a North Pole expedition. Be prepared to put in the time and learn the skills needed to survive on the Arctic Ocean. It could take many years and smaller expeditions before being ready to undertake a Geographic North Pole expedition and be successful.'
— Antony Jinman,
who skied from land to the North Pole in 2010
and founded Education Through Expeditions

From client to guide

In 2005, Helen Turton was running a residential outdoor centre in the Peak District National Park. After years of saving, she fulfilled a lifelong ambition and joined a Last Degree expedition to the North Pole. She got on so well with her guide that she went back again two years later to help on another expedition.

Since then she has given up her day job, completed over a dozen more expeditions including skiing all the way to the South Pole and now works for her original North Pole guide as the company's UK expedition manager.

Easier, Harder, Different

- Kayak or row there – In 2006 two Americans, Eric Larsen and Lonnie

Dupre, walked and canoed to the Geographic North Pole, and in 2011 a team led by Jock Wishart rowed to the Magnetic North Pole.

- Visit all four Poles – It is possible that people have visited all four Poles by plane but no one has yet achieved it overland.
- Ski across Lake Baikal – a lot cheaper, fewer people have done it and it's easier to do off your own back. Good training for the Pole too.
- Do it in winter – The sun rose just before Børge Ousland and Mike Horn reached the Pole from the coast but a re-supplied team of Russians made it all the way in darkness. Winter will be perpetually dark and bitterly cold but it is possible.
- Do a return journey – Before planes were available, this was the only option besides a traverse. It has been repeated once with dogs and once on foot but is getting harder with the sea ice melting earlier every year.
- Complete a traverse – From one coast to another. This has only been completed a handful of times.

Resources

- RGS Polar Expeditions Manual – Incredibly detailed handbook for operating in polar environments and it's free to download – see: www.rgs.org.
- Adventure Stats – Wonderful records of every full distance North Pole expedition in history – see: www.adventurestats.com.
- Ben Saunders' website – British polar explorer with lots of hidden gems in his blog posts including detailed kit lists – see: www.bensaunders.com.
- Explorers Web – News, interviews and features on all things polar – see: www.explorersweb.com/polar.
- You can find companies offering Last Degree expeditions online by simply searching for 'north pole expedition last degree'. Some of the expeditioners quoting advice throughout this chapter also offer trips.

Contributors

Alex Hibbert

Alex is a world-record holding polar expedition leader and photographer. Only 25 years old, he has spent over 165 days unsupported in the Arctic and has crossed the second largest icecap on Earth four times.

See: www.alexhibbert.com.

Helen Turton

Helen has skied to the North Pole three times on Last Degree expeditions. She has also skied the Last Degree to the South Pole as well as crossing the Greenland ice cap. In 2009/10 she joined the Women's Commonwealth Antarctic Expedition skiing the full distance to the South Pole and now works as the UK expedition manager for Norwegian company Newland (www.newland.no).
See: www.polargirl.co.uk.

Special thanks

Thanks to the ExplorersWeb team for maintaining:
www.adventurestats.com.

How to Row an Ocean

'Simplify, simplify, simplify. Yes, seek advice and take
what you consider to be wise sentiments. But surely
part of the reason you are rowing an ocean is for the
beautiful simplicity of the concept. Get a boat, make
her seaworthy and put her in the ocean where you
want to begin.'

– Olly Hicks,
the first person to row solo from America to England

Setting the Scene

To row an ocean means to take a specially designed boat and power it by oar from one shore to another. Solo or in a team, you will be at sea for many weeks and months, at the mercy of the weather with all of your supplies sealed behind hatches. It is as intensely physical as it is mental, dealing with long days of rowing and great stretches of isolation. What used to be the preserve of the independent adventurer is now increasingly becoming a recognised sport with regular organised races.

Statistics

USP:	Crossing an ocean by human power alone.
Difficulty:	Moderate to difficult.
Cost:	£30,000–£70,000+.
Hurdles:	Weather, capsize, isolation.
Purest style:	Independent (rather than an event).
Who's done it?:	500+.
Glory potential:	Reasonable.

Background

The first recorded ocean crossing in a rowing boat was completed by two Norwegians: George Harbo and Gabriel Samuelson. In 1896, they rowed from New York to the Scilly Isles over a period of 55 days before continuing to France. This journey was the first of what the Ocean Rowing Society calls the 'Historic Ocean Rows'. All of these journeys were completed without GPS, satellite phones, emergency beacons, water makers or life rafts.

The 12 historic rows included several more crossings of the Atlantic along with the first crossing of the Indian Ocean by Swede, Anders

Svedlund. He travelled alone in a plastic boat with no books or radio for entertainment. Also in the historic category is the epic year-long first crossing of the Pacific from San Francisco to Australia by John Fairfax and Sylvia Cook.

Since then, with the introduction of modern equipment to improve navigation, safety and quality of life at sea, many more crossings have taken place. The Atlantic is by far the most popular stomping ground with a few hundred crossings now having been completed. In contrast, however, the Pacific and Indian have seen fewer than 20 successful crossings each.

The high volume of Atlantic trips is accounted for in no small part by the introduction of organised races in which several teams compete to reach the far shore. This has made the sport – as it is now becoming recognised – considerably easier to access with an increase of information now available for the aspirant rower and a market in second-hand ocean rowing vessels.

Russians rowing the Arctic

Eugene Smurgis rowed all his life. Growing up in Russia he copied the design of a boat he saw an old lady rowing down the river and used it to row on the Volga, the Amur and across the Caspian Sea, racking up hundreds of days at the oars.

He dreamed of rowing further and set off from northern Siberia in 1988. He covered several thousand miles in the Arctic Circle along the northern shores of his country where he frequently had to drag his boat across ice. Eventually he left Russian water and headed across the North Sea.

It took him two and a half months in the open seas before he reached the UK. Upon arrival in his tiny wooden rowing boat, the British Coast Guard took some persuading to believe that Smurgis was not a Russian defector.

See: www.oceanrowing.com.

Introduction – Oceans and Routes

There are generally considered to be up to five oceans in the world:

1. the Atlantic Ocean;
2. the Indian Ocean;
3. the Pacific Ocean;
4. the Arctic Ocean;
5. the Southern Ocean.

Of course, they each flow freely into one another and could just be considered a single 'World Ocean'. The geographical subtleties, however, are not important in this context. They are relevant only to the extent that you know what you have got to row across.

The Arctic tends to be largely frozen (though watch this space as the globe warms) and the Southern Ocean has a continent in the middle: Antarctica. So whilst there remain plenty of options for rowing in these waters, this chapter will not dwell on them.

As such, that leaves three oceans, of which two have been crossed in both directions:

1. the Atlantic – east-west and west-east;
2. the Pacific – east-west and west-east;
3. the Indian – east-west.

There are infinite variations, shorter options and combinations possible but these five routes are the focus for most ocean rowers and will be the focus of this chapter.

Options – Styles

Entering an organised race

The first ocean rowing race was held in 1997. It ran east-west across the

Atlantic from the Canary Islands to Barbados.

Atlantic rowing races have been organised every few years since then and the event calendar now includes the Indian Ocean and a race around Great Britain. There is at least one event most years.

'Woodvale' organise most ocean rowing events. Typical entry costs for an Atlantic race are:

- single – £13,000;
- pair – £16,000;
- four – £18,000.

This price includes support and emergency cover throughout the event, and covers a lot of the red tape required for crossing an ocean by rowing boat. It does not include a boat.

Events vary from year to year but some other current races include:

- The Bouvet Guayane – Solo across the Atlantic from Senegal to French Guyana. £13,500 entry – see: www.ramesguyane.com;
- La Route du Nord – West-east across the Atlantic. £15,000 entry – see: www.routedunord.com;
- GB Row – 2,000 miles around Britain. £4,000 entry – see: www.gbrowchallenge.com.

Compared with researching and organising everything for yourself, entering a race is a comparatively easy way to get your toe in the water. There are certain rules about equipment: what is required and what is not allowed in such races. Check the specifics of a race before committing to a boat.

Joining a team

It is not uncommon to find teams who are looking for extra members. Either to make up numbers in a boat or to replace last-minute drop-outs, advertisements appear frequently. Such opportunities are most commonly in organised races but not always.

Some pros and cons of this option:

- On the plus side, some or all of the organisation may already have been taken care of.
- A potential risk, however, is that you are committing to undertake a long and difficult journey with people you don't yet know.

Check what has already been obtained and prepared before committing to join a team. Also note that if you pay to join a group then it could technically be considered a commercially chartered vessel which has legal implications.

The Ocean Rowing Society is a good place to start looking for such opportunities.

Rowing to the North Pole

Jock Wishart is the only person to have both walked unsupported to a Pole and rowed across an ocean. One day, whilst combining these two loves by training on a rowing machine outside on the Arctic ice, a friend joked 'What are you going to do next Jock? Row to the Pole!'

On 26 August 2011, Jock Wishart and five team members arrived at the 1996 position of the Magnetic North Pole with an ocean rowing boat.

They had to navigate past floating ice blocks, extricate their boat after it got stuck in the ice and walk the last two miles to the Pole dragging the boat over the frozen ocean.

As difficult as this may sound, such a journey would not have been possible at all only a few years ago. Until recently the surrounding water would have remained frozen all year round. It is assumed that the reduction in ice is the result of global warming.

See: www.rowtothepole.com.

Rowing independently

The alternative to joining an event or someone else's team is to do it all yourself. Physically, there is no difference between an organised event and going independently. However, there will be an increased logistical burden which will include:

- buying your own boat;
- deciding on the best start and finish points for your crossing;
- shipping the boat to the start line and arranging a return shipment or onward sale;
- arranging port clearances and permissions from authorities;
- researching timings, currents and weather, and/or hiring a meteorologist to help through the trip.

You also have an increased responsibility as no one else will be responsible for your safety. On the plus side, however:

- You will learn more through completing all of the preparations yourself.
- You get the satisfaction of knowing that you have done everything yourself rather than having it done for you.

This independent approach will be the assumed approach for the remainder of this chapter unless otherwise stated.

Rowing solo or in a group

The number of people on ocean rowing boats stretches from one to eight or more but solo, double and fours are the most common sizes.
    The advantages of a team:

- you can share the rowing between more arms and legs;
- you can work in shifts offering more respite whilst the boat keeps moving in the right direction;
- you will have other people to keep you company for the otherwise long and lonely weeks at sea.

The advantages of the solo rower include:

- no risk of conflict from being in the same personal space for weeks at sea;
- working to your own schedule and following your own methods;
- extra sense of achievement from having completed something on your own.

The differences in durations of crossings between solo, double and larger groups are not as great as you might anticipate. The speed records are usually held by teams but, otherwise, there is often not that big a gap between them.

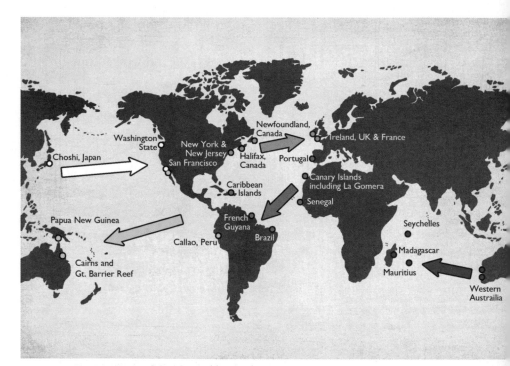

Map 3: World map showing ocean rowing routes

Options – Routes

Crossing the Atlantic Ocean
The M1 of ocean rows, the Atlantic was the first to be completed and has seen far more crossings than the others.

- Typical distance rowed: 3,000–3,500 miles (varies based on route choice and where the weather takes you).
- Most common route: East-west.
- East-west start/finish areas: Canary Islands and North Africa to the Caribbean and northern edge of South America.
- West-east start/finish areas: North America to the UK and Northern Europe.

Of the possible combinations, the only major route across the Atlantic that is yet to be completed is from South America to Africa.

As well as being the shortest option, the Atlantic is becoming increasingly well trodden which should make it easier to find out more information.

Crossing the Pacific Ocean
The Pacific Ocean is the biggest of the three and some people opt to make the crossing in stages, hopping between islands.

- Typical distance rowed: 5,000–6,000 miles.
- More common route: East-west.
- East-west start/finish areas: North America and Peru or Chile to Papua New Guinea and north Australia.
- West-east start/finish areas: Japan to North America.

Only 19 people over 16 boats have crossed the Pacific.

Crossing the Indian Ocean
Just 12 successful crossings of the Indian Ocean have been completed.

- Typical distance rowed: 3,600–4,000 miles.
- Only route completed: East–west.
- East–west start/finish areas: Western Australia to Mauritius, Madagascar and Seychelles.

Alternative ocean rowing routes

As well as the big three oceans, there are many other large bodies of water that can be rowed across in much the same manner. Few will be as large as an entire ocean but the same approach can be applied.

Options are endless but some possibilities include:

- the North Sea between Norway and the UK;
- the Tasman Sea between Australia and New Zealand;
- the Bering Strait between America and Russia;
- the Mediterranean, Black or Caspian Seas.

Around the world by human power

To travel around the world by human power, rowing is a logical choice for crossing the large bodies of water.

There is some debate in the adventure world about the technical definition of what constitutes a circumnavigation of the globe. However, keeping the finer details to one side for a moment, here are some adventurers who have completed round-the-world expeditions of varying sorts which involved crossing oceans:

Colin Angus – Rowed across the Atlantic with his fiancée (now wife), Julie Wafaei, on a two-year trip starting and finishing in Vancouver. He biked, hiked, canoed and skied the rest of the way including crossing Siberia in the winter. See: www.angusadventures.com.

Jason Lewis – Spent over a decade cycling, skating and walking a circumnavigation with an international team for different legs of the journey. Rather than row the oceans, his boat had pedals to make use of his cycling fitness. See: www.expedition360.com.

Erden Eruç – Already having become the first person to row

across all three oceans on his expedition, Eruç is still going because he also intends to climb the highest mountains on each of the six continents he reaches. See: www.around-n-over.org.

Sarah Outen – Currently part way through a loop of the planet which involves west-east crossings of the Pacific and Atlantic. She also kayaked across the English Channel and several straits between Russia and Japan. See: www.sarahouten.com.

Practicalities

Where do you sleep?

Ocean rowing boats have cabins where you can sleep, sealed shut from the elements, usually at the back of the boat. This is where you will hide in bad weather and get whatever down time there is to be had. They are not spacious and can be tough in choppy seas but as with all of these things, you should hopefully adapt.

Shift patterns are normal at sea for groups. As such, sleep tends to be in short bursts of a few hours at a time. Solo or on a less arduous itinerary, there may be times when you follow a more normal sleep/wake routine, rowing during the day and sleeping at night. Other times, this may be far from the case. You may need to row for long, unearthly hours, or simply not be able to sleep through the fear and discomfort of an angry sea tossing you about.

What do you eat and drink?

Food is stored in a small cabin for several weeks or months at sea. As such, you mostly want food that has a reasonable calorie-to-weight-and-space ratio that will keep for a long period and be easy to serve.

- Snacks: Easily accommodated with whatever you like to eat such as chocolate, biscuits, dried fruit, nuts and cakes.
- Meals: You will probably have a small camping stove for cooking. It

is often easiest to rely on **ration packs** as the neat little packets make rationing over time easy. However, you could just as well take more common foods like pasta, rice and cous cous with packets of sauce.
- Supplements: Vitamins, minerals, protein powders and sports drinks or home-made equivalents might be considered. They are not necessary but can be useful to ensure your body gets what it needs.
- Fishing line: Some people take a line to catch fresh fish too although it would be difficult to rely on this.

As with so many endurance expeditions, getting enough calories on board can be difficult so you should plan accordingly or be prepared for potentially significant weight loss.

The first few ocean rowers had to carry a supply of fresh water and plan refill stops along their way. Nowadays, rowers use a desalination machine to take water from the sea. Rowing boats tend to also have a large ballast of fresh water too which can be used in an emergency and refilled at the first opportunity to maintain the boat's ability to self-right.

'I grow my own beansprouts on board. It's great to have a change from freeze-dried food and snack bars, and they're packed with fibre, vitamins and minerals to keep me healthy. I use a Sproutamo sprouting pot, and grow sprouts from chickpeas, lentils, peas and peanuts. Yummy mixed up with tahini and soy sauce!"
– Roz Savage,
the only woman to have rowed all three major oceans

Where do you go to the loo?
Bucket and chuck-it is the preferred technique for toileting at sea.

Washing can also be done with a bucket so you will want to carry at least two of these.

Bear in mind, however, that fresh water can be a rare commodity. Either use it sparingly or take cleaning products that will work in sea water. Many normal products don't lather well in salty water. Wet wipes are another common option.

How long do you actually spend rowing?
- Two or more rowers: You may row in shifts for up to 24 hours a day, particularly if you are in a race. Shifts can be as long as you want but between one and three hours is fairly typical. You might do longer shifts at night so your team mates get some rest, or shorter ones when the going gets tough.
- Solo: You can still expect an average day to involve somewhere around 8–12 hours of rowing. To fight a current or winds, or to make the most of the calm before a storm, however, you may end up rowing for much longer stretches. Equally, bad weather may restrict you to your cabin for days at a time.

Unlike a 20-minute session on a static rowing machine at the gym, ocean rowing is a long, slow marathon event. Rowing for eight hours a day may seem unfathomable but your body should slowly adjust.

How do you know where to go?
In the big picture, navigation is quite simple: you need to head in a given direction for many weeks until you hit shore. The detail, however, is a little more complicated.

- GPS: Most ocean rowers will rely on GPS to give their exact location. Some boats will have GPS trackers that automatically broadcast their location every few hours.
- Wind and currents: The course you take will be significantly influenced by currents and winds, and thus far from a straight line. Even if you ultimately want to head due west, some days you may

end up rowing closer to due north or due south to compensate for external elements threatening to push you off course.

- Meteorologist: It is quite common to have a weather expert back on land who will look at the meteorological data for you and advise on your best route.
- Setting a course: With all of the above information compiled, you will work out a bearing that you can set on your compass and follow until it comes time to check your navigation again.

'The proximity of land can be given by a GPS, but also by the colour and shape of clouds, the species and behaviour of birds, the motion of the swell, the amount of flotsam, the altitude and heading of aircraft, the smells in the air, the colour of the water and even its temperature.'

– Tristan Gooley, author of the *Natural Navigator*

When to go

Ocean rowing is best done outside of storm seasons on the oceans. Exact timings depend on the hemisphere, from which side of a continent you depart and who you ask for advice.

The Atlantic Ocean has been crossed many times and the trends for departure dates are:

- East-west from Canary Islands area: November to January;
- East-west from Senegal area: November to March;
- West-east (from North America): May and July.

Having seen far less action, the other two oceans have less of a precedent for timings. However, this is when past expeditions have set out across the Pacific:

- East-west from North America: Mostly June to August;
- East-west from South America: Only a few crossings, between February to June;
- West-east (from Japan): Only completed three times. Departures May to July.

The Indian Ocean has only been crossed a few times:

- East-west (from Western Australia): Mostly April.

What if something goes wrong...?

Many situations at sea will be scary with some element of risk but the most likely scenarios that would require assistance are either:

- becoming incapable of rowing any further through illness or injury;
- your boat taking significant damage.

You can signal for help with whatever communications you have, including an EPIRB but it may take hours or days to arrive. If your boat is intact then sit tight and wait for help.

If your boat is having some problems then you would normally:

- get into your **immersion suit** to keep you warm and dry;
- throw a life jacket over the top;
- get your emergency grab bag which is filled with all the essentials for survival.

Most ocean rowers will carry a life raft – indeed, they are mandatory in races – but some boats retain the ability to float regardless of the level of damage so can be used without a raft. Either way, you should end up floating. From there it is just a case of continuing your communication and waiting for the nearest boat or helicopter to help.

'Bear in mind there are only three main ways to die on a human powered ocean crossing: 1) hitting land, 2) hitting ships and 3) falling overboard. So as long as you stick with your boat and avoid the hard stuff (a fortifying slug of whisky now 'n then notwithstanding), you'll have a grand adventure and live to tell the tale.'

— Stevie Smith, author of *Pedalling to Hawaii*

Difficulties

Getting caught in heavy weather

The weather can cause many hardships for ocean rowers:

- rendering it impossible to row for days at a time;
- pushing you off course or backwards;
- generally making life very unpleasant. It might be funny the first time you spill your soup down your front but can quickly become draining when even the simplest of tasks requires three points of contact between body and boat to maintain balance.

This can migrate from being a hassle to being a real problem if:

- you get taken so far off course that you can't get back to where you need to be;
- it delays you sufficiently enough that you risk running out of supplies;
- it wears you down physically or mentally to the extent that you can't carry on;
- it causes damage to you or your boat.

You can help matters by monitoring what lies ahead. If bad weather is a few days off then make the most of the good weather by trying to row further. It will help keep overall progress up and you may get some rest from rowing in the rougher weather.

However, rowing boats are too slow to outrun or avoid most weather systems so there will be times when there is nothing you can do but wait for bad weather to catch you up.

Capsizing your boat

Any ocean rowing boat worth its sea salt will be designed to self-right in the event of being tipped up or over. However, there are still risks involved.

If you are caught outside when it happens then there is a good chance you will be thrown overboard. If you are not clipped on with your harness then this can spell real trouble.

Even if you are safely inside your cabin when you start to roll then there is still a danger of injury from tumbling or impact from any of the many items around you that will get sent flying. You can improve the situation by:

- stowing away as much kit as possible;
- some rowers use a helmet and straps to protect themselves.

Possible causes for your boat losing its ability to self-right include:

- leaving a hatch open to one of your cabins so it fills with water;
- failing to refill your ballast after drinking the emergency supply;
- the boat suffering significant damage.

Needless to say, a small boat on the open ocean without the ability to self-right is a disaster waiting to happen. Should any of these things happen then you will want to address them as quickly as possible so that you are prepared for a capsize.

> ### How does a tiny boat survive in a big ocean?
>
> Like any sea-worthy vessel, ocean rowing boats are designed to stay upright as much as possible but also to quickly self-right should they get flipped.
>
> Some features of modern ocean rowing boats that help achieve this include:
>
> - low centre of gravity due to a heavy ballast at the bottom of the boat. Usually a large volume of fresh water;
> - completely sealed deck and cabins to avoid swamping or water getting inside the holds;
> - maintaining buoyancy, in part through the large air-filled cabins on top of the boat;
> - the boats are made from many small compartments so a single hole won't cause the whole thing to fill with water.

Failure of electrical equipment

As much as expeditions are about getting away from the trappings of modern life, the truth with ocean rowing is that unless you are trying a drastically different approach, you will be reliant upon electricity.

Power is normally generated through solar panels although wind turbines, fuel cells and petrol-fuelled generators have also been used. If you're in a race then you'll need to check what is and is not allowed.

To avoid running out of power you can take a few basic measures:

- include more than one source of power;
- mount solar panels facing in different directions so they catch the sun whatever direction you are travelling;
- use batteries that can store a charge rather than plugging the panels directly into devices;
- take lots of spare batteries, fuses and other parts as well as a wiring diagram and a basic understanding of electronics.

These are simple measures but it pays to think the whole system through as something as basic as a spare fuse could scuttle your trip otherwise.

Running out of drinking water

Despite being surrounded by the stuff, getting enough water to drink can be a problem. You will use a **de-salinator** to convert sea water into something drinkable which usually requires a lot of power and, like most things, is susceptible to breakage.

That means if you lose power or get a malfunction then you lose the ability to make water. You should have a ballast filled with fresh water but that is only for emergencies as it helps keep your boat upright.

Make sure you have a way of making water manually as a back up. Some electric pumps allow manual operation; otherwise, take a second pump.

Corrosion from salt water

You will spend the vast majority of your time at sea wet. What may be a novelty on the seaside can be a real issue on a long row. Sores and boils can easily develop on your bum from the repetitive motion of rowing, and blisters and skin loss on your hands and feet will likely arise from being constantly damp.

Additionally, salt water is corrosive over time. You will find a lot of your equipment wearing out at an alarming rate unless you take precautions such as sealing precious bits of equipment in dry bags and washing and rinsing the deck regularly.

'Love your bum! Look after the areas you know you're likely to have problems with – prevention is better than cure.'
– Rachel Smith,
who has rowed the Atlantic and holds a Dragon Boating world record

Aches, pains and other bodily injuries

Rowing for many hours a day over several weeks can obviously cause your body to suffer. Some discomfort is almost inevitable but it threatens to become a problem when it persists and gets worse over time.

You can help this by:

- conditioning your body in advance with a good training programme;
- learning and practising good rowing technique;
- warming up and down and stretching are good practices even at sea;
- maintaining a good diet to help fuel and repair your body.

Collisions with other boats

You are likely to be considerably smaller than any other vessels you encounter out at sea. There is every chance that other boats will not see you, even with a **radar reflector**. As soon as you pick something up on your radar, hail them with your radio. You can set your radar to sound an alarm to wake you at night if it picks up another vessel.

Dealing with the isolation

Last but not least, you will be separated from the world for a long period. In a team with a good satellite internet connection, the feeling of isolation may be less intense than it is for the solo rower with limited battery on their phone. Either way though, it will probably be a unique experience.

Some people may revel in the solitude and time to reflect whilst others may go stir crazy.

You can prepare for this however you want – working with a coach, talking it through with other people or buying extra credit for your satellite phone – but do not underestimate the strain such a trip can put on your mind as well as your body.

Pedal power

On 6 October 2007, a small yellow pedal boat crossed the Greenwich Meridian. It had left that same line 13 years earlier with Jason Lewis at its helm.

In the intervening years, Lewis had pedalled the boat to France, across the Atlantic to America and the Pacific to Australia, up through Indonesia, from India to Djibouti and finally back across the Channel and up the Thames.

Although Lewis was joined by other people for many parts of his trip, he was clearly struck by the long weeks when he was alone at sea. Speaking after the event, Lewis described both moments of epiphany and slightly crazed conversations with fictional characters whose voices would motivate him to keep moving.

See: www.expedition360.com.

Kit

Choosing a rowing boat

Your first, most important and most expensive piece of kit is a boat.

- Design: Compared to sailing, the number of ocean rowing boats in the world is tiny. Some boats are one-of-a-kind. Many, however, are similar or identical in construction and all built from the same set of plans.
- Materials: Plywood and fibreglass are common materials for making boats and usually the cheaper options. Kevlar and carbon composites are more expensive choices but are stronger and lighter.
- Purchasing: Your options are buying new, buying second-hand or building one yourself.

Getting a boat built for you

The easiest option, albeit the most expensive, is to buy a new boat. Ocean

1. Wind turbines for power.
2. Aerial for radio communication.
3. Watertight hatches.
4. Solar panels for power.
5. Cabin for sleeping and shelter in rough weather.
6. Heavy water ballast - maintains self-righting
   capability but can be used for drinking in an emergency.
7. Storage for food and equipment.

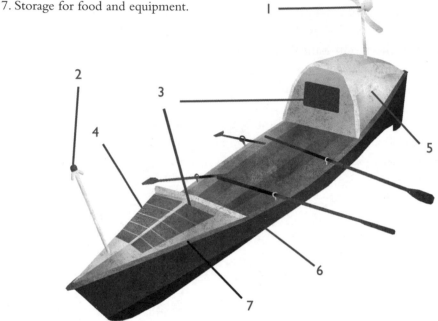

Fig. 4: Typical ocean rowing boat

rowing boats are still fairly niche, however, so no one keeps a supply of
pre-built boats in stock. As such, buying new means having a boat built
for you.

You can either have a boat built to an existing plan which will
probably be cheaper and quicker; or you can commission a boat to be
built including your own specifications. The latter option comes with the
risk of trying untested design elements but allows you to customise the
boat to your own liking.

Boat builders in the UK include:

- Global Boatworks;
- Rossiter Yachts;
- Woodvale.

Buying a second-hand boat

Since most people use boats for just a single trip, there is a reasonable market in second-hand boats. This is cheaper and can save a lot of time and effort if the boat comes fully equipped. However, boats weaken over time, particularly plywood, so it would pay to have someone with experience check out any purchases first.

The following organisations list boats for sale:

- The Ocean Rowing Society;
- The Association of Ocean Rowers;
- Woodvale.

It is sometimes possible to rent these boats too.

Building a boat yourself

In the early races, it was standard practice for teams to buy a flat-packed boat kit and assemble it themselves. This is still possible. Some options include:

- Woodvale – Makers of the original 'Pairs Class' boat for the Atlantic Rowing Race in 2001. They now sell kits for solo, pairs and fours boats.
- The Association of Ocean Rowers – Have a free set of plans you can download.

This requires a lot more effort than the other options as well as more skill. It also places a lot of responsibility on you to build it properly as your life will be in this boat's hands. However, building it yourself means you will know your boat intimately and may be very satisfying.

Across the Bering Straits in a sailing boat with oars

There aren't many ocean rowing boats in the world but there are plenty of ocean-worthy sailing boats about the same size. Canadian adventurer Colin Angus picked up one such yacht from eBay on the cheap.

He took off the sailing gear, sealed the hatches and added the necessary parts for rowing. Including modifications but not the onboard equipment, he estimates that the boat cost $3,400 US dollars.

He used the boat to row from Alaska to Russia across the Bering Sea with his friend Tim Harvey.

See: www.angusadventures.com.

Navigation and communications equipment

You may be alone at sea but that doesn't mean that you're out of touch.

- **VHF radio (Very High Frequency)**: The standard method of communicating between ships and ports. The range on a rowing boat is less than other boats which sit higher in the water. Four or five miles is typical.
- **Satellite phone**: You can expect reception on a satellite phone wherever you are. Not strictly necessary but usually prudent.
- **GPS**: This will tell you and the rest of the world where you are, helping you navigate and track your route.
- **Internet connection**: Some form of internet connection is also common. Most rowers use the marine equivalent of dial-up internet which is very slow but good enough to send and receive emails. If you have the money then you can get faster broadband speeds via satellite.
- **EPIRB**: Always carried but only pushed in a life-threatening situation with no other communication.

Sea anchor to slow you down

Shaped like a parachute and with a similar action, a sea anchor is used to slow you down if the wind is blowing you in the wrong direction. It also helps ensure that your boat is perpendicular to waves which is the most stable position.

Radar reflector and Automatic Identification System (AIS)

Rowing boats are tiny objects on a vast ocean. Barely rising 2m above sea level when you stand and wave, your visibility is never going to be good and you will be too small to appear on people's radar.

You can help yourself by carrying an:

- Active **radar reflector**: Also known as a transponder, this device takes incoming radar signals and re-transmits them back. This means you are more likely to appear on other people's radar.
- **Automatic Identification System (AIS)**: Technology that shares location, course, speed and other information between vessels using VHF signals. It can have better range and reliability than radar.

Grab bag for emergencies

Filled with all your basic supplies should things go awry, an emergency grab bag is simply the bag you should grab in an emergency. It will include:

- flares, signalling mirror, torch and whistle to aid in calling for help;
- VHF radio and satellite phone for communicating;
- GPS and EPIRB to track your location and signal for help;
- food, fishing line, water and manual desalination pump to keep you going.

And don't forget to bring...

Don't forget the following:

- several oars in case any should break;

- a harness with connecting line to avoid becoming separated from your boat;
- bilge pump, buckets and sponges to remove water from the boat;
- an electric de-salinator and a manual option should that fail;
- a good range of clothing to cover the variety of conditions that you might face although, on warmer seas, many rowers prefer to go naked.

'Always tie on. Your boat is your life support machine. Without it, a human cannot expect to survive long surrounded by thousands of miles of empty ocean. After my co-pedaller, Steve, was thrown overboard following a sudden capsize on the Atlantic, we secured rope leashes to our ankles and kept connected at all times.'
– Jason Lewis,
who completed a 13-year circumnavigation of the globe
using a pedal-powered boat

A Day in the Life of an Ocean Rower
by Sarah Outen

Sarah Outen was the first woman and youngest person to row solo across the Indian Ocean, a journey of 3,100 nautical miles from Australia to Mauritius over 124 days. She has recently embarked on an expedition to travel around the world by human power alone which will include rowing both the Pacific and Atlantic Oceans.

'Life on an ocean rowing boat is so simple and seemingly unpressured, with time and space to really live and breathe in the moment and just be – yet, in spite of this, I really find routine (albeit a flexible one) helpful to ensure the hippy tendencies are controlled and I do actually get down to some useful rowing. After all, the miles won't row themselves.

Everything is lived out by the energies of the ocean and the weather and shaped by the need to maximize mileage when the conditions allow. It's about efficiency really — of mind, body, boat and spirit: it's a marathon, not a sprint, remember.

So with this in mind, I tend to split my day between the natural pattern of light and darkness hours — getting up before dawn to start the day and get to the oars, and stowing them again for the last time around sunset, unless the weather is good for night time rowing. That way there is time to row and rest as much as possible so that one enhances the other.

My first glance in the morning is to the compass, to check the boat's direction and tell me what's going on. Your body becomes attuned to the wind and waves so sound and motion all feed into the picture of outside.

Clipping my harness on is second nature now so I'm leashed up before I open up the hatch and head outside to take in the morning air. After a night in the cabin I'm usually gagging for a lungful of fresh air.

I use the bucket and head inside again to log our position and start on breakfast — nibbling at a bar or some dried fruit, or perhaps even a bar of chocolate if I'm lucky. I get dressed for whatever the weather is doing (anything from nothing to lycra to foulies) and then head outside for a full breakfast — boiling water in my little stove to mix into oats and dried fruit. If it's a lovely morning, it can be a beautiful moment of peace and if it's gnarly then it becomes a race to wolf it down before saturation — both of me and the porridge — ensues.

Then it is emails (via the satphone) while I'm brushing my teeth, before lathering thick zinc sun cream all over my face. There's no excuse to get burned out there so personal admin is key.

My morning ritual over, it's time to start rowing. If it's been a rough or particularly strenuous day before, I am likely to take a while to get going and warm up, but once I've found my rhythm it feels good and strong. I row and eat and rest alternately throughout the day, resting or eating more or less according to the weather and how tough the rowing is. Some days I can row for hours and not notice whereas others are punctuated by twenty-minute bursts of rowing and resting as I battle into the waves.

Through the hottest or brightest part of the day (if there is one) I switch on the water maker to fill up the day can and will often break after lunch to catch up on chores or have a quick nap. Sometimes there are things to be fixed or cleaned or washed and at others there is an interview to do over the satellite phone. After a few weeks at sea your body is pretty tuned in to itself, so it is easy to know what your body needs and when, even if it's not always possible to take it. For instance, when you're battened down in the cabin during a roaring storm, it's sometimes tricky to rest at all, let alone properly. (I find adrenaline and fear aren't conducive to rest until you're so rag tired that nothing will wake you.)

Sunset is my favourite time of the day – an opportunity to pause and reflect on whatever thought is filling my head or to just enjoy the peace and quiet of not having to think about anything in particular. If the weather is good I whip up some dinner (maybe pasta/rice or something freeze dried) and then row on into the night. It is one of the most beautiful places to be on a calm evening with bright skies, looking up into a three dimensional starry blanket, with the boat trailing swirls of bioluminescence. After three bashes in the chest with the oars as I fall asleep on my rowing seat, or after the first wave over my head, I call it a day and turn in for the night.

Just as with the morning there is the night time routine of the log, the blog, a comms check via email or SMS and my weather router to see what the weather is doing and forecast to do, before tending to sores and aches with creams and powders and resting.

The boat drifts over night, either freely or on a parachute anchor. I tend to sleep in bursts, waking to check that all is well, and to nibble and drink until dawn. Then it starts over again and is repeated for as long as needs be through whatever trials and tribulations and wonders the ocean presents. From my experience, I'd say a day on the ocean can be many things – magical, energizing, demoralizing, intimidating, encouraging, boring, mind boggling and always, in its own salty way, incredible and interesting and, ultimately, life affirming.'

Find out more and follow her journey around the world at: www.sarahouten.com.

Costs

Boat costs
- DIY kit: £5,000–£10,000+. Could be less if you buy materials yourself and just work to a plan.
- Second-hand: £8,000–£40,000+. Varies significantly based on the quality of boat, how many crossings it's done, and how desperate the owner is for a sale. It is normal for boats to come with much of the necessary equipment already installed.
- New build: £15,000–£40,000+. The cheapest option will probably be a standard design from Woodvale. Custom designs, carbon and kevlar construction and larger boats cost more.

Other costs
- Equipment: £10,000–£20,000. Vast array of unavoidably expensive equipment for keeping you and your boat safe at sea.
- Shipping: £2,000–£6,000. Sending by container ship. You may also need a trailer to move the boat around.
- Flights, supplies, insurance: £1,000–£3,000.

Lowest total cost – £30,000 (£15,000 each)
Picking up a second-hand bargain rowing boat that's well equipped, avoiding long-haul flights and shipping, and splitting the costs between two people.

More typical total cost – £60,000 solo, £70,000 pair
Buying a new but popular boat design, kitting it out from scratch and entering a race.

Training

Building rowing fitness
Rowing machines will instantly spring to mind for training. They are

certainly the easiest way of developing strength and fitness but it always pays to make your training as close as possible to the real thing. Rowing on open water where possible will be an improvement as it better mimics what you will put your body through.

Improving rowing technique

Remember, that it is not just about big muscles and endurance but also technique. A rowing club would be a good place to start.

Learning procedures and about your equipment

You will need to learn how to operate all of the equipment on board, including:

- operating the radar, AIS and GPS systems;
- reading ocean charts and the basics of navigation;
- what procedures you follow in an emergency;
- a few nautical terms for communicating with sea folk.

Sea safety and marine navigation courses would be a good place to start.

Getting your head straight

Last up is giving some thought to the fact that you are going to be out at sea for weeks if not months which can be tough on the head. You may not be able to train directly for this but you can:

- seek guidance from a professional;
- prepare yourself with supplies, e.g. books, music, audio books and letters from home;
- devise deployable tactics for those moments when morale is low.

First Steps

1. Join a rowing club to see how you find the experience of rowing.

2. Try spending extended periods on a rowing machine to test your body and mind with the monotony.

3. Undertake some journeys down rivers, along the coast, or across lakes in a rowing boat, or enter some rowing events.

4. Get some experience of sea travel by trying a sailing course or offering yourself as a crew.

5. There are not many more steps after this before the big one – buying a boat – so make sure you have done plenty of them before committing.

6. Buy a boat, pick your ocean and start planning.

'Trust me when I say that experience is overrated. And ignore the cynics: they never attend the sendoff nor show up at the finish line; they are irrelevant to your success.'

– Erden Eruç, who has rowed the Indian, Atlantic and Pacific oceans, spending over 600 days at sea

Easier, Harder, Different

- Row all the oceans or all the way around the world. Erden Eruç and Roz Savage are the only people to have rowed across each of the Indian, Pacific and Atlantic Oceans.
- Row the South Atlantic from west to east, or west-east across the Indian Ocean. Neither have been done.
- Row continent-to-continent across the Indian Ocean instead of from island-to-island. It has never been done.
- Row the Southern Ocean in a journey around Antarctica. This was attempted by Olly Hicks in 2009 but never completed.
- Row through the Arctic Ocean. A team made it to the Magnetic North Pole in 2011 and, if the ice continues to melt, more options may become available soon.

- Row some of the smaller bodies of water around the world in a day. For example, the English Channel, Gibraltar Straits or Tatar Straits. They may be shorter but the currents and traffic in such areas can make them tricky.
- Pedal. Ocean-worthy pedalos exist and have been used successfully on more than one occasion. Most notably by Stevie Smith and Jason Lewis, documented in the book *Pedalling to Hawaii*.
- Row a river instead. Do this in either in a smaller boat or by taking an ocean rowing boat down a big river.

Resources

- Ocean Rowing Society International – Fantastic database of statistics, as well as a news archive and second-hand boats – see: www.oceanrowing.com.
- The Association of Ocean Rowers – Good, simple site with information on many areas of ocean rowing – see: www.oceanrowers.com.
- *Angus Adventure Handbook* – Useful basics from experienced rowers Colin and Julie Angus – see: www.angusadventures.com/oceanrowing.
- Explore Rowing – Find local clubs, suggested routes and challenge events – see: www.explorerowing.org.
- Woodvale Challenge – Races, new and second-hand boats and other services – see: www.woodvale-challenge.com.
- Boat builders in the UK – Global Boatworks (www.globalboatworks.com), Rossiter Yachts (www.rossiteryachts.co.uk) and Woodvale (www.woodvale-challenge.com).
- Old websites of the many ocean rows that have taken place in recent years can be a useful source of information.

'No two ocean rowing trips are the same. Everyone who has rowed an ocean would do something different the next time around. So tap into that advice. Chat to as many ocean rowers and ask their advice as possible.'
– Chris Martin,
half of the first team to row west–east across the Pacific Ocean

Contributors

Chris Martin
Chris is a world record setting ocean rower. After rowing as part of the British Squad, he rowed solo across the Atlantic Ocean in 2005. In 2009, he joined Mick Dawson and they became the first team to row across the North Pacific Ocean. Chris is now director of New Ocean Wave which operates ocean rowing races from California to Hawaii.
See: www.newoceanwave.com.

Rachel Smith
Rachel (and rowing partner Lin) hold a Guinness World Record for rowing across the Atlantic in 2007. She has won 25 World and European medals and two world records in Dragon Boat Racing and will be a Torch Bearer for the London 2012 Olympic Games. Rachel now runs her own company, Big Blue Projects, providing marketing & PR services, business/life coaching, writing and motivational speaking.
See: www.bigblueprojects.com.

Special thanks
Thanks to the Ocean Rowing Society International, The Association of Ocean Rowers and Angus Adventures.

How to Cycle Around the World

*'Just go. Any bike, any tent, anywhere. It's true, the
toughest step is always the first one!'*
−Matt Bridgestock, @55n[1]

[1] Tips for this chapter were gathered through Twitter by posting the question: 'What one
piece of advice would you give someone considering a round-the-world bike trip?'. The
Twitter username for each commentator is given after the @ symbol.

Setting the Scene

Picture setting off from your front door, fresh-faced on a shiny new bike laden with still-labelled equipment. Now imagine returning several years later with wiry legs, filthy clothes, a sorry excuse for a bicycle and a book-load of stories to tell at the pub. Cycling around the world is a wonderfully simple adventure that requires little skill, training or money yet holds huge potential for a journey that can last as long as you are willing to keep turning the pedals.

Statistics

USP:	Circumnavigation with your own two legs.
Difficulty:	Easy to moderate.
Cost:	£2,500–£10,000+.
Hurdles:	Learning to ride a bike and finding the time.
Purest style:	Independent and low-budget.
Who's done it?:	Hundreds.
Glory potential:	Low.

Background

The first record of someone pedalling around the world is Englishman Thomas Stevens' 13,000 mile journey by penny-farthing in 1884 carrying little more than a spare shirt, a change of socks and a pistol. Much has changed since then – in particular there is less need for firearms – but the essence remains much the same: you can go a long way with a bicycle and a sense of adventure.

Skipping forward a hundred years or so to Valentine's Day 2008, a Scotsman by the name of Mark Beaumont completed a high-profile circumnavigation of the globe by bicycle and in so doing set a world record for the fastest such journey. He was not the first to set such a record and in fact held it for only a short period of time, but he is certainly responsible for a greater public interest in the idea and practice of pedalling oneself across continents.

For its weight, the bicycle converts energy into movement more efficiently than any other machine or animal on the planet. In the twenty-first century they are easily and cheaply obtained, and even the most basic are capable of covering huge distances in relative comfort. The internet is littered with information and stories about those who have upped sticks and pedalled off towards the horizon. With the concept of big cycling trips slowly seeping into the national consciousness and the increasing number of stories appearing in the papers, you might get the impression that such journeys happen every day. This is probably an exaggeration but it does highlight one crucial fact: an around-the-world bicycle tour is open to almost anyone.

Introduction – What Constitutes Cycling Around the World?

Guinness World Records has a set of rules which define what constitutes an around-the-world cycle. These include:

- cycling at least 18,000 miles in a given direction, i.e. east or west;
- crossing every line of longitude around the world and two antipodal points (opposite points of the globe);
- travelling a total distance – including flights and boats – of at least as much as 24,900 miles, the earth's circumference at the equator.

If you want to break the record then you will need to abide by these rules. Should you complete such a journey then few would dispute, in the technical sense, that you had indeed cycled around the world.

But to apply such a clinical approach to a venture like this seems to rather miss the point. One of the great beauties of the long-distance bicycle tour is the freedom it grants you and setting out with the sole intention of breaking a record flies in the face of that idea.

For the purposes of this chapter, cycling around the world will be defined less by a set of rules and more as a philosophy: the idea of riding a bicycle to and through many different places on our planet with the vague aim of ending up back where you started. That journey may take you across each line of longitude largely by power of pedal or perhaps you will have just travelled the world in the more metaphorical sense.

Options – Routes and Styles

Touring with a company

There are a few organised tours that take in the length or width of a continent on a bicycle. Two examples are the competitive Race Across America (RAAM) and the largely non-competitive Tour d'Afrique, who actually do trips in other continents as well as Africa.

An organised event like this will typically see you paying a significant entry fee. For that you will have the organisation taken care of and be supported by vehicles throughout. The experience is, of course, not the same as undertaking such a trip independently but might be a good option for those daunted by the idea of going it alone or simply preferring to focus on the physical elements of the challenge.

Approximate costs:

- Tour d'Afrique, Cairo to Cape Town: £8,000 fully supported;
- Tour d'Afrique, single stage: £800 upwards;
- Race Across America (RAAM): £2,000 solo entry fee, cheaper for teams. Normal to have a vehicle support team which can make it significantly more expensive.

Going for the world record

Ever since Mark Beaumont broke the world record, a spate of challengers to the throne have launched their own bids. His record has already been bested several times and all record breakers so far have been enthusiastic amateurs cycling largely unsupported carrying their own kit. So while the challenge becomes tougher each time the record is broken, it is still open to anyone with a bike and a pair of legs.

If you are considering this then you will want to have a high level of cycling fitness and be willing to sacrifice detours and experiences in favour of hours in the saddle.

Advice from a record breaker – Mark Beaumont
Circumnavigation completed February 2008 in 194 days.

Mark's record attempt was made into a BBC documentary called 'The Man Who Cycled the World'. He has since cycled the length of North and South America, climbed the highest mountain in each, and rowed to the Magnetic North Pole. See: www.markbeaumontonline.com.

'Anyone who wants to cycle around the world tends to be good at the cycling bit but the missing link that really stumps people is how to get to the start line. Most great enterprises never become more than the dream.

If you need sponsors, whether that be money or kit, the fastest method is by direct networking. In my experience, cold calling, emailing, and phoning wastes a lot of time and tends to be very demoralising. If a company or person is well enough known for you to consider approaching them, then they will be used to being regularly asked and are unlikely to be able to help everyone. When I started out I reasoned that I didn't have any money or network so I had to cold call for support. But that is not true, we all know people who know people. Each of my major capital sponsors came on board through a second point of contact. Follow every lead, and ask for introductions, it's by far the best way to get the start any expedition needs.'

Independent

For the vast majority of people cycling around the world will be a personal journey without stringent rules or constraints. Going it alone means setting your own agenda, going at your own pace and doing it in your own style.

Within the broad definition of circumnavigation as set out in the introduction, there are a thousand different routes that you could follow. However, here is a brief overview of some common options to get your brain whirring:

The most straightforward route, if any route for cycling across the globe can be described as such, is probably:

- head east from the UK, across Europe;
- continue through Russia, Kazakhstan and China to the Pacific;
- hop across to North America, cycle the width of that and head home victorious.

Obtaining a visa for any of these countries is, at present, routine. Foreign and Commonwealth Office (FCO) travel advice is good for the vast majority of regions and roads of varying degrees exist throughout.

An alternative would be:

- take a right-hand-turn halfway across Europe;
- head down through Turkey, Iran and Pakistan; or
- turn right in Kazakhstan and travel through Central Asia;
- either way, continue towards India and South-East Asia.

Some countries on this route might warrant a little research into the safer areas but most places have a safe route through for the cyclist. From there you could hop across some Indonesian islands, and perhaps Australia and New Zealand before continuing your journey to either of the Americas. Another angle on the around-the-world idea would be to cycle the length of each of the continental land masses:

- cycle down the length of Africa;
- up South and North America;
- and back across Eurasia, perhaps squeezing Australia in there too.

You will never be able to see the whole world on a bicycle – or any other means of transport for that matter – but a route like this feels a little more encompassing.

Another option would be a high-latitude trip through Scandinavia, northern Russia, Alaska and the Canadian Territories.

The world is the cyclist's oyster. You do not need to follow a predetermined route of someone else's creation. Just use the suggestions above to get yourself thinking or, even better, don't use them at all.

Aimless adventure

There is absolutely no reason that you need to set off with a specific route plan. Many are the cyclists who leave home on a bike trip only to fall in love with travelling on two wheels and live for many years as wandering bicycle nomads. If you are not constrained by time then stopping to work

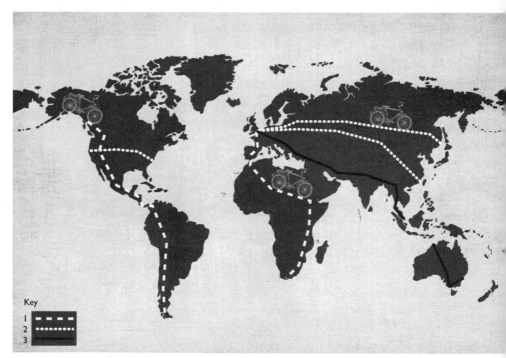

Map 4: World map showing possible cycle routes

and earn money as you go may help perpetuate your journey.

This approach arguably goes closer to the heart of a round-the-world cycling journey than any other approach. It ignores all rules and criteria for a technical circumnavigation and embraces the freedom of the open road on two wheels.

You could begin such a thing yourself by simply setting off with only the vaguest of plans and seeing where the road takes you.

Cycling off the beaten track

Two cyclists who took a different approach to cycling around the world are Andy Welch and Tom Allen. They decided to undertake their tour using mountain bikes geared up for off-road cycling. That meant front suspension and carrying kit on a trailer rather than just with panniers. This allowed them the freedom to get away from the main roads and explore a bit more of the world.

In Mongolia, for example, where many cyclists on bikes built for roads will curse the uneven, unmaintained dirt tracks, Tom and Andy could carry on as normal and enjoy the experience.

Their angle on travelling around the world was less literal too as, despite being away for a few years, clocking up some 40,000km through 40-odd countries, Mongolia was the furthest east they got.

Tom and Andy each maintain websites about their experiences at: www.tomsbiketrip.com and: www.slowquest.co.uk respectively.

Practicalities

Where do you sleep?

On a long cycle there is almost certainly just one sleeping option available: wild camping. It may be possible to use hotels in many places but it is unlikely you would manage that the whole way around without significantly constraining your route, not to mention breaking the bank. Being able to sleep anywhere goes to the very core of bicycle touring and grants a far greater freedom than reliance on bricks and mortar. That said, when the offer of a bed from a new friend presents, no doubt it will rarely be declined.

On a hammock, under a **tarpaulin** and in a waterproof **bivvy bag** are all options but tents are the most common.

What do you eat and drink?

On a cycle tour you can pretty much eat anything you can fit in your panniers and cook on a camping stove; aside from those long stretches without civilisation where weight and shelf-life may become more critical.

It takes a long time to cycle around the world and you will tire quickly if you try to rely on 'expedition food'. The world over, fresh, local produce should do you well and each region will bring new offerings: bread and salami through Russia, coconuts in India, cabbage and beans throughout Africa and bananas from Central America.

Of course, there is nothing stopping you from tapping up the many cafés and restaurants you will pass on the way when time and money allow. Besides, experiencing local cuisines and meeting people is surely as important to a bike trip as the miles you crank out each day.

As for drinking, if you are in a country with safe tap water then use that – pubs, cafés, public toilets, drinking fountains or knocking on someone's door if need be. Other places you will need to purify it or buy bottled water. When you get more remote you will rely on streams, rivers and lakes, again, purifying where necessary.

The hungry cyclist

Tom Kevill-Davies loves riding his bike and loves to eat. In search of the perfect meal he has spent two and a half years cycling through the Americas, pedalled the length of the Mekong river, cycled from Cairo to Jerusalem, and completed a tour of the Monopoly board in London.

Collecting recipes and photographs as he goes, he shares them online through his blog and in his book *The Hungry Cyclist*.

See: www.thehungrycyclist.com.

Where do you go to the loo?

Going to the loo on a cycle trip need not be complicated. If you are in a civilised place then be civilised and use a toilet. If you are in the wilds then go wild.

Advice from a record breaker – James Bowthorpe

Circumnavigation completed September 2009 in 175 days.

James used his record attempt as a way to raise over £100,000 for the charity 'What's Driving Parkinson's?'. He (unofficially) broke Mark Beaumont's record by 19 days. See: www.jamesbowthorpe.com.

'When I first imagined cycling around the world I was 18. I thought that it would probably take around four years to do it properly and to work a bit along the way. Although I did a lot of touring in the subsequent years I always returned home, back to university or work, that particular dream on a distant back-burner. Thirteen years later I was able to reignite the idea, whilst looking for something to do to raise money for the charity that I work for, "What's Driving Parkinson's?". The ideal four years went out the window; speed was now the aim, with that urgency intended to reflect the importance of the cause I raise money for.

My advice therefore to anyone considering an entire circumnavigation or section thereof, is this... Be flexible, remember your reasons for being out there (be they idealistic or pragmatic), and adapt your way around the world.'

How long will it take?

The Guinness record for cycling the necessary 18,000 miles to qualify for an around the world journey was set at 163 days by Vin Cox in 2010. In contrast, Heinz Stucke set off on a bike tour in 1962 and has yet to finish.

A world tour can be as long or as short as you want depending on your definition and your approach. A reasonable starting point, however, for a fairly direct route across Eurasia and North America would be six months to a year.

> **Fifty years in the saddle**
>
> On 4 November 1962, the 22-year-old Heinz Stucke departed his home town in Germany on a three-speed bicycle. Fifty years later, he is still pedalling.
>
> Stucke has now covered nearly 600,000km through over 200 different countries. He used the same bicycle – which weighed a whopping 25kg – for the first 44 years of his travels but has since acquired two folding bikes to help him travel to the more remote corners of the globe in an attempt to set a Guinness World Record.
>
> To find out more about Stucke and help with his world record, visit: www.heinzstucke.com.

How long do you actually spend cycling?

You can cycle for as little or long as you like each day but anywhere between five and eight hours of actual pedalling time would be typical. Once your body and mind have adapted to life on the road, churning out revolutions day after day will become second nature. In moderate conditions, this often means simply rising soon after the sun and pedalling until dark.

Daily distances vary greatly but, as a rough indication, 50 miles would be quite a short day while 90 would be quite long.

'Factor in some rest days so you actually get a chance to *see* the places you're cycling through.'
– Steve Crawford, @MrStevious

How do you know where to go?

Your options are boundless. If a country has roads then you can cycle there. And even when there aren't any roads, with a fat-tyred mountain bike and a bit of preparation, you can probably still cycle there.

On a daily basis, you can rely on maps, compass and road signs. Alternatively, asking whoever happens to be standing by the side of the road is another cyclists' fail safe. A picture book, translated letter explaining your journey in foreign languages and a willingness to mime can all be helpful for this. Similarly, carrying a phrasebook and learning a bit of the local language or alphabet will help with road signs. A map case mounted onto your **bar bag** can be really helpful too.

Be prepared for scepticism and incredulity when you ask for directions to the next town/region/country. Cycling to a village 50 miles away may be perfectly routine on such a trip but in everyday life it is relatively uncommon. As such, some locals, with no ill intent, may try to convince you that it is too far or not possible on a bike. Combine their advice with your own judgement.

The natural navigator
by Tristan Gooley, author of *The Natural Navigator*
'Long distance cyclists get to know the direction of the prevailing winds quite well. These winds so often make the difference between a grimace and a smile! It is quite satisfying to note that nature is tuned to these winds too. The tops of trees will be bent over by the prevailing winds. If you are cycling in the direction the tops of exposed trees are pointing it is likely to be much easier going.'

When to go
Setting off on a bike trip is feasible at any time of year. Cycling through Alaska in winter would be tough as would spending much time near the equator during summer. But even these two extremes of season are far from impossible, they just require some extra planning.

Some basic planning ahead could help you avoid the countries with the coldest winters, hottest summers and wettest rainy seasons at the wrong time of year. But if you are going for a long time then there is a good chance that at some point you will encounter weather at either extreme.

As such, the best answer to the question of 'When to go?' is probably: 'As soon as you are ready'.

Cycling home from Siberia

As if to prove that cyclists can handle whatever climate the world throws at them, Rob Lilwall and Alastair Humphreys set out to ride the notorious 'Road of Bones' in Siberia, in winter. They were repeatedly told that it was impossible, their plastic pumps kept snapping because it was too cold and they constantly found themselves getting 'wiped out' by icy roads. But, despite all of this, they managed to cover some 3,000 miles in temperatures down to at least −40°C (the lowest their thermometer recorded) and even took in a couple of swims on the way.

Both Rob and Alastair have written books about their trip which you can read about at: www.roblilwall.com and: www.alastairhumphreys.com.

What if things go wrong...?

Accidents can happen on bikes and incidents can occur whilst cycling around the world, just as they can anywhere. If things go wrong, your options will really depend on where you are and how remote it is.

The majority of places that have roads now have mobile phone signals so most times you can probably just call for help. If you anticipate getting further off the beaten track then letting someone know where you are going (an email home or telling whoever you last stayed with) would be a start. And if you are really heading into the unknown then you could consider a satellite phone or an **emergency beacon**.

Remember that just because a country looks a long way off on a map and sounds exotic, it is still filled with people and the roads have been built for cars to go along. As such, the chances are that you won't be ever be too far from help. A first-aid kit, a roll of duct tape and some cable ties will probably get you through most incidents long enough that you can pedal to safety or call for help.

'Avoid flat land! Much better to work hard, be stimulated and rewarded with descents than not.'
– Alistair Pearson, @alistairpearson

Difficulties

Cycling all day and up big hills

Most people could pedal a bike for a few hours. And, if push came to shove, they could probably do the same again the next day. Well, cycling around the world is really no different from that. You keep pedalling until you need a rest then get going again once you have done so. Cycling of this sort is a low impact, low intensity exercise. That means that even an unconditioned pair of legs can adapt to a life of constant pedalling, getting stronger each day.

The second most common apprehension is probably hills. There is no reason to assume that hills in other countries are steeper than the ones in your local town. And, even if they are steeper and longer than anything you have seen before, and even if your legs haven't been conditioned sufficiently by the time you reach them, you can always push. If the world's steepest street in Dunedin, New Zealand, has people cycling up it every day then the rest of the planet's roads must be achievable.

'Don't take yourself too seriously and just keep at it. Every uphill is followed by a downhill!'
– Jolandie Rust, @JolandieRust

The steepest streets in the world
by Tim Moss

Hills are interesting things. When I say that I cycled a thousand miles through Scandinavia, it probably sounds a lot tougher than riding through Essex. But in three weeks' cycling through Norway, Finland and Sweden, I didn't come across a single hill that was steep enough to make me use the lowest gear on my bike.

In contrast, however, five minutes after cycling away from Stansted airport back in the UK on my way home, I hit the steepest hill of the whole trip, quickly dropped to first gear and spun the pedals furiously to get to the top.

Suffering from saddle soreness

It is almost inevitable that your bum will hurt at some point if you cycle long distances. There are a few steps you can take to help ensure it is not too uncomfortable but it is probably not worth worrying about too much. It is unlikely ever to be excruciating, has probably never been responsible for a failed round-the-world ride and it tends to be something that improves over time.

- Shorts: Lycra, Spandex and other similar tight-fitting garments are common for cycling as they reduce rubbing. Padded shorts, too, are often used. However, they are certainly not necessary for avoiding discomfort and you might not want to wear synthetic fabrics next to your skin for an extended period. You are best advised to test out different underwear and legwear combinations before setting off but focus most of your attention on your saddle.
- Saddle: Big squishy saddles are not usually appropriate for longer journeys as there is more to rub against and the very small, hard ones used on racing bikes tend to be a little harsh. Something in between the two is likely what you are after. Many tourers swear by Brooks saddles – old fashioned looking leather seats with spring suspension. These latter types in particular can take time to break-in for comfort. You can also improve your riding experience by playing

with the tilt of the saddle, moving it back and forward a little on the seat-post, and adjusting its height relative to the handlebars.

• Vaseline: Use this for emergencies.

Getting flat tyres

You would be a very lucky person indeed if you made it around the world without a single puncture but the method for replacing or repairing them is easily learned and the whole process will only take a couple of minutes once you have practised on half a dozen. Repair kits and inner tubes cost a few pounds each and step-by-step instructions are easily found online. Good, puncture-resistant tyres (e.g. kevlar lined) can make a big difference too.

Falling off your bike

Any time you ride a bike, there is a risk that you could crash. This may be increased by many factors on a long tour: a heavily laden bike, erratic driving styles, cycling when exhausted, long mountain descents and worn out bicycle parts to name but a few. It is unlikely, however, that these things will make the danger unacceptable or even what might broadly be considered 'high'.

If you find yourself in such a situation – e.g. cycling late in the dark on a windy track with reckless road users – then you can always just walk for a bit, look for another route or set up camp for the night.

Wearing a helmet and gloves will give you some protection should you fall.

Obtaining visas

Getting visas can be a pain when the information is confusing: they take time to process and you have to keep paying for them. However, obtaining them is possible for most countries with a little bit of research and patience.

Try the following:

1. Check the FCO website for travel advice.

2. Find the website for the embassy of the country you want to visit. Most will have instructions and forms to download.

3. If it is not clear from the embassy, try searching travel and ex-pat forums online.

4. Alternatively, it is often possible to pay a company to help. You can buy the 'invitations' that some countries require and have them do all your paperwork for a fee.

Transporting your bike

Whatever route you take, you are likely to cross a substantial body of water at some point and a plane journey is often the easiest way of dealing with that. Most airlines have a system for handling sporting goods including bikes. You normally just pay a little extra.

To package your bike for travel, your options are:

- Buying a purpose-built bag or box. This offers good protection but they are too big to carry with you on your bike afterwards.
- Carry a thin plastic cover bag that fits in your panniers and pad your bike with whatever disposable materials you can find.
- Find a local bike shop and ask for an old cardboard box from their last delivery. You can pack it out with other bits of kit or ask if they can throw in some bubble-wrap.

To fit your bike into a box and onto a plane, you may need to do some or all of the following:

- Remove the pedals. This requires a narrow spanner or large Allen key (usually bigger than the one you have on your **multi-tool**) depending on the bike. Also, remember that the left-hand pedal unscrews in the opposite direction from normal – turn it clockwise to loosen.
- Remove the front and/or back wheels. You will need a spanner if they don't have quick-release latches.
- Remove or adjust the handlebars by loosening the nuts with Allen keys.

- Remove or adjust any lights, bells or computers to stop them getting damaged.
- Deflate the tyres to stop them bursting at altitude.

Kit

'Pack less! Whatever you think you might need, you don't.'
— Kelsey Wiens, @Bella_Velo

Buying a bike

There are innumerable books and websites that discuss the pros and cons of every last part of a bicycle. But most of it is really not that important. Take any bicycle that is reasonably comfortable, can carry the necessary kit and is not about to fall apart and you are pretty much there. A second-hand mountain bike with a rack bought on eBay, for example, could well be fine.

Here are some basic elements to look for in a touring bike:

- Comfort. Comfort comes from an appropriate riding position. That usually means not being hunched over on a small bike designed for racing or sitting bolt-upright on a bike built for cruising around town. You can work out what size frame you need online using your height and leg length then try it out for size in a shop.
- Strength. You need a bike that can take the weight of you with all of your kit. The weaker they are, the higher the chance of parts breaking as you rack up miles and go over potholes. Check your bike can be fitted with a rack too, front and back ideally.
- Gears. Most people will want a good range of gears (27 is usually the maximum) and particularly the low ones to get them up big hills. Hub gears keep all the mechanics hidden inside the wheel removing the need for maintenance. However, they are very expensive and, if something does go wrong then there is not much chance of getting

it fixed locally. In contrast, the more common external gears are open to the elements but intuitively repaired.

- Made of steel. Bikes are typically made from steel, aluminium, carbon or titanium. Carbon is fragile so not great for touring. Titanium is strong and light but expensive and rarely used in touring bikes. Between aluminium and steel there is much debate about weight, strength and ride quality. Either would be absolutely fine. Aluminium's usually a bit lighter but, probably more important for a tourer, steel is far easier to weld making emergency repairs much easier while travelling.

- Extras. Other useful features include mudguards to help deal with inclement weather, space for two or more **bottle cages** (carriers for your water bottle), and handlebars that offer a variety of riding positions to help with comfort while riding over long periods.

Unless you are a bike mechanic and perhaps even if you are, it pays to keep things simple. Complicated parts mean complicated repairs and you won't always be near a well stocked bike repair shop.

Which bike is best?
Different bikes will suit different people in different situations but some broad rules apply. Below are some general attributes of different types of bike.

Road bikes
Lightweight bikes with thin tyres designed for travelling fast on roads.

- Fast and lightweight.
- Least comfortable for long distance.
- Thin, light frames not designed to take extra weight.
- Not great off tarmac.

Good for shorter or faster tours in well developed countries. Not generally ideal for round the world.

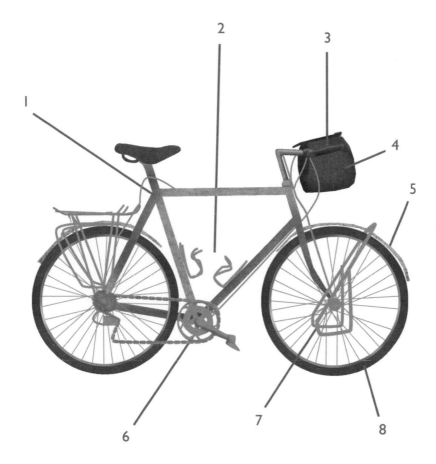

1. Steel frame for easy repairs in less developed areas.
2. Space for two or more bottle cages.
3. Handlebars that allow different riding positions for comfort.
4. Handlebar bag for access whilst cycling, and a map case mounted on top.
5. Mudguards for inevitable wet weather.
6. Low gears for steep hills.
7. Front and back rack.
8. Tyres wide enough to take weight and grip on the occasional dirt track,
   but slick enough for efficiency on roads.

Fig. 5: Ideal touring bike

Mountain bikes
Originally conceived for off-road riding with fat tyres but now
ubiquitous and often used on tarmac with thin tyres.

- Large second-hand market.
- Tough frames.
- Can't always take front and back racks.

Good option for building your own and a cheaper alternative to a
purpose-built touring bike.

Hybrid / Touring bike
A hybrid is broadly any bike that is not an out-and-out road or
mountain bike. Touring bikes are those designed specifically with long-
distance cycling in mind.

- Most comfortable riding position.
- Long wheel base (gap between front and back wheel) for maximum
  stability.
- Often come fitted with mud guards, two or three bottle cages, and
  racks.
- Handlebars often offer variety of riding positions.

> **1,000 miles in a rickshaw**
> by Tim Moss
>
> I hold the world record for the longest distance cycled in a
> rickshaw: 1,000 miles. I spent a month pedalling one around the
> UK from Scotland back to London. It is an obscure record and one
> that could easily be beaten by anyone who put their mind to it but
> my experience taught me a few things about cycle touring.
>
> The most important lesson was that even the heaviest of bikes can
> get up steep hills. I have no idea how much my rickshaw weighed
> but I would guess it was about as much as me. And that was before

I had any of my kit on it, let alone passengers. I wouldn't exactly race up hills – people would effortlessly walk past me – but I never had to get off and push, even up a three-mile hill in the Highlands.

Rack for mounting panniers

Even if you opt for a trailer, there is a good chance you will still have a rack. You can get them for the front as well as the back. Not all bikes are set up to take a rack so check before you buy – it is easiest if you have mounts on the frame (small attachments for screws).

The key attribute in a rack is strength.

Panniers, trailers and other kit carriers

The main options for carrying your equipment are panniers or a trailer. Trying to carry it all in a backpack is unnecessarily uncomfortable compared with letting your bike take the burden.

Panniers: These are bags that clip onto your rack and hang either side of your wheels. Two at the back and, if you need them, two more at the front. They are the most common method of carrying kit on a bike. Look for:

- Robustness. You don't want clips breaking or material tearing, you just want something you don't have to worry about it each time you lug your bike over a fence or go over a pothole.
- Waterproofing. If you can afford it, waterproof panniers with a roll-top closure (one that folds over several times to ensure it is watertight) are good. Waterproof dry-bags or even bin liners will suffice if not.
- Saddle bags. An even cheaper alternative are old-fashioned canvas saddle bags that sit over the rack.

Trailer: An alternative to panniers is a trailer attached to the back of your bike. On the plus side:

- they offer more storage;
- they take the load off your bike.

On the downside:

- it's another large and heavy piece of kit to move around;
- they are more expensive than panniers;
- it is another thing that may need repairing.

Extra storage options
In addition to panniers and/or a trailer, you might also take:

- Bar bag: A small bag that attaches to your handlebars. It is highly recommended for access to your map, snacks and camera whilst cycling. Baskets are a more basic alternative.
- Bungees: If you take some bungee cords then you can strap things on top of your rack between the two panniers. This is handy for a single large item like a sleeping bag or tent, or to accommodate overflow.
- Saddle bag: A tiny bag that fits underneath your saddle. Not strictly necessary when you have so many other bags available but many cyclists keep their repair kit in one.

'Don't mention the P word! Every time we said "puncture" we'd be stopping in five miles with a burst tyre.'
– Bryn Davies, @BrynATmag

Spares and repairs
by Rob Thomson

Rob Thomson cycled 12,000km from Japan to the UK on a **recumbent** bicycle and although he decided to return to Japan by skateboard – he holds the record for the longest such journey – he is still an avid cyclist. Here he shares his advice on bicycle maintenance for a long tour.

'I know of at least one around-the-world cyclist who "breaks out in a cold sweat at the thought of having to fix a puncture" (his words). The moral of that and other mechanically disinclined cyclists is that you don't need to be a bike mechanic to successfully bike around the world. That said, some spares and skills might be the difference between being able to manage a road-side repair (yes, you are amazing), or having to hitch a ride to the nearest town or city, where there's bound to be a bike shop (a great opportunity to interact with the locals, which is equally fantastic).

Bare minimum spares to take

Lube for a squeaky chain.

Puncture repair kit, tyre levers and pump, for the all-important puncture repair.

Multi-tool *which fits all the bolts and nuts on your bike.*

*A variety of **hose clamps**, cable ties, and gaffa tape. These items will afford a temporary fix for most issues such as a broken rack, ripped pannier or wayward bottle cage.*

Simple skills to learn

Bicycle cleaning – Knowing how to effectively clean the moving parts of your bike can vastly improve its life-span.

Tyre puncture repair – Believe it or not, though, there exist around-the-world cyclists who don't know how.

Brake pad adjustment – A month of cycling through Denmark and the Netherlands can deceive you into thinking your brakes are just fine, until you hit the Swiss Alps.

And some useful extras

While it's generally bombproof, a bike chain will gradually wear out, and

> breakages may occur. Carry a few extra links of chain (to replace the mangled bits), a **master link** (a magic chain link that can be attached/detached by hand), and a chain-breaker tool (very often found on bicycle multi-tools).
>
> Also useful would be a cassette tool, **chain whip**, and spanner. A **cassette** refers to the stack of cogs on the back wheel of a bike, and very occasionally, the chain can derail from the biggest cog and get hopelessly lodged between the cassette and the spokes. If this happens, a cyclist is going nowhere fast. Using a chain whip to lock the cassette in place, the cassette tool can be used to screw the cassette off the wheel, thus freeing the chain (and, if you're really smart you can then fix any broken spokes). This process is easy once you know how, so give it a go at home before you leave.'
>
> Read more about Rob's adventures at: www.14degrees.org.

Equipment for camping

If you are planning to camp – and you surely are – then you are going to need a few bits of kit: tent, sleeping bag, mattress, stove and so forth. There are not many camping equipment requirements peculiar to the cycle tourist other than wanting a reasonable degree of comfort given the duration of your trip – saving a hundred grams on a sleeping bag only to shiver every night is probably not productive – keeping weight down where possible and ensuring it is small enough to fit in your bags.

- Stove: you will probably want a **multi-fuel** variety that can burn petrol. That means you can refill at fuel pumps which you will find the world over. This is far easier than having to hunt for methylated spirits or gas canisters which are not readily available in many countries.
- Shelter: Alternatives to tents such as tarpaulins, bivvy bags and hammocks tend to be lighter and all have their place. However, they don't offer as much protection from the elements which may be wearing on such a long trip.

And don't forget to pack ...

- a bicycle computer (or **odometer**) to measure how far and fast you are going;
- a map of the world or inflatable globe to show people where you've come from and where you're going;
- a bell for warning stray pedestrians and a horn for entertaining kids;
- a large collapsible water bladder to fill up before dry spells or a night's camp;
- a flannel for when showers and bodies of water aren't available;
- lights for when you inevitably get caught out after dark and reflective gear if your bike and panniers don't already have enough;
- a helmet.

Advice from a Record Breaker – Julian Sayarer

Circumnavigation completed June 2010 in 169 days.

Under the bold title of 'This Is Not For Charity', London cycle-courier Julian set a new unofficial record less than a year after James Bowthorpe's circumnavigation. He argued that cycling is a step in the right direction for improving modern society.

See: www.thisisnotforcharity.com.

'Make sure you fall seriously in love with the prospect of the ride, and so long as that's taken care of then everything else is just common sense and will just fit into place. Diet, mechanics, foreign cultures, baggage, navigation … none of it is at all problematic once riding becomes daily reality rather than far-off undertaking that would seem to require careful planning.

Other basic points, less idealised and more pragmatic:

Have a decent bike, not fancy, but solid. Riding against a heap of junk isn't the way to fall in love with riding as a mode of transport. Pack less luggage than you think you need. All of the things that you scratch your head about whether or not to take, once on the road, it transpires that you didn't need them after all. And don't take much money… the more comfort and plenty you can afford, the less interesting your trip becomes, and the more it stops you appreciating simple things as they truly should be appreciated.'

A Day in the Life of a Round-the-World Cyclist
by Alastair Humphreys

Alastair spent four years cycling 46,000 miles around the world. He funded the trip with £7,000's worth of accumulated student loans. Since then he has walked across India, completed a crossing of Iceland using inflatable rafts, and run the Marathon des Sables. He is now a full-time adventurer and author, and has written five books about his experiences.

'A day in the life of a long distance cyclist. Or should that be a life in the day of a long distance cyclist? For once you embark on a long journey time and distance all warp rather weirdly. A ten-mile climb up a mountain pass may take an eternity to complete, the camp at day's end and respite from a gale seems to arrive with glacial slowness, and yet in the blink of an eye you realise you have been on the road for a month already, you're thousands of miles into the experience, and you're rightly feeling smug, competent and proud.

So you've made the decision to undertake a long cycling expedition: what can you expect from a typical day on the road? Although the thrill of a big bike trip is the freedom to be spontaneous and do whatever the day inspires you to do, and although you will have odd and memorable and frustrating distractions galore (the memories that will live with you forever), most days on the road are founded on a framework of routine so rigid it will make the life of a commuting accountant appear wildly bohemian. All long distance cyclists will feel comfortable with their own specific routine (a point worth noting for those not planning solo journeys). Here is mine.

Whilst I would not set a morning alarm (indeed I never even wore a watch), I did rise early. I enjoyed the cool, peaceful dawns, the feeling of having the world to myself for a short while, and I was also quite a mile-hungry cyclist unlike some.

So I'd normally be up at first light. As I would have been asleep since dusk this early start was not a painful one. What happened next depended on the climate. If it was cold I'd pack my tent, stuff a couple of things into my panniers (I always tidied most things away the night before – a relic perhaps of a brief military phase), jump on my bike and ride hard to warm myself up. Once warm I'd stop for food. In warmer places I would be more relaxed. I'd pack, eat a banana or a jam sandwich, and then get riding. I used to brush my teeth as I pedalled: I read once you're meant to brush your teeth for two minutes. Only on the road do I ever have patience to make it through the full two minutes. Plus two minutes concentrating on brushing is two minutes not having to think about something to think about!

For the rest of the day my routine was pretty standard. I'd ride for an hour or two then stop, relax for a few minutes and eat, then ride again. Repeat until sunset ...

My round the world ride was not a race. If I saw something interesting I would stop to investigate. If I met someone nice I would stop and chat (I tried to say hello or wave to every single person to pass the time) and perhaps accept an invitation for tea or lunch in their home. If I saw a river I would swim. If I saw a shop or a petrol station I would stock up on food and water.

And that's about it. It's not a complex life. I would daydream a lot, plan logistics, dream of girls and food and football. I'd calculate miles and speed and average speeds and ETAs over and over. I sang songs and learned poems. I listened to music and shouted at the wind or idiot drivers. I mooed at cows (in all languages), waved at children, practised riding with no hands. I daydreamed of home and wished I was anywhere but "here". I looked around and felt privileged to be out "there".

As the sun slowly sank across the sky I would start looking for somewhere to sleep. This was almost always wild camping or serendipitous invitations into strangers' homes. When wild camping I would start looking for a good spot about an hour before nightfall. The art of wild camping is essential for long distance riders. It's fun, liberating and free. Ideally you find a spot out of sight of the road, away from houses, with a bit of flat land. If you're lucky there may be grass. If you're really lucky there's water – a lake or river to wash in, and there is always a sunset to enjoy and stars to stare at as you gobble down a filling pan of pasta, write your diary by the light of your headtorch, read a couple of pages of your book to generate tomorrow's toilet paper, and then you're falling asleep. And before you know it the dawn is breaking and you get to do it all again. Repeat a few hundred or a few thousand times and you'll have made it round the world ...'

Read more and buy Alastair's books from:
www.alastairhumphreys.com.

'Talk about your experiences to inspire the rest of us.'
– James Borrell, @James_Borrell

So, You Want to Make a Movie?

Tom Allen spent three and a half years filming himself cycling around the world. After his return to the UK, his footage was turned into the feature length film 'Janapar'. Here he shares some advice on filmmaking on expedition.

'It is very easy to film an expedition nowadays as the equipment required to do so is cheap and accessible. What takes more effort, however, is making your footage more than just something to show your friends and family.

Filming an expedition is a full-time job, and requires a huge level of commitment. More than any other medium, the end result of a filmmaking project belies the sheer breadth of planning, labour and expertise behind it. There are a few critical pieces of knowledge which will dramatically increase an expedition film's chances of success. Here are the most important:

1. At its core, a successful film is a good story well told. This has nothing to do with stunning visuals or fancy cameras. If you take one piece of advice, make it this one.

2. Every piece of storytelling advice for writers is equally applicable to filmmakers. Work out what the story is – or at least, what the story's beginning is – before you leave. Follow it through its twists and turns until the end. And be prepared for the story to change.

3. Especially in this relatively eccentric field, a story will be driven by its characters. Make sure you explore the psyche of the expeditioners. Anticipate that one character will probably emerge dominant.

4. An audience won't care about what the characters see or do until they're emotionally invested in their hopes and fears and can empathise with them. Cover this early in an expedition, or before it begins.

5. Audiences have incredibly sensitive bullshit detectors. Any character who plays to the camera or attempts to be the "TV presenter" will inevitably come across as unnatural and false. Finding the true voice is easy for some, but difficult for most. Practise. A lot.

6. Self-shooting a solo expedition means that you'll have to bear all of this in mind as well as spending most of your time setting up tripod shots and pointing the camera at yourself. In a team, one (diplomatic) member should assume a directorial role to ensure consistency and completeness.

7. Stories can be broken into sub-stories. During shooting, focus on capturing one complete sub-story at a time. Later, review what you have, and consider how these sub-stories fit into the bigger picture.

8. No good film was ever shot chronologically. Remember that you're shooting for an editor. For each sub-story, establish the dilemma or challenge. Capture the action and the story's resolution. Get your characters' immediate responses to what happened. Then go back and shoot the cutaways, establishing shots and general views.

9. Your equipment is important, but nowhere near as much as the content of your film. It's a tired cliché, but consider why the Blair Witch Project was so successful. It had nothing to do with cameras or budget, and everything to do with story.'

Find out more at: www.janapar.com

Costs

'Sell your telly and set a date. You don't need fancy kit.'
– Fearghal O'Nuallain, @Revolution_Ferg

With accommodation (tent), transport (bike) and cooking facilities (camping stove) all carried with you, costs for a bicycle journey can be kept very low.

- Bike: £200–£2,000+. Purpose-built touring bikes start from around £400 new and go as high as your credit card limit will allow. You could get a second-hand mountain bike for less.
- Panniers, clothing and camping kit: £200–£3000+. Huge scope.

- You could buy all of your equipment new and get higher end stuff – waterproof panniers, cycling-specific clothes, lightweight tent and so forth – and see a couple of thousand pounds disappear. Or you could do it as cheaply as possible by holding out for eBay bargains, using an old pair of shorts and some t-shirts from the cupboard, picking up an own-brand tent and borrowing from friends.
- Living costs: £5–£20+ a day. You can control how much your daily expenses are. Apart from the occasional hostel or campsite, food will be the main expenditure. If you are willing to cycle an extra ten miles for a cheaper lunch and are happy to pitch your tent in the pouring rain instead of pay for a hostel then costs can be very low.
- Extras: In addition to the above, you should budget for some combination of transportation, visas, insurance and some maintenance for the bike.

Lowest total cost – £2,500
Make do with cheap kit, live frugally and avoid long-haul flights.

More typical total cost – £10,000
Buy better equipment, splash out on a few hotels and take a couple of flights.

Training

Getting cycling fit
You don't need to be fit enough to cycle around the world when you set off. You just need to be able to cycle. You can build fitness over time. That said, you could make your life easier by spending plenty of time on a bicycle before you depart.

The more cycling you can do, the better. That can be on a commute, with a club on the weekends or whenever you can fit in a short tour. As well as getting you stronger for hills and long days, it should

Table of round-the-world cyclists' costs

Name	Duration	Route	Cost	Notes from the rider
Mark Beaumont – www.markbeaumontonline.com	6 months	Across Europe, India, Australasia and North America in pursuit of the world record.	£25,000	'I don't think that is a good guide as I had a lot of costs that most wouldn't as I went for the record and filmed a doc for the BBC.'
Julian Sayarer – www.thisisnotforcharity.com	6 months	From Europe to Shanghai, up New Zealand and across North America in an attempt to break the world record.	£3,000 on the road. plus £2,000 on flights.	'This was more than necessary because time constraints meant I was paying other people to cook for me but it could definitely be done for comfortably less.'
Peter Gostelow – www.petergostelow.com	3 years	From Japan, through South East Asia, Middle East, North Africa and Europe.	£6,000–£6,500	'Don't use this figure or anyone else's as a benchmark. The beauty of cycle touring is that it offers you flexibility. Once you're set up it's you who makes the decisions according to your budget.'
Friedel and Andrew Grant – www.travellingtwo.com	3 years	From Canada, through Europe, Middle East, South East Asia, Australasia and back to North America.	$25,216 each for everything including transport, gear, insurance, medical and visas.	Complete and detailed breakdown of all their costs available on their website.
Matt Bridgestock – www.55northarchitecture.com	1 year	Across Eurasia, up half of South America and across the USA.	£12,000 including new bike, kit, flights, visas.	'The usual answer I give is: everything, you will cash in all your favours, sell all your old stuff and eke out all your savings! I still think it was cheaper than staying in the UK!'
Alastair Humphreys – www.alastairhumphreys.com	4 years	Length of Africa, Americas and Eurasia working on the premise that less money spent meant more time on the road.	£7,000	'I saved my loans through university and left home with about £7,000. This easily lasted more than four years. A diet of bread and bananas, sleeping rough, and focused, disciplined ascetism mean you can travel most of the world very cheaply.'
Fearghal O'Nuallain – www.revolutioncycle.ie	1.5 years	Across Eurasia and South America.	€ 7,000 each including flights. € 5,000's worth of high-end kit donated by sponsors.	'I could have comfortably done the whole thing - kit, camping, bike, flights - for € 7k. Having sponsors gave us more cash but imposed constraints and tied us into certain itineraries.'
Rob Thomson – www.14degrees.org	2.5 years	From Japan through China, Central Asia and Europe to the UK. Return journey by skateboard.	£11,000 on the road. £3,000 on kit.	'If we're just talking monetary costs, it is extremely expensive if we add in lost income. Something not insignificant. Of course, I consider it worth the sacrifice.'
Dorothee Fleck	2.5 years	Across Eurasia, Australia and South America.	€ 15,000	'What do you need money for, if you travel on a bike with a tent?'

also make you less prone to strains and injuries on the way and condition your bottom to life in the saddle.

Learning some basic mechanics

Teaching yourself some simple skills for looking after and fixing your bike on the road will be time well spent. You could:

- Attend a maintenance course. Try a local shop or club, the Cyclists' Touring Club (CTC) or Cycle Training UK.
- Use online tutorials. Instructional videos are easily found for most aspects of tinkering with your bike. Just search for the key words (e.g. 'bicycle puncture repair' or 'fix broken chain'). Sheldon Brown's website has good tutorials too.
- Do it yourself. Buy a cheap second-hand bike, take it to pieces and put it back together again.

Join a club or enter some events

You could consider joining a cycling club. It can be a good place to learn from more experienced people and motivate you to get outside more. CTC and British Cycling have regional lists.

Another option is to enter an event or two, such as:

- A large organised rally like the London-to-Brighton and frequent London-to-Paris rides.
- The regular and very cheap weekend **sportive** rides run by Audax.
- Signing up for races. They are not always competitive. British Cycling has an event calendar.

First Steps

1. Get a bike, any bike, and start riding it everywhere you can.
2. Test yourself and see how far you can ride in a day. Aim high. You can always catch a train back.

3. Plan a trip. Fly overseas or start from your front door. Do it in a weekend or take a month off work. The details don't matter, just give yourself a taste of life on the road.

4. If you are left hungry for more then you can start planning the big one. Work out a route you would like to follow, start accumulating the gear, apply for some visas if you want and set a date.

You could plan and prepare for months and years for a trip like this and still not be 100% ready. But even if you set off tomorrow with no preparation whatsoever, you would probably pick it up as you went.

> *'Enjoy it! Don't lose your calmness.*
> *Somehow it always goes on.'*
> – Dorothee Fleck, @DoroFleck

Easier, Harder, Different

- Use a different type of bike – single speed, recumbent, tandem, rickshaw, penny-farthing or similar.
- Forget about getting around the world and just plan a route that interests you.
- Take a mountain bike and get off-road.
- Complete the journey entirely on the earth's surface (i.e. no flights).
- Complete the journey entirely by natural power (e.g. sailing across the oceans).
- Complete the journey entirely by human power by rowing, pedalling or swimming across the necessary water bodies. Jason Lewis, Colin Angus and Erden Eruç have completed such trips.
- Do it in stages. For example, cycling through Europe one holiday, across Kazakhstan the next, head to China after that and keep going.
- Skateboard instead. 'Longboards' are much easier to ride than the ones typically used for tricks, you can still cover reasonable distances

each day and, if you carry your kit in a rucksack then you are much more mobile than a fully laden cyclist.

Resources

- Adventure Cycling Association – American association with useful PDF downloads on touring – see: www.adventurecycling.org.
- *Adventure Cycle Touring Handbook* by Stephen Lord – Practical advice and route planning for cycling in the developing world.
- Adventure Cycling Guide – Simple website with useful expedition touring advice – see: www.adventure-cycling.co.uk.
- Audax – Long-distance cycling association who run regular and cheap sportives across the country – see: www.aukweb.net.
- British Cycling – Lists events and local clubs – see: www.britishcycling.org.uk.
- CTC – The Cyclists' Touring Club is a membership organisation offering advice, events, insurance and maps – see: www.ctc.org.uk.
- Sheldon Brown's website – Great down-to-earth explanations of many technical bike-related matters – see: www.sheldonbrown.com.
- The Travelling Two – Information from cycle touring and camping basics to country-by-country resources and kit advice and reviews – see: www.travellingtwo.com.

How to
Sail the Seven Seas

'Keep the rig up and the water out!
And, just go ...'
– David Nicelys, www.mylifeafloat.com[1]

---

[1] Tips in this chapter come from online sailing forums. I posted a question asking for advice or a piece of equipment or resource users would recommend. They are acknowledged by their username, website and/or the name of their boat.

Setting the Scene

To sail the Seven Seas is to explore the world's great waters by wind power alone. Be it an organised rally, a gruelling high-speed yacht race, volunteering your hands on deck in exchange for discounted passage or simply cruising at your own pace from port to port, the oceans are as ripe for adventure today as they were in centuries past.

Statistics

USP:	Travelling the world by wind power.
Difficulty:	Easy to difficult.
Cost:	£25,000–£120,000+.
Hurdles:	Learning to sail, getting a boat, avoiding storms.
Purest style:	Independent ocean cruising in a small yacht.
Who's done it?:	Tens of thousands of ocean crossings.
Glory potential:	Moderate.

Background

Seafaring is an old tradition. It may have started with canoes and paddles but there are records of boats with sails in the Arab empires from as far back as several hundred, if it not a thousand, years BC.

In the first millennium, Polynesians relied on sailing for transporting people between islands. The North Europeans did the same using boats with a single square sail alongside a large set of oars, while the Chinese relied on large junk ships with multiple masts. Meanwhile, the Indians joined the Arabs in exploring the Indian Ocean and Persian Gulf using dhows with triangular sails which were more efficient for sailing upwind.

Not long into the second millennium, the magnetic compass was invented and sailing expanded significantly. The Europeans – largely

France, Britain, Spain and the Netherlands – led the way with trading, exploration and colonisation.

Then, sometime around the 17th century, the richer members of society began to embrace sailing as a pastime for pleasure and recreational sailing has grown ever since. And whilst technological advances have made many aspects of sailing easier – most notably communications equipment and GPS navigation – when far out at sea in a small, floating vessel with sails, much of the experience remains the same.

In the world of adventurous sailing, a few names will always stand out, including:

- Joshua Slocum – who completed the first solo circumnavigation of the globe over a period of three years, returning to North America in 1988 and subsequently writing the classic travel book *Sailing Alone Around the World*.
- Robin Knox-Johnston – who won the Sunday Times Golden Globe Race in 1968 to become the first man to sail around the world solo and non-stop.
- Bernard Moitessier – who gave up half way through the Golden Globe Race to sail to Tahiti instead and whose many travels at sea are documented in a series of popular books.
- Ellen MacArthur – who broke the world record for sailing solo around the world in under 72 days.

There are many, many more notable sailors, of course, but what sets sailing apart from the other expeditions in this book is the fact that ordinary people undertake sailboat adventures every day.

There will always be those who push the boundaries in races and daring but for every one of them, there are a hundred more who will simply choose to cross the Atlantic in a sociable rally, take an extended holiday to sail to the Mediterranean or embrace the nomadic life of a **live-aboard**, indefinitely cruising from port to port.

Introduction – What are the Seven Seas?

This chapter will treat sailing the Seven Seas as anything that gets you across a sea or an ocean through your own skill, the power of the wind and the blessing of the Gods. That might mean a few weeks spent crossing a single, large body of water – like sailing across the Atlantic – or it could mean many months and years, cruising the world from port to far flung port.

Sailing is a popular sport and oceans are crossed all the time. It is unlikely that you will break any records or achieve a great expedition 'first' but the oceans are vast and the opportunities infinite. You do not need to follow set itineraries or stick to designated routes. You can travel as far and fast, or as little and slow as you like.

The beauty of sailing lies in the freedom to roam. Some 70% of the earth's surface is covered in water and the vast majority is just waiting to have your hull glide over it.

The actual term 'Seven Seas' may stem from Ancient and Medieval Europe and refer to the Mediterranean, Adriatic, Black, Red, Arabian and Caspian Seas, and the Persian Gulf. However, the phrase was used earlier in history in reference to a different collection of water bodies.

Modern variations have also been created to give a greater coverage of the globe, either by referring to the largest seven bodies of water or classifying the world's oceans such that there are seven of them. Others would argue that the phrase is really just used to indicate experience and skill in seafaring, or having crossed many of the world's large bodies of water, as in: 'Aye, he's certainly sailed the Seven Seas, alright'.

'My recommendations for sailing – or any other risky undertaking for that matter – can be summed up in one word ... PREPARE.'
– Izzy1414, AnythingSailing.com user

Options

Sail with a company

There are plenty of organisations that will get you out on the Seven Seas for a fee, from a short trip cruising down to the Mediterranean, to a crossing of the Atlantic.

Unless you are paying for real luxury, you will be mucking in with tasks and playing a hand in the voyage. Such a trip will be an experience in itself but also a good stepping stone on the way to setting out independently.

- A week's sailing – £500 to £1,500 for a week.
- Atlantic crossing – £1,500 and upwards.

Work on a tall ship

Tall ships are large, traditional sailing boat. They look a bit like the *Cutty Sark*. To mark the end of an era, the remaining 20 tall ships were brought together for a race. It was so popular, however, that the races have continued ever since and many new tall ships have been made.

These days, the ships are primarily used to train people in sailing, either during races or in sessions that take place between them. There is an emphasis on younger participation but there are still plenty of opportunities for all ages.

Here is an idea of some basic costs:

- single day outings – £100;
- multi-week trans-Atlantic voyages – £1,500.

There are various commercial operations offering trips but many of the courses are run by charities, including:

- Jubilee Sailing Trust;
- Tall Ships Youth Trust;
- Ocean Youth Trust.

Volunteer as a crew member

There are always ships that need to be sailed from one place to another but don't have enough crew. Sometimes it is just lending a hand on a weekend trip, other times you can help deliver a boat across an ocean. Opportunities exist for both those with experience and qualifications, and for complete novices.

The cost is usually just your own expenses (e.g. travel, insurance and kit) and perhaps a contribution to food and fuel.

Methods for finding crew positions include:

- crew-finding websites;
- cruising forums (both listed under 'Resources' below);
- asking around at a marina, particularly in busy areas like Panama or Las Palmas in the Canary Islands.

Crewing offers a fantastic opportunity for a cheap and easy entry to sailing. Be prepared for long waits though, particularly if you have a specific journey in mind. You should also bear in mind that you are not joining a commercial operation so it is your responsibility to determine the worthiness of boat and skipper.

Join a rally

Sailing rallies are large organised events, like a race but with a focus on the fun and the experience of crossing a large body of water rather than actually competing.

These are a few example rallies:

- Atlantic Rally for Cruisers (ARC) – Best known and biggest rally.
- World ARC – Same organisers for an around-the-world rally.
- Eastern Mediterranean Yacht Rally – From Turkey to Egypt, £350 per person.
- Sail Indonesia – Three-month annual tour departing Darwin, Australia. £350 per yacht.

The advantages of joining such an event are that most of the organisation is done for you and you get a degree of support and backup.

They require some experience – usually a certain number of miles' sailing rather than a string of qualifications – but less than you would need to go independently.

Enter the Clipper Round the World Yacht Race

The Clipper race is a somewhat unique event set up by the well-known sailor Sir Robin Knox-Johnston. Each yacht in the race has a fully trained skipper in charge but the rest of its crew is made up of amateurs.

Comprising several smaller races, the entire circumnavigation takes the best part of a year to complete. It is not cheap but training is included and you really can enter as a complete novice and sail right the way around the world.

- Individual stages – £8,000 upwards.
- Round the world – £40,000.

Ellen MacArthur

The name Ellen MacArthur is synonymous with round-the-world sailing.

MacArthur was only 24 years old when she came second in the Vendee Globe circumnavigation race. But it was a trip she undertook a few years later that really fixed her place in sailing history.

In November 2004, MacArthur departed Falmouth in a 75-foot trimaran on her own. After less than 72 days, without sleeping for more than 20 minutes at a time, she returned having sailed around the world. She beat the previous record by one day and eight hours.

MacArthur has now retired from competitive racing to run her charity: The Ellen MacArthur Foundation.

See: www.ellenmacarthurfoundation.org.

Independent cruising on your own schedule

The final option is to buy a boat and be your own captain. It is a big investment that requires a strong foundation of experience. However, once your sails are up – weather permitting – you can go wherever you want, whenever you want.

Boats can be fitted for several months at sea if need be. There are few stretches of water that would actually necessitate that length of solitude but Neptune's siren song may exert its lure.

There are many ways to wander the world's waves but independent cruising is the purest. As such, it is this approach that will be the focus of this chapter.

'Remember your camera and batteries ...
Those memories are so much more tangible
when you can see them!'
– Kate Tee, 'Aaza Dana'

The youngest solo sailor

Recent years have seen a spate of young sailors taking to the waves in an attempt to become the youngest person to complete a solo and unsupported circumnavigation. There are debates about which journeys were made entirely unsupported and those which were non-stop but the sailors include:

• Both 18, Australians Jesse Martin and David Dicks had only a few weeks' difference in their age when they finished their journeys around the world in the late 90s. Dicks was slightly younger but deemed to have received help fixing his rig thus not travelling fully unsupported.

• In July 2009, Zac Sunderland arrived home at the age of 17 after a one-year voyage on a boat he bought for $6,500.

• Although her route is not officially recognised, Jessica Watson completed her loop of the globe just three days before her 17th birthday.

• Finally, despite attempted intervention by the Dutch government to stop her departing, Dutch sailor Laura Dekker began her own attempt in August 2010 when she was just short of her 15th birthday. Completing the journey in stages, she needs to finish by September 2012 to claim the record.

The World Sailing Speed Record Council governing body does not recognise record attempts by those under 18 years old.

Practicalities

Where do you sleep?

The onboard accommodation will depend on the size of your vessel and how you rank amongst any crew on board. You could have anything from your own cabin with a proper bed that feels like a small hotel room, to a seat converted into a bunk in the main cabin, or a tiny berth best described as a coffin which allows little more than lying flat on your back.

Most beds will have a **lee cloth** to stop you falling out. They are typically large sheets attached to the open side of your bed which strap to the ceiling, effectively forming a wall.

What do you eat and drink?

The days of sea biscuits and scurvy are long gone. You need to give some consideration to space and shelf life on longer journeys but can otherwise follow a reasonably normal diet. You will have a stove for cooking.

Tinned, dried and packaged foods are normal. Most **cruising ships** will actually have some onboard refrigeration or even a freezer. They are nice perks but it is probably better not to be reliant upon them as power can run out. You could supplement your food with a fishing line too.

Typically, you will just take enough fresh water from shore as you anticipate needing on your journey. **De-salinators** for converting salt-water are a possible addition. They are often viewed by sailors with scepticism – just another gadget that can let you down – but they are routinely relied upon by ocean rowers. Collecting rainwater is also possible if you are prepared.

You can store your water in large tanks – they will require cleaning and you may want to install a filter to improve the taste – or you can rely on bottled water.

Where do you go to the loo?

Most boats these days will have some form of toilet (or **head** as they are known at sea). Bigger boats may have automatic loos that require fresh water and electricity but smaller ones tend to operate with a hand pump and salt water.

If you are close to shore then regulations may dictate that your **black water** be stored until some miles out to sea, otherwise it will be down to when common sense dictates it is okay. Peeing over the edge carries the risk of falling overboard.

Washing can be anything from a proper electric shower in a cubicle, to a solar shower heated by the sun, or a bucket of cold water and a sponge. If your water supply is limited then you may wash with salt water, drying off quickly afterwards to get rid of the salt. Soap does not lather well in salt water. Lots of liquid soap tends to do the job or you can buy special salt-water soap.

What do you do with your rubbish?

Rubbish on a cruising ship is important to manage. It will take up space and can smell and attract pests if you are not careful so minimise what you bring on board.

What you do with your waste will depend on where you are and what you are doing:

- Shorter journeys in first world areas – store your rubbish and take it to the next port to be disposed of responsibly.
- Longer voyages in less developed areas – storing becomes less practical. Some countries do not have good refuge management systems, however, and delivering your rubbish may put a strain on a community.

There is some debate about what is and is not acceptable to throw overboard. As a rule of thumb:

- Plastic – never throw overboard. It floats and does not decompose.
- Food waste – throw over once away from shore in deep water.
- Cans, glass bottles and paper – debatable. Once in very deep water, some will break items or fill them with water to ensure they sink. Others are against this on environmental grounds.

For whatever remains on board, wash it where necessary and squash it down as much as possible.

How long do you actually spend sailing?

Weather and crew permitting, a sailing boat will usually be moving 24 hours a day while at sea. This invariably means working in shifts which will vary depending on how many crew there are and where you are located:

- With a larger crew – you might be able to sleep a reasonable number of hours at a time with some degree of regularity.
- With a smaller crew – this might see you taking shifts of, say, two or four hours, on and off, around the clock.
- Solo out at sea – you might allow a few hours' sleep at a time and rely on your equipment to wake you if anything comes too close.
- Solo in a busy shipping channel – at times it will be necessary to navigate continually. In such situations, solo sailors might sleep in the **cockpit** for just a few minutes at a time. This is hard to sustain for long periods so unless you are trying to win a race, you would probably try to keep such crossings to a minimum and break them up with rests in port.

How do you know where to go?

Navigation these days is largely completed with GPS and **charts** (maps of the sea). On a day-to-day basis, you will typically just set a course and keep heading in that direction for several hours or even days at a time.

However, the route you follow from A to B is rarely a straight line. Instead, sailors usually go with the prevailing winds. This sometimes means going hundreds of miles out of your way but can still save time as the wind is on your side.

As such, many crossings have well-established routes and boats all tend to follow very similar paths. In less popular areas, however, you will have to research currents and winds, and talk to other sailors to work out the best route to follow.

'The traditional Pacific Islands navigators could sense which way their canoes were heading with their eyes shut, just by lying on the deck and sensing the movement of the swell. It is tricky, but one of the most fun ways to fill a quiet period, whilst simultaneously tuning to your surroundings.'
– Tristan Gooley, author of *The Natural Navigator*

Direction of prevailing winds
A simple rule of thumb for working out where prevailing winds – also called **trade winds** – blow, is that rotating areas of high-pressure tend to dominate the centre of each ocean in each hemisphere. They rotate clockwise in the north and anti-clockwise in the south. These drive the prevailing winds and currents in a reasonably predictable direction and thus dictate the most popular sailing routes.

How long will it take?
Sailing the Seven Seas is an open-ended endeavour. A cruiser will typically travel between 100 and 140 **nautical miles** in a day. This obviously drops with bad weather or no wind, and tends to be higher when following trade winds.

From this you can work out basic calculations of how long any

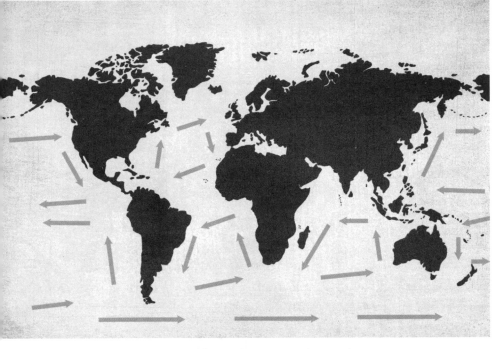

Map 5: World map showing prevailing winds

given passage might take. For journeys of more than a couple of weeks you will probably make stops, not only to re-supply but also for a break and, perhaps, to explore a new country.

1,000 days at sea

American sailor Reid Stowe set out to spend 1,000 days at sea without touching land or being re-supplied. Despite his girlfriend returning to land part way through the trip, a collision with a freighter, and an incident involving a US Navy firing range, Stowe returned to New York City in June 2010 having been aboard his boat for 1,152 days.

When to go

Most recreational cruisers will cross the major oceans outside of storm seasons. These are the times of year when **tropical cyclones** are most likely.

People do head out during storm seasons: the risks of getting caught in heavy weather are just higher. To do this, aside from needing confidence in your abilities and your boat, you will want to:

- monitor forecasts more closely than normal;
- study local patterns to know where the safest places tend to be;
- carry extra fuel so you can motor quickly away from an approaching storm.

Cyclone, hurricane and typhoon seasons

A tropical cyclone is a large area of low pressure containing lots of storms. It is called tropical because it forms at sea in the tropics and the cyclone part refers to its spinning – clockwise in the southern hemisphere and counter clockwise in the north.

They are given a variety of different names based on their location and intensity. The names for the severest types are given for different regions in the table below.

Region	Known as	Season	Notes
North Atlantic (including Caribbean and Gulf of Mexico)	Hurricane	1 June–30 November	
South Atlantic	Cyclone	None	Cyclones are rare
Eastern Pacific	Hurricane	1 June–30 November	
Central Pacific	Hurricane	1 June–30 November	
Western Pacific	Typhoon	All year	Most storms of any region, worst from June to November
North Indian	Cyclone	April–December (approximately)	
South Indian	Cyclone	November–April (approximately)	

What if things go wrong...?

It takes a lot to sink a ship. It is more likely that you will sustain damage such as a broken mast. If a boat does start taking water on board then you need to do everything you can to plug the leak.

In the case of a problem, your options include:

- **Jury rig** – doing whatever you can to create a makeshift sail from any spare or damaged parts you have on board to keep you moving.
- **Pan-pan** – signal given to indicate a problem but not one that is life threatening.
- **Mayday** – for a life-threatening scenario. This is put out by VHF, either manually or automatically with a feature known as DSC (Digital Selective Calling). You can also use an EPIRB.
- Life raft – always a last resort as even a heavily damaged boat tends to be more sea-worthy.

If you are close to a country with good rescue facilities then your signal may trigger a rescue by helicopter. Otherwise, it will be down to other boats to come to your rescue. On a popular route in the North Atlantic, that might happen within a few hours. Away from frequented areas and if you are less lucky, it could be several days or worse.

'I would simply reiterate that "one hand for the boat", "always tether on" and "maintain situational awareness", while clichés of cruising, are in fact commandments.'
– Marc Dacey, 'Alchemy', see: www.alchemy2009.blogspot.com

Difficulties

Suffering from sea sickness

As with altitude sickness in the mountains, there is no way of knowing in advance who will suffer from sea sickness. Just because you were fine on one boat with one type of motion, that does not mean that you will be fine on a different one.

It is not something to underestimate either. Sea sickness can be truly debilitating and the combination of losing water and not taking on food can easily become dangerous if ignored.

Preventions and cures are myriad but often include some combination of:

- staying in the middle of the boat which should rock less;
- fixing your eyes on the horizon;
- consuming ginger in the form of tea, beer, biscuits and other supplements;
- wearing wrist bands that act on pressure points;
- taking over-the-counter **antiemetic** drugs to treat motion sickness or more expensive prescription-only patches.

Getting caught in a storm
The threat with a storm is that:

- high winds and/or large waves catch you side-on and knock you over;
- you surf down a wave so fast that you bury your **bow** in the next one and **pitch pole** (cartwheel);
- wind and waves damage equipment on your boat.

Such situations are quite rare and you have a number of options to keep the risk to a minimum. Prevention is better than cure, of course, so the first way to deal with storms is to avoid them in the first place by:

- travelling outside of storm seasons;
- monitoring weather forecasts and patterns;
- asking about and researching local conditions.

If you still get caught then the question is how to get through it:

- Drop sails – It is hard for waves alone to topple a boat. High winds catching sails from the wrong direction is far more dangerous. As such, it is often prudent to leave up just enough sails to allow you to steer.
- Go with the flow – Even if it means travelling in the wrong direction, you are less likely to come to harm if you don't fight against the weather.
- Slow yourself down – This can be achieved with specially designed equipment or by dragging rope or similar off the back of the boat. This also helps minimise how far off course you go.

Names for scary things that can happen to a boat
- **Broach** – Excessive rolling to one side as a result of waves or wind.
- **Knockdown** – The boat being tipped onto its side such that the mast is horizontal to the water. Most boats should recover from this.
- **Capsizing** – Getting rolled over and upside down. A good monohull may recover from this but a catamaran will not.
- **Pitchpoling** – An end-over-end capsize like a cartwheel which usually results from surfing too fast down a wave.

Keeping calm in calms

Although battling a storm may be more dramatic, you are likely to spend a lot more time struggling against light winds in an attempt to keep the sails full.

Calms will make progress slow. They will also mean you have to spend more time navigating in an attempt to pick up the strongest breeze; especially since self-steering equipment doesn't function in really low winds.

If there is no wind at all then unless you have sufficiently short a distance that your engine will cover it, there is not a lot you can do besides sit back and wait.

Running your boat aground

There is a possibility of running aground any time you are close to land in an unfamiliar area or an area with poor charts. When calculating the best route for a safe passage, you can take account of all the usual variables, e.g. wind, depth, tide, but still get stuck.

If that happens the focus will be getting away swiftly without inflicting more damage on your boat. A careful reverse with the engine or rocking the boat may do the trick.

Collision with other boats and objects

There is always a risk of colliding with another boat or object while sailing.

The chances are lower while far out at sea than they are while navigating a busy shipping area but then you probably won't be quite as alert as a result.

Also, because storm seasons and prevailing winds conspire to put boats on similar routes at similar times, the chances of coming across another vessel in the middle of the Pacific are not as remote as you might think.

Possible collision risks include:

- huge container ships that can't see you or are not checking their equipment properly;
- floating debris;
- another lonely cruiser who has left their auto-pilot in charge;
- even a curious whale surfacing at the wrong moment.

Maintaining an around-the-clock watch is your basic protection against this. Additionally, monitoring your radar or setting it to sound an alarm if anything comes within a certain distance will help.

Hijack by pirates

They may have replaced cutlasses with automatic weapons but pirates are still a risk in the 21st century. They tend to cluster around certain areas and usually go for boats which they believe have valuable cargo or crew. Hopefully, and with all due respect, you won't have either.

Nonetheless, it would be prudent to read up on the areas you plan to visit. To get advice and the latest reports, visit: www.noonsite.com.

> ### Sailing alone around the world
>
> In the late 19th century, Canadian born Joshua Slocum found himself the proud owner of a dilapidated 37-foot wooden sailing boat named 'Spray'.
>
> After a few years restoring the boat, Slocum set sail from Boston. Navigating using a basic sextant, through choice, his voyage covered 46,000 miles over three years and made him the first person to circumnavigate the globe single-handed.
>
> Returning to North America, Slocum was able to live off the earnings of the book he wrote about the journey – *Sailing Alone Around the World*. He continued to spend most of his time living aboard 'Spray' until 1909 when Slocum went out to sea one final time. He was last seen heading for South America.

Kit – Choosing a Yacht

There are myriad different vessels that you could take onto the deep blue sea. Entire books, websites and heated debates have been dedicated to the subject. Explained below are just some of the common types and the basic features you might want to look for.

Types of boat

Type of boat	Description
Sailing dinghy	The smallest type of boats. Often used for learning to sail and short trips and races typically up to a few hours. Normally just one or two people on board, their weight and position is important for steering. Small enough to transport by trailer.
Other dinghies	The term 'dinghy' is also used for small inflatable, rowed and engine-powered boats. Small enough to be carried on board larger yachts and used to give easier access to land.
Yacht	General term for recreational sailing and power boats of a certain size, typically around 7m and upwards. This chapter focuses on the sailing variety. The term yacht includes the following types:
Racing yacht	Designed for speed by minimising weight and the surface area in contact with the water. Generally achieved at a cost to the comfort of the crew.
Day sailer or weekender yacht	A yacht at the smaller end of the spectrum (e.g. less than 10m) with a couple of berths and some storage, enough for making short trips up to a few days.
Cruising yacht	A boat designed for longer, slower journeys with more room for storage and sleeping. Cruising yachts designed for ocean crossings are usually known as offshore cruisers though are also called blue water boats or passage makers. This is the assumed boat type for this chapter.

1. *Mast.*
2. *Main sail.*
3. *Jib or headsail.*
4. **Boom**.
5. *Helm – steering mechanism and where you stand to control the boat.*
6. *Jackline – rope to clip onto in bad weather.*
7. *Motor – for marina entry and exit.*
8. *Keel – keeps boat from being blown sideways and provides ballast to avoid capsize.*
9. **Rudder** *for steering.*

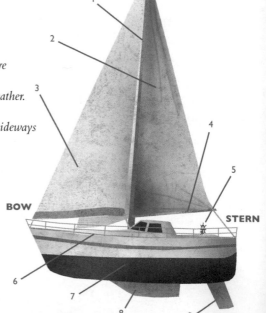

BOW STERN

Fig. 6: Typical sailing boat

Choosing between a catamaran and mono-hull

Catamarans have two separate parallel hulls connected in the middle by a bridge deck, and are the most common type of **multi-hull** boat. Mono hulls are the more traditional design of boat with, as the name implies, a single hull. Pros and cons of catamarans:

- They are generally faster (though perhaps less significantly so when cruising fully laden).
- They don't **heel** (rock from side-to-side) like a mono-hull and thus cause less sea-sickness and spilt coffee.
- They are harder to capsize but will not self-right when they do, which a good mono-hull can.
- Their width can make them harder to accommodate at a marina.
- They tend to be more expensive.

The cut of your jib

Different boats are propelled by different combinations of sails, masts and ropes known as **rigging**. Below is a brief overview of the masts and sails on some of the more common rigs.

- Sloop – One mast and two sails: a mainsail and a foresail (called a jib or genoa).
- Cutter – One mast and three sails: a mainsail and two foresails (called a staysail and jib).
- Ketch – Two masts and three or more sails. A taller forward 'main' mast and a shorter **aft** 'mizzen' mast. The forward mast has sails like a cutter and the aft sail is called the mizzen. The less common 'yawl' rig also has two masts and three sails.
- Schooner – Two or more masts: The aft 'main' mast is as tall or taller than the other(s). Various options for sails but typically four or more.
- Cat – One mast and two sails.

The position of the mast(s) on a hull also differs between rigs and it is sometimes possible to configure a given boat in a few different ways.

A boat's rigging will affect how easily it is controlled and its versatility in different conditions.

The sails can also be changed for different conditions. Sails such as spinnakers and gennakers can be used on any rig when winds are light, as can a storm sail during heavy weather.

Picking what your boat is made of

Boats come in a number of different materials including:

- Fibreglass: Tough, lasts a long time and can be easily repaired, fibreglass is often called GRP which stands for glass-reinforced plastic.
- Metal: Steel is the most common. This is the strongest option but heavy, particularly for smaller boats (e.g below 10m), and prone to rust. Aluminium is rarer but it is lighter and does not rust.
- Wood: Many boats are still made from the traditional seafaring material. It is cheaper initially although can be more time-consuming and expensive to maintain.

Selecting your boat's size

A boat's size is measured by its length. For two or three people on a fairly typical ocean crossing you will probably be looking at something between about 9 and 14m.

Bigger boats are better for:

- safety in avoiding being tossed around too much at sea;
- comfort;
- more storage space.

However, bigger is not always better:

- they cost more;
- they are harder and more expensive to maintain;
- they are harder to handle with a small crew which can make passages harder work or mean waiting around in port for extra crew.

> ## Across the Pacific on a wooden raft
>
> Norwegian Thor Heyerdahl believed that Polynesia was originally populated by travellers from the east, specifically South America, rather than from Asia as was widely thought. To demonstrate that this would have been possible, he travelled to Peru, built a raft from tree trunks and sailed it across the Pacific.
>
> Heyerdahl largely relied on tools and materials that would have been available at the time for the construction of the raft which was named 'Kon-Tiki' after the Inca Sun God. In 1947, he and five companions spent 101 days at sea sailing over 4,000 miles to French Polynesia.
>
> The book of the journey – *Kon-tiki*, written by Heyerdahl – has become a classic. A film has been made and several others have attempted to repeat the journey.

Kit – On Board Equipment

Motor for port entry and exit

It may come as a surprise to learn that sailing boats almost always have a motor. They are not designed for crossing oceans – that would require a lot of fuel – but they are very useful for entering and exiting ports, and over short distances when the wind disappears.

They are also very useful for generating power.

Power generating methods

Almost all cruisers will require power for some combination of the following:

- GPS and navigation equipment;
- radio and communication kit;
- radar and AIS;
- lights;
- refrigeration;
- de-salinator;
- electric shower, sound system and even air conditioning.

On shorter voyages, you can rely on a motor but it would be impractical to carry enough fuel on a long journey. Besides, it is better not to put all of your eggs in one basket. Other options include:

- Wind turbines – You usually get more wind in the higher latitudes.
- Solar panels – Tend to be better close to the equator.
- Towed turbines – Dragged in the water.

In theory you could simply add as many panels and batteries to power everything you need. However, the downsides of this are:

- Monitoring power levels of many gadgets can be hard work.
- The large batteries can take up space (they are similar to car batteries).
- It will make you heavier. The batteries can weigh 10 or 20kg each.
- It can be expensive.

As such, it is usually prudent to give some thought to what is actually necessary and when, and make decisions about your priorities. Perhaps foregoing a freezer to save power for your auto-pilot, or only playing music when batteries are full.

Equipment for navigation
To navigate at sea your boat will be equipped with some of the following:

- Charts – Maps of the sea; either on paper or computer, or both.
- GPS – It is very rare that anyone will go out to sea without at least one GPS.
- Chart plotter – Computerised navigation system that combines GPS with electronic charts. It can be used to plot and calculate complex routes, and some will interface with your radar and **Automatic Identification System**.
- Laptop – An alternative to a chart plotter is to hook up a GPS to a laptop.

- Compass – This is what you will use to maintain your course most of the time you are at the helm.
- Sextant – An understanding of celestial navigation and how to use a sextant is rarely necessary in an age of GPS but it can be a useful backup and give a deeper appreciation of where you are.

'You need backup navigation systems and information. Luckily new smartphones and tablets like the iPad can offer that extra level of certainty.'
– Hugh Moore, 'Shannon'

Self-steering wind vanes and auto-pilots

It is not normally necessary to spend your whole time steering a boat. Either through the use of mechanical **wind vane self-steering** or an electronic **auto-pilot**, you can set a course and stick to it in most decent conditions out at sea.

Auto-pilots are increasingly popular. Some pros and cons:

- They allow intricate route programming on a computer or chart plotter.
- They are often more efficient than a decent helmsman.
- They require power so are not always ideal for long cruises.
- They can remove you from the navigation process which some may find boring or disconcerting.

The mechanical wind vane option is simpler and just allows you to maintain a given angle to the wind:

- It can take longer to set up but out at sea, where winds tend to be more constant, it can keep your direction for long periods.
- They are hard to fit on catamarans because of the need to mount the wind vane in the centre of the boat at the back.

It is not uncommon to have both on a cruiser, using the electronic option for more complicated passages and where electricity is more readily available, and the mechanical option for longer passages.

Radios and phones for communication

Equipment for communicating at sea includes:

- **VHF (Very High Frequency) radio** – Like a more powerful walkie-talkie, they are used for talking to nearby ships and harbours. Their range at sea is typically around 20–50 miles. Should be carried by all vessels.
- **SSB (Single Side Band) Radio** – These units are a lot more expensive than VHF but allow you to communicate with boats many miles away. They can even be hooked up to a laptop for slow but free internet the world over. Variously referred to as 'amateur' and 'ham' radio, the technology is the same as High Frequency (HF) radio. You need a General Operators Certificate from the Royal Yachting Association (RYA) to operate one.
- **Satellite phone** – An addition for contacting the rest of the world although, unlike with radio, you have to pay for your calls. They can give coverage anywhere in the world.
- **EPIRB** – An emergency beacon that is a must at sea.

'A good system for wifi connection. Might include SSB radio, sat phone, remote antennae, internet stick.'
– AndrewB, YBW.com user

Radar and Automatic Information System (AIS) to avoid collisions

- Radar: This can both help you avoid collision and aid you when entering harbours in the dark. It usually features an alarm that will sound when anything comes within a certain range. They can also be used for spotting incoming **squalls**. They cost money, however, and are power hungry so are not always used.

- Automatic Identification System (AIS): This displays the position, size and speed of other vessels in the area. It communicates the information using VHF signals and adds another layer of safety for a small ship.

Sea anchor or drogue to slow you down

A sea anchor acts to slow a boat down by creating drag through the water. There are a few scenarios in which you might use one but they are most useful during a storm.

If the wind is too high to steer your boat with the sails, you can use a sea anchor to keep yourself at the best angle relative to the waves to avoid being rolled. On larger ships, you can drag a spare sail behind the boat for a similar effect.

A drogue is a smaller variety of sea anchor that is primarily used to slow a boat's descent in high waves which makes it easier to control and less susceptible to damage.

And don't forget to bring...

Don't forget the following:

- life raft – although a last resort, should almost invariably be carried;
- de-salinator for longer voyages if you do not want to carry all of your water;
- harness to clip onto the **jackline** cable that runs along the deck of your boat;
- red and green lights on your **port** and **starboard** bows respectively, and a white one at the stern. These are legal requirements;
- snorkelling mask for conducting repairs under the boat and even a wetsuit if you are in colder waters;
- emergency grab bag with enough essentials to last you a few days, as well as flares, a radio, satellite phone and EPIRB;
- buoyancy aids.

'A remote wifi antenna; ours snaps into a cheap fitting on the boom – we can often get internet on the boat.'

– Bruce Clark, 'Ainia', www.OnAinia.blogspot.com

A Day in the Life of a Sailor
by Skip Novak

At the age of 25, Skip Novak navigated the British cutter 'Kings Legend' to a second place in the Whitbread Round the World Race. Since then he has taken part in the competition three more times as skipper and also co-skippered the maxi catamaran *Innovation Explorer* to a second place in 'The Race' – a non-stop circumnavigation at the turn of the millennium. Skip has two high latitude expedition sailing vessels, *Pelagic* and *Pelagic Australis* and since 1987 he has spent every season in the Antarctic where he combines sailing with his love of mountaineering.

'My typical day on a sailing expedition in the Southern Ocean might go something like this. Note: For the tropics, substitute coral reefs for ice bergs, and hurricanes for Southern Ocean storms.

It is 0145. The off going watch wakes our gang of four up about 15 minutes before the 0200 to 0600 shift. From a deep sleep within seconds I can sense the boat's motion and feel that she is slightly overpowered while I struggle out of the leeward bunk against the force of gravity anticipating the violent pitching motion. We are beating into a frigid southwesterly wind on a moonless night about to cross the Antarctic Convergence, mid Drake Passage. I struggle with mid-layer thermals, foul weather gear and boots, verify I have my hat and gloves at the ready and ascend into the pilot house. All quiet there as a crew member hands me a cup of tea. The off going watch captain, without ceremony, briefs me on direction, speed and the sails we have flying. He makes his last entry in the logbook, and remembers to tell me about "so and so" who is in his bunk down with sea sickness, but still breathing. The radar is on with a clear screen, but we are now in ice berg country so this piece of electronics backed up by a look out on deck is essential. Fully dressed, with life harness and PFD (Portable Flotation Device) de rigueur in these conditions, I slowly emerge on deck and get a feel for it while shining a flashlight around the rigging, sails, and sheets. All's well, but we have too much sail.

We decide to take a reef to play it conservative – a half hour's job with no hang ups. The off going watch stay to lend a hand. The colder it is the longer these maneuvers take. Wrestling with the gear in gloves and mittens doubles the time it normally takes barehanded. With wind chill sub zero, we scuttle back into the pilot house nursing freezing fingers and faces, while a few linger for the seconds needed to verify and admire the Southern Cross – a key moment to affirm all this struggle and pain is worth it!

As the grey dawn comes on four hours later, the mood relaxes as the "day" begins. Our watch prepare the breakfast for the oncoming watch. More cups of tea and coffee to start off. The watches are maintained throughout, but the "business day" has begun and there is little lounging around for me. First checking the service battery levels, I fire up the satellite communication system, download a GRIB file which is the weather analysis showing wind strength and direction for the next five days. Depending on the urgency of the circumstances, this might be downloaded twice per day, as the information is updated every six hours. Based on this information tactics for getting to the destination are modified to suit – slow up, speed up, or change course in anticipation of a shift in conditions. Then the inescapable email traffic… sadly gone are days of peaceful isolation at sea when there was time to indulge in and absorb Joyce's "Ulysses". Instead of succumbing to airport novels, I steal precious free moments and stare out to sea. Well, it is the only way to see whales!

By 1100 the wind has dropped and so has boat speed. To stick to our ETA on the Antarctic Peninsula I decide to go with the engine and "motor sail" to maintain a desired speed. But first all systems must be checked: no leaks, coolant topped up, belts OK, engine bilge dry. The fuel "day tank" must be pumped up from the main tanks, to feed the diesel engine by gravity. Lastly a quick look over the side to make sure no running rigging is trailing that can foul the propeller. With engine on tick over, the jib must be furled up, the mainsail brought to the centerline and again, all rigging checked there is no chafe between sails, shrouds and the sheets. Now the on watch will focus on the engine gauges, making visual checks in the engine room every hour and monitoring the consumption via the day tank sight glass.

Most of the crew will be up by lunch, skipping their "off watch" and doing odd repair jobs, cleaning below decks, or just having a natter. Everywhere one looks on a boat there are things to fix, adjust and monitor. It is the nature of the beast.

During early afternoon, the evening meal is mulled over and "volunteers" are coaxed out for culinary inspiration. Throughout the afternoon several more sail changes take place as the wind shifts back behind us to the north, and with this warm air flowing over a cold sea we are enveloped in thick fog. Once again, tension builds with lack of visibility. Nevertheless, a crew member is baking bread, taking advantages of an upright and relatively calm galley while we run downwind. Cooking smells migrate to the forward cabins and by 2000, all hands are in the pilot house, bowls of stew balanced in laps, cups in hand.

While washing up, the watch captain shouts down to me he has three bergs on radar off the starboard bow. We reduce speed and the lookout switches the auto pilot off and hand steers, now aware of bergy bits and growlers close aboard, invisible to our radar. The off watch goes below, reluctantly. They won't sleep tonight.'

Find out more about Skip and his yachts at: www.pelagic.co.uk.

Antiki and Plastiki

As well as imitators, Thor Heyerdahl's legendary journey across the Pacific has inspired other expeditions, including:

'Plastiki' – An 18-metre catamaran made from recycled bottles and other plastics that was sailed from San Francisco to Sydney. Expedition leader David de Rothschild and his team were aiming to highlight rising water levels from climate change and the amount of waste in the world. They reckoned that their boat was made from 12,500 plastic bottles and that same amount of bottles is thrown away every 8.3 seconds.

'Antiki' – 84-year-old Anthony Smith led a team of mature sailors across the Atlantic on a raft made from four plastic pipes. His four-man team, the youngest of which was 56 years old, spent 67 days building the raft and 66 more sailing it 2,700 miles across the Atlantic.

Costs

Buying a boat

Buying a boat is a significant investment and by far the biggest outlay for a cruiser. However, once bought and sufficiently equipped, you will have far greater control over the costs of your travels and be able to keep them low if desired.

- New boat: £45,000–£500,000 upwards. Purchasing a new boat gives you better flexibility to pick the exact boat you want, equipped exactly as you want it. You also have the reassurance of a guarantee. However, as with cars, you pay a premium for these benefits.
- Second-hand boat: £20,000–£300,000 upwards. There is a large second-hand yacht market. You might consider paying a surveyor to check a boat before you commit.
- Extra equipment: £5,000–£30,000 upwards. Most cruisers, second-hand or new, will come with at least some equipment already installed. However, there will invariably be more that you need, particularly if you get a second-hand bargain or are particular about the equipment you want.

Cruising costs

During a passage from A to B, you may not incur any costs at all. The expenses come from buying supplies and time spent on the coast.

Cruising costs include:

- supplies, e.g. food, water and fuel;
- mooring fees;
- fees for entering new countries;
- maintenance and repairs;
- communications such as phone, satellite phone and internet;
- insurance for yourself and the boat (unlike cars, this is not mandatory).

For continual cruising, a £500/month budget might be suitable for:

- a smaller boat which requires less maintenance and lower mooring fees;
- anchoring off-shore to avoid paying marina fees;
- a willingness to look after your boat and ability to make repairs yourself;
- cruising in less developed areas of the world where costs are lower;
- happy to live on a shoe string, not eating in restaurants and avoiding expenditures in port.

Cruising on £1,200/month budget could allow:

- a larger boat;
- occasionally paying for a marina or enjoying a trip onto land to explore;
- ability to afford repairs and replacements when necessary without having to make do.

It is quite possible to spend significantly more than this while cruising and many people operate with much higher budgets.

Lowest total cost – £50,000 (£25,000 each)
Finding a bargain boat with equipment you like and repair work you can do yourself. Split the costs with a team mate then spend six months cruising your way to Australia, anchoring off-shore and living frugally.

More typical total cost – £120,000 (£60,000 each)
Buying a second-hand boat with a bit more freedom to pick the equipment you want and pay for any repairs then spending a year or so sailing slowly around the world, making use of the occasional marina and local entertainment.

Training

Courses and qualifications
You don't need any qualifications to sail a boat but going through the process can be a good way to learn. Qualifications can also be useful for getting crew positions or earning money.

The Royal Yachting Association (RYA) have a series of qualifications and courses for complete beginners right through to advanced offshore cruising. Similarly, attending a course on sea survival would be recommended.

Reading up on seafaring
Reading books and training manuals can help with understanding techniques and best practice. Internet forums can also be great resources for finding out about particular areas or pieces of equipment.

'Sail Away by Nicola Rodriguez'.
– Jonic, www.jryachts.com

'It's hard to find but Circumnavigation: Sail the Trade Winds by Sue Moesly is a two-volume treasure.'
– Janet Groene, www.boatcook.blogspot.com

'Roth's book How to Sail Around the World is getting a bit dated but it has still got some good tips.'
– Danny Dukes

'Any book by Beth Leonard. Compulsory reading for potential liveaboards.'
– Bob and Lin, 'Ile Jeudi'

Accumulating sea miles
Once you have access to a boat, there will be few better ways to prepare yourself for a big sailing trip than to get more nautical miles under your belt. The more time spent at the helm, experiencing different conditions the better.

First Steps

1. Sign up for a course, convince a friend to take you out or try through a marina or sailing forum.
2. Accumulate more time on a boat. Join a club or do some more courses, or you could learn through a tall ships voyage or by volunteering yourself as inexperienced crew for a passage.
3. Buy a boat. A big investment but part of the learning experience: researching different vessels, selecting and operating the equipment, and maintaining your own boat.
4. Now you are the captain. Start with day trips in sheltered areas then follow that up with longer coastal journeys. Build to an overnight voyage.
5. Try a Channel crossing to France and back. Perhaps do another trip to Spain.
6. Enter a rally. You can complete your first trans–oceanic passage with the comfort blanket of an organised event.

7. Sail back to where you started with other vessels from the rally. You're not in an event any more but you have the combined experience of several boats for support.
8. Make the next voyage independently. Follow a well-known route, perhaps across the Atlantic or round Spain to the Mediterranean.
9. Continue the voyage to wherever your sails see fit.

Easier, Harder, Different

- Go old school and ditch the electronics, or as many of them as your safety threshold allows. Navigate by stars and paper charts, communicate in person, and learn to park without a motor.
- Break a world record. Plenty exist for long-distance sailing in all sorts of categories.
- Forget about the oceans and sail down some rivers instead.
- There are many types of smaller boats with various names like pocket cruisers, trailer sailers and day sailers. Use one of them for coastal cruising, shorter hops or a more ambitious journey.
- Travel by powered boat instead. Motor cruiser, RIBs and jetskis have all been used for long journeys.
- Swim. As well as 'short' crossings like the English Channel and Straits of Gibraltar, people have swum across the Atlantic (see Beno Lecomte and Jennifer Figge) and the length of the Yangtze and Amazon rivers (see Martin Strel).

Resources

- Royal Yachting Association (RYA) – local clubs, beginner and advanced courses, advice, publications and qualifications – see: www.rya.org.uk.
- Online sailing forums – a strong community, useful for both research and getting questions answered – such as: www.cruisersforum.com, www.anythingsailing.com and www.sailnet.com.
- Crew finding websites – see: www.crewfinders.com, www.crewseekers.net and www.crewfile.com.
- Cruising Resources – large collection of articles for cruisers – see: www.cruisingresources.com.
- *Around-the-World Sailing Guide* by Alan Phillips.
- *Care and Feeding of the Sailing Crew* by Lin Pardey.
- *How to Sail Around the World* by Hal Roth.
- *The Voyager's Handbook* by Beth Leonard.
- *World Cruising Routes* by Jimmy Cornell.

'Talk to other cruisers either in person or research blogs. There is no better resource than someone who has been there, done that.'

– Kiwis, CruisersForum.com user

Contributors

Andreas Julseth

Andreas first fell overboard from a moving sailboat when he was three years old and has been in love with them ever since. He learned the art of sailing when he bought his first sailboat and sailed solo in the Mediterranean for a year. Since then he's crossed the Atlantic five times, and recently captained a boat sailing from Norway to Australia on an adventure that took two and a half years.
See: www.julseth.com.

Ben Davitt

Captain Ben has sailed across the Atlantic six times, competed in Trans-Atlantic and World championship yacht races and cruised the Baltic, Mediterranean, North American and Caribbean waters. Ben has been involved in International Yacht, Super Yacht and Americas Cup Racing Campaigns for the past ten years.

Scotty Johnson

Scotty has been sailing for over 25 years in a variety of craft. His experience includes the challenge of teaching students in the waters of West Scotland in open traditional cutters, running small group charters around the world, and skippering at Caribbean Regattas. He is a RYA commercial Yachtmaster and runs S3 Adventures.
See: www.s3adventures.com.

Special thanks

Thanks to the users of CruisersForum.com, AnythingSailing.com, YBW.com and SailNet.com, Robbie Briton and Tom Brearley.

How to
Get to the South Pole

'*Respect those in whose footsteps you follow, the real explorers, and respect the place you are in ... or it might just have you.*'
– Robert Swan,
the first person to walk to both the North and South Poles

Setting the Scene

The South Pole was a highly sought after prize for many years. Although now easily reached by plane, Antarctica is still a great stomping ground for the adventurer. From entering the annual race, to a week spent skiing the last degree or months of sled hauling in an old-fashioned slog from the coast, there are many different ways to reach the iconic red-and-white striped pole that marks the bottom of the world.

Statistics

USP:	Photo at the world's most famous barber's pole.
Difficulty:	Easy to difficult.
Cost:	£36,000–£70,000+.
Hurdles:	Cold, terrain, isolation, and altitude.
Purest style:	Skiing unsupported from the coast.
Who's done it?:	Thousands visited, 200–300+ walked all the way.
Glory potential:	Moderate.

Background

On 17 January 1912, Captain Robert Falcon Scott's British expedition reached the South Pole. Upon arrival, however, he discovered the flag of Norway flapping in the wind. It had been planted by Roald Amundsen's team one month prior. Scott never made it back.

Shortly after this, the fondly recalled 'Heroic Age of Antarctic Exploration' came to an end as technology increased allowing planes to land at the Pole, first achieved by the Americans in 1956. They were the first people to set foot there since Scott and they set up the Amundsen-Scott South Pole Station which has remained in varying forms until the present day. The next team to reach the Pole overland was the

Commonwealth Trans-Antarctic Expedition led by Sir Vivian Fuchs and including Everest veteran Sir Edmund Hillary. Their journey was completed using special tractors making it the first time land vehicles had made the trip. It was also the first crossing of the Antarctic continent.

The arrival of Robert Swan's team in 1986 marked the first unassisted journey to the Pole – no dogs, no motors – and a few years later, Norwegian Erling Kagge completed a similar journey from the coast on his own without support. Meanwhile, Reinhold Messner and Arved Fuchs completed the first on-foot crossing of the continent in 1989, and Ranulph Fiennes and Mike Stroud used windpower and parachutes to help them on their own, unsupported traverse a few years later. Since then, all sorts of variations on these themes – solo or team, with or without re-supplies, human, natural or motor power – have been completed.

There are now camps used for commercial expeditions in Antarctica occupied every summer. They offer a wide variety of trips from flying straight to the Pole, to being dropped at the coast so you can ski the whole way, and everything else in between.

Introduction – Finding the Coast of Antarctica

The South Pole is located in the heart of Antarctica at 90-degrees south, the bottom of the world. It is marked by a nearby barber's pole, a collection of flags from the nations that originally signed the Antarctic treaty, and a large American research station.

The vast majority of expeditions use the Geographic South Pole as their destination. As such, that is the focus of this chapter. The other three South Poles are briefly described below.

Fixing the Geographic South Pole as the finish point makes things easier but you still need to work out where you begin your expedition. The coast is a good place to start but, in Antarctica, it is not straightforward to work out exactly where the coast is.

Consider first that there is always land beneath the sea. Under normal

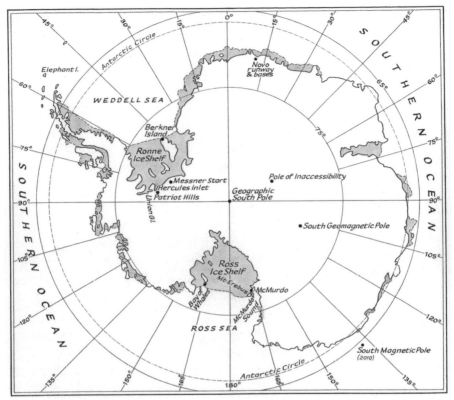

Map 6: Map of Antarctica

circumstances, a coast can easily be identified as the point at which that land protrudes above sea level. However, given that the vast majority of Antarctica is permanently covered in ice, sometimes a mile or so thick, it becomes a little more complicated to define what constitutes the coast.

For an expedition travelling to Antarctica a hundred years ago by ship, when the bow hit solid ice, the only real option was to get out and walk on the assumption that you'd reached the coast. However, the first few hundred miles would then be conducted on the icecap with any actual land mass well below sea level. As such, it has become commonplace to start expeditions at the point at which the ground beneath the ice is at exactly sea level.

Such start points have no doubt gained popularity due to the fact that they are located conveniently close to a commercial camp which makes them far cheaper to access. The result is that the bulk of expeditions in the last 50 years have started from a technically defined coast several hundred miles closer to the Pole than the one where you can hear waves crashing behind you. Some would dispute whether such a journey constitutes travelling from the coast or is just a compromise of convenience. This chapter covers all of the options. You can decide for yourself how you balance purity with practicality and purpose.

The Geographic South Pole

This is the bottom of the world and the point through which the globe's axis runs. It is the location of the iconic barber's pole and the goal of almost every 'South Pole' expedition. Unless otherwise stated, this is the Pole referred to throughout this chapter.

The Magnetic South Pole

Your compass points at the Magnetic South Pole. It is slowly moving over time and currently lies somewhere off the coast of Antarctica.

Several expeditions attempted unsuccessfully to sail to the Magnetic South Pole in the 19th century. Amongst them was James Clark Ross who led the first expedition to reach the Magnetic North Pole. At the time, however, the Magnetic South Pole was located on land and it was not until 1909 that members of Shackleton's expedition made the first claim to have reached it.

The Geomagnetic South Pole

The Geomagnetic South Pole is located where the earth's magnetic dipole touches the planet's surface. Like the Magnetic Pole, it is slowly moving. Close to this location is the Russian research base called Vostok which is best known for having the lowest ever recorded temperature: −89.2°C.

The Southern Pole of Inaccessibility

This is the point of Antarctica which is furthest from the sea. Its exact location is subject to debate. A key problem with pin pointing it is whether you take measurements from the edge of the ice or the edge of land (which is often hundreds of metres beneath the ice and many kilometres 'inland'). Even though it is no longer a very accurate measurement, the expedition world sometimes uses an old Soviet station – now indicated only by a statue of Lenin – as a marker of the Southern Pole of Inaccessibility.

All the locations are in the same broad region of Antarctica. By definition, an expedition to any of them should be a longer overland journey than an equivalent trip to the Geographic South Pole.

In 2005, a Spanish team skied with the aid of kites to two possible locations of this Pole, and in 2007 a British-Canadian team used similar methods to reach the location of the Soviet station.

Options – Transport

Flying to Antarctica and the Pole

As with most places on Earth these days, it is entirely possible to fly to the South Pole with almost no hardship except for enduring a long flight that is almost invariably delayed by weather. Even if you don't want to fly the whole way, you will almost certainly take a plane at some point.

- Departures: Flights depart from the bottom of the other continents. Punta Arenas in Chile and Cape Town in South Africa are common and trips from Australia and New Zealand are possible too.
- Arrivals: Planes arriving in Antarctica usually land on **blue ice runways** near permanent research stations or temporary seasonal camps such as Union Glacier, Novo and White Desert.

'Patience!'
– Mike Sharp,
Operations Manager for Antarctic Logistics & Expeditions

Antarctic camps and runways

Most introductions to Antarctica will begin at a semi-permanent camp. These camps have large heated catering tents offering about as much luxury as you will get on the coldest and windiest of continents. A stay there provides an opportunity to acclimatise with a degree of comfort.

Union Glacier camp

This is the destination for most flights from South America. The camp used to be located at **Patriot Hills** and known by that name, but it moved to Union Glacier for the 2010–2011 season in anticipation of better weather conditions.

Union Glacier is closer to both the South Pole and the more common expedition start points so is the best bet for most expeditions. It is run by Antarctic Logistics & Expeditions (ALE).

Novo runway

Flights from South Africa tend to land on a runway known as Novo. Novo is short for Novolazarevskaya, the name of a nearby Russian research station. The runway actually belongs to the South African company Antarctic Logistics Center International and its official name is the ALCI airbase. There is a camp nearby called White Desert which is run by The Antarctic Company.

Novo and the surrounding camps are a long way from the South Pole. They are typically used as a base for onward flights or for exploration in the surrounding area.

Sailing to Antarctica

It is possible to visit Antarctica by boat. Cruise ships frequent Antarctic islands and but only tend to reach the northern end of the peninsula – a long way from the South Pole even if they were allowed to drop you off. In theory, you could start an expedition by chartering a yacht to drop you at the coast. Unfortunately, much of the coast is sheer ice cliffs. The peninsula can provide easier landing spots but access to the Antarctic interior from there is difficult as many areas are mountainous and crevasse filled.

Entering a race

Extreme World Races organise a race to the South Pole every year. The start line is at a convenient inland spot and teams of three spend a few weeks racing the 500 miles to the Pole. The cost is around £60,000 per person. Training is included, most of the organisation is done for you and support is provided throughout. It can still be physically gruelling, especially with the competitive element, but is otherwise an easy way into an Antarctic expedition.

Alternatively, a marathon is held each year in Antarctica. No specialist training is really required beyond being marathon fit, getting some experience running in cold conditions and following the advice provided. The same company also offers a 100km Antarctic ultra marathon. Entry costs around £8,000. However, these races are actually conducted close to Union Glacier, a few hundred miles from the South Pole. If you want to fly to the South Pole afterwards it will probably cost you the same or more again.

Race to the Pole

British TV presenter Ben Fogle and Olympian James Cracknell entered the inaugural South Pole race in 2008 with doctor Ed Coats. Despite losing their rope in a crevasse field, Fogle suffering frostbite on his nose and Cracknell losing three stone in three weeks, the trio finished in second place. Like the unofficial race 100 years prior, they were pipped to the post by a team of Norwegians.

The BBC TV series, 'On Thin Ice' followed their progress and Fogle and Cracknell wrote a book about it called Race to the Pole.

Dogs in Antarctica

One of the tactics that may have helped Amundsen beat Scott to the Pole in 1911 was the fact that his team slowly ate their sled-dogs as the journey went on. Providing a good means of transport and a potential source of food, dogs might seem like the ideal expedition partner. Unfortunately for you, if not for the canines, dogs have been banned in Antarctica since 1994 to avoid spreading diseases and otherwise interfering with the wildlife. If you want to use dogs then you are better off going to the Arctic.

Driving to the South Pole

The planes that fly to Antarctica are large enough to fit many types of vehicle on board so motorised expeditions are not uncommon.

Crevasses pose a significant risk if you are travelling at speed with a loud engine and the implications of a breakdown could be serious but, otherwise, a vehicle-based expedition should be far less demanding than anything on foot. Of course, it is not really the same as going under your own steam but there is still a lot of potential for adventure.

Antarctica with an engine

The first crossing of Antarctica was completed in 1957 using a variety of vehicles including small tanks built for snow travel, three tracked Sno-Cat vehicles and an adapted tractor. The expedition was led by British explorer Sir Vivian Fuchs. His team-mate, Everest summiter Sir Edmund Hillary, was just supposed to be laying supplies but took an opportunity to be the first person to reach the Pole by vehicle.

Ranulph Fiennes traversed Antarctica with Charlie Burton and Oliver Shepard as part of their three-year Trans-Globe Expedition. After overwintering near the coast in temporary shelters made from cardboard, they crossed the continent in 67 days using skidoos.

Subsequent motorised excursions to the South Pole include: Japanese adventurer Kazama Shinji driving there on a motorcycle; a six-wheeled truck that took just 69 hours to reach the Pole; a 'bio-inspired ice vehicle' that crossed the continent with skis and propellers.

On foot, with snow shoes and using skis

The simplest method, but by no means the easiest, is to travel on foot. This generally means skiing with the odd bit of ski-less footwork on trickier terrain. It has also been known to walk all the way in snowshoes. Probably the slowest of your options, travelling by foot is arguably also the purest and most straightforward method. It is the most common means of travel for South Pole expeditions and is the assumed method for most of this chapter.

Flying by kite

Finally, an increasingly common technique for Antarctic travel is the use of kites – the basic principle being to hold on tightly to a kite whilst wearing skis and use the wind to drag you along. This method may not be human powered but is more natural than a vehicle and can be very fast in good conditions. Since the winds blow quite consistently away from the Pole, kite-skiing is really only an option for the return leg of a journey.

Differences between the Arctic and Antarctica:

The Arctic	Antarctica
The Arctic is an ocean surrounded by continents.	Antarctica is a continent surrounded by oceans.
It is typically defined by the Arctic Circle at 66.5-degrees north which marks the edge of 24 hour days and nights.	There is an Antarctic Circle at 66.5-degrees south but Antarctica refers to the continent.
North Pole expeditions are largely conducted on the frozen sea ice surface of the Arctic Ocean. Water is always flowing beneath your feet and in many areas there is a constant threat of falling through the ice.	South Pole expeditions operate on ice but largely with land beneath it.
Polar bears live only in the Arctic. Seals of varying types live in both the Arctic and Antarctica.	Penguins live in Antarctica. They live outside the Antarctic Circle too but never in the Arctic. The aggressive leopard seals live in Antarctica but not the Arctic.
There are trees, roads, villages and shops inside the Arctic Circle but nothing permanent exists on the Arctic Ocean as it constantly moves and melts.	A few permanent and seasonal bases exist in Antarctica, mostly research stations, including one at the South Pole. There are no roads, villages or trees though.
The North Pole is only ever a metre or two above sea level depending on the thickness of the ice.	The South Pole is at an elevation of almost 3,000m.
There is nothing at the location of the North Pole.	The South Pole is marked by a nearby research station, circle of flags and a stripy pole for posed photographs.
The Arctic Ocean is very humid. Managing moisture inside a tent is critical during North Pole expeditions.	Antarctica is the driest of the seven continents and technically a desert. Any 'snowing' that you experience is almost certainly the result of snow on the ground being blown by wind.
On average, the Arctic is not as cold as Antarctica. However, most North Pole expeditions cannot operate at the Arctic's warmest because the sea ice melts so, in practice, it can be just as cold.	Antarctica is colder than the Arctic but most people will plan their expeditions for the warmer summer and the dryness also makes it easier to handle the cold.

Options – Routes and Styles

Given that a plane can drop you almost anywhere in Antarctica, it follows that you could travel to the South Pole from any start point and follow whatever route you desire. However, there are a few common itineraries and start positions.

Ski the Last Degree

Starting from the 89th degree of latitude gives you just 60 or so miles to cover and is a very good introductory route for those without the time, money, experience or inclination for a longer trip. It still costs upwards of £30,000 but the whole trip can be done in three weeks with about a week to ten days on the ice.

Clearly very short, and usually under supervision – although there is no reason you couldn't do it yourself – Last Degree trips offer a genuine experience of Antarctic travel and the satisfaction of reaching the Pole under your own steam. Many companies offer this itinerary and variants of it (e.g. skiing the last two degrees).

Journeys from the technical coast

As discussed in the introduction, there are different ways to define where the coast of Antarctica begins. It has become increasingly common to start expeditions from the point at which the land beneath the ice is at sea level. It is an abstract concept rather than the coast in any real sense – the sea may be hundreds of miles away – but provides start points conveniently located near camps that avoid long, expensive flights.

Two popular start points are:

1. Hercules Inlet. Starting from here gives you 730 miles to the South Pole. This is slightly shorter than the trips from the actual coast but is still officially recognised by the record keepers as a coastal start, so is very popular for speed records.
2. The Messner Start. This one is not recognised by the record keepers but is only 580 miles from the South Pole and thus the shortest 'coastal'

option. It is named after the explorer Reinhold Messner's 1989 Antarctic crossing.

Full distance from the real coast

For the more puritanical, you can start your journey from the undisputed coastline of Antarctica as the early explorers did. You could start from anywhere really but the ones used historically offer the shortest distances:

1. McMurdo Sound is where Shackleton and Scott both had bases at the start of the 20th century. It is about 800 miles from the Pole.
2. Berkner Island is 900 miles away from the South Pole and was Scott's starting point in 1911.

Both of these points are a long way from the camps so tend to require far longer flights. As such, you can expect this to cost notably more than the other options above.

Antarctic traverses and return journeys

Finally, it is entirely possible for an expedition to traverse the whole continent or to make a return journey to the coast. Indeed, before regular plane access was possible, these were the only options.

Obviously, now that planes can pick you up from pretty much anywhere, this is primarily for novelty and challenge. But, it also offers some good possibilities and the closest adherence to an old-fashioned Antarctic expedition.

The last great challenge?

Expeditions arise every year that claim to be the 'last remaining great challenge on earth' or similar but there is one simple Antarctic itinerary that remains to be done.

Very few expeditions have completed traverses or return journeys. Perhaps just a dozen of the former and a handful for the latter. Only one of those traverses was completed by human power alone – most opting to use at least wind power for part of the journey – and that was only achieved in 2009–2010 by Norwegian Cecilie Skog and American Ryan Waters.

What is still to be done is an unsupported, unassisted return journey. That is walking or skiing from the coast of Antarctica to the South Pole and back without kites or dogs, and without being resupplied by plane. To achieve this, a team would almost certainly drop caches of supplies on their outward journey that they could collect on their return to save weight. When they reached the South Pole, purists would also have to refuse any offers of tea or a spare chocolate bar from the base or any other expeditions they encountered for fear of breaking the unassisted rule.

This journey is what Captain Scott died attempting in 1911 – the successful Amundsen was using dogs – and, 100 years later, it is still left untouched.

With or without resupply

The last big decision to make for those longer journeys is whether or not you will have a plane bringing you supplies. This can cost extra – potentially a lot if you are not following a convenient route – and adds another small logistical consideration to your itinerary but has the huge advantage of reducing the weight that you have to carry. Some will prefer to go without resupply for the sake of purity, simplicity or in pursuit of an unassisted record.

Practicalities

Where do you sleep?

An expedition in Antarctica almost certainly means sleeping in a tent. The cold and wind are likely to deter even the keenest of bivouacers. But with the ground tending to be reasonably level, if not smooth, none of the fear of falling through the ice that you have on a North Pole trip – assuming you haven't inadvertently pitched in a crevasse field – and not much chance of shelter no matter how hard you look — picking a spot for the night is at least a fairly easy task.

What do you eat and drink?

Food options at the South Pole will be limited to what you can bring with you. The chances are that you will have to carry all of your supplies with you in a pulk (sled). You will be burning a lot of calories too so it makes sense to carry food that packs a lot of calories for its weight. Food that can survive the cold and is easily prepared is good. That might be a just-add-water dehydrated meal in the evening or defrosting a chocolate bar in your pocket while skiing.

Water for cooking and drinking comes from melting the snow and ice that lies beneath you. It is a time-consuming ritual that may take several hours every day but can at least be hastened slightly by adding a splash of water to the bottom of the pan rather than starting with just dry snow. Having an insulated thermos or two is another useful trick, allowing you to store heated water whilst melting your next pan-full in the tent, and keeping it from freezing whilst out skiing.

Where do you go to the loo?

Few are the prying eyes in Antarctica and minor are the differences from one kilometre to the next. Wherever you lay your trousers is your toilet. Some expeditions have tried removing their human waste by bagging it up, carrying it in their pulks and having it flown out. No doubt the sub-zero temperatures make this experience more pleasant than it might otherwise be but even this practice raises environmental questions of its own. The only place such a removal policy is actually enforced is in the final degree of latitude surrounding the Pole where expedition activity is more focused.

As a final note for those worried about such things, if you're in a race, then the location, frequency and shade of your yellow snow may be used against you by competitors on your tail.

How do you know where to go?

A compass will point you to the Magnetic South Pole rather than the geographic one so you will need to make a significant adjustment for the variation. Additionally, they often get stuck by the needle wanting to point directly downwards to the North Pole or end up spinning unhelpfully.

So, in addition to some clever interpretation of your compass, a GPS checked a couple of times a day can help you keep track of progress. Battery life can be an issue with the cold and length of journey so expeditions often rely on:

- The sun – You can make the most of the long daylight hours by using your shadow to tell you what direction you are facing depending on the time of day.
- **Sastrug**i – These ice ridges tend to consistently run in the same direction. Once you have worked out that direction, you can simply keep going at the same angle.

'The angle the sun rises can be worked out by taking your latitude and subtracting 90 degrees. 90 minus 90 is zero, so when you reach the Pole the sun moves parallel to your horizon. This is also why you get such short sunsets in the tropics and long ones at high latitudes.'

– Tristan Gooley, author of *The Natural Navigator*

How long will it take?

The duration of a South Pole expedition depends on your approach:

- Flights: It may only be a few hours to Antarctica and a similar length to the Pole but weather delays are very common and you may have

to wait for a plane to be available.
- Last Degree: A week to ten days on the ice. Two or three weeks away from home.
- Messner Start: 30–40 days skiing might be typical with another week or two on top for transfers and delays.
- Coastal starts: Going the whole way is likely to take around 40–70 days of skiing. This can be reduced by using kites and resupplies.

How long do you actually spend skiing each day?
Even in the mildest of conditions, you probably won't want to take lengthy breaks from skiing unless you are in your tent, as it is simply too cold to hang around. As such, if you are not stuffing food into your mouth or fiddling with the zip on your flies (tip: tie big loops of cord to zips so they are easily operated when wearing mittens), during the day you will probably be heading southwards.

Since the sun is likely to be up for the entire duration of your trip, your day can really stretch for as short or long a period as you fancy. Somewhere around eight to ten hours skiing in a day might be typical. In competition or pursuit of records, you could do twice that or more. But, aside from the importance of sleep on an endurance test like this, morning and evening tent routines can take a couple of hours and you should leave enough time to do them properly.

'Build up slowly to 9–10 hour days of skiing. On longer expeditions, the temptation is to get as much distance under your belt as soon as possible but a gradual increase is much more likely to maintain endurance.'
– Helen Turton,
Logistics Manager and team member for the Women's Commonwealth Antarctic expedition.

When to go

Being in the southern hemisphere, the seasons are the reverse of what you get in the northern half of the world. They are also a little more extreme than in lower latitudes. Areas of Antarctica will see the sun disappear for as long as four months in the winter. Indeed the South Pole itself has just one day and one night per year, each one six months long.

As such, it is generally prudent to go during the summer months when it is warmer and your pictures come out better. For most people, this means somewhere between November and February with the prime time being roughly in the middle of that (i.e. Christmas and New Year). Winter journeys, despite being colder and likely to be conducted largely in darkness, are possible.

What happens if things go wrong?

If something goes wrong on the ice then your priority in most situations will simply be to keep warm, fed and hydrated in your tent while you await rescue. You won't be travelling without the means of contacting whoever has provided your logistics – and if your communications equipment breaks then they will have your last GPS fix and a plan if you go silent – so you can call for help if that is what you need.

Much of Antarctica's frozen landscape can provide a decent runway so your chances of a nearby pick-up are high but the weather is notoriously volatile and can keep planes grounded for days or weeks at a time.

Commonwealth Women at the South Pole

Just before midnight on 29 December 2009, a team of six women arrived at the South Pole on skis. All from different Commonwealth countries, most of them had little or no experience of expeditions or cold environments just a year earlier.

British adventurer Felicity Aston came up with the idea to mark the 60th anniversary of the Commonwealth. Application forms were sent around the world and Felicity flew out to interview applicants from Jamaica, Brunei, Cyprus, India, Ghana, Singapore and New Zealand. The application forms made no reference to fitness or prior experience so the team were largely trained from scratch.

Difficulties

High winds and low temperatures

Unsurprisingly, Antarctica is cold and covered in snow and ice. The South Pole itself doesn't often get above −20°C. In summer, when you're likely to visit, you can probably expect temperatures down to about −40°C elsewhere on the continent. If you are doing something particularly tough that will take you further into spring or autumn, then prepare for worse.

Antarctica is also well known for its **katabatic winds** that bring cold dense air down from the South Pole, hastened under gravity. Great for kite-skiing back but a pain to ski into, this will also make it feel a lot colder than the ambient air temperature.

> *'Get out and travel every day.*
> *The wind always sounds worse inside the tent.'*
> − Conrad Dickinson,
> who completed a return journey to the South Pole with kites

Thin air from the altitude

Getting to the South Pole is an uphill struggle. Your finish line lies at over 2,800m above sea level. This means that you can throw into the mix of difficulties the complications of decreased atmospheric pressure. And, because of the extreme cold there, the pressure is lowered further and the effects are exacerbated.

For those who fly straight to the Pole, shortness of breath and headaches are not uncommon. On Last Degree trips, which start at close to this altitude, lack of acclimatisation is one of the highest causes of evacuation. If you travel there overland, then your body should slowly acclimatise but don't be surprised to find any exertion that little bit harder than it might otherwise be as your body struggles to get the oxygen that it needs.

Avoiding crevasses

Given that you will be travelling largely across a huge ice cap, your route may occasionally take you through fields of **crevasses**: splits in the ice that can be many metres deep and many more wide. Falling into them is best avoided.

Heavily crevassed areas tend to be reasonably well known in Antarctica. A combination of satellite imagery and fly-bys in planes can give forewarning of any developments from year to year. If for some reason you find yourself in such an area, it may be prudent to tie yourself to a colleague by a length of rope to give you a fighting chance of extraction should you take a fall. Crevasse rescue is a well-established technique for which you are best advised to carry a few pieces of specially-designed kit and practise the routine in advance.

(There is more detail on crevasse rescue and the effects of altitude in Chapter 7 'How to climb an unclimbed mountain'.)

Struggling over sastrugi

The snowy equivalent of sand dunes, sastrugi are ridges of compact snow formed by wind. They can be metres high at their worst and tend to be rock solid. This makes travelling across them on skis towing a pulk frustrating and physically demanding. This is made worse if the visibility is low enough to make make route finding difficult. Mercifully, as with crevasses, the worst areas are often flagged up in advance by planes and satellites.

The desolation and isolation of a bleak continent

The regularity of conditions underfoot may aid your progress but the environment can also be mind-numbingly repetitive. While some may never fail to appreciate the beauty of a 360-degree white vista, others will go stir-crazy at the monotony.

Compounding the solitude is the fact that it is common practice to ski in single file so that only one person has to navigate and break trail through the snow. It can also help maintain a good pace and reduce the risk of getting separated or falling into a crevasse.

Kit

Pulk for towing your supplies

If your intention is to ski any significant distance to the South Pole, then carrying all of your supplies in a rucksack would be impractical if not impossible. You will almost certainly need a pulk. This is a sled that you will fill with kit, attach to your waist and tow.

With slick runners on smooth ice, pulks can make comparatively light work of very heavy loads. Uphill and across sastrugi they require a lot of effort but are still the best method for hauling supplies.

Whereas the early explorers relied on wooden creations, fibreglass is more common today and plastic options are springing up too. As a rule of thumb, fibreglass pulks are stronger, heavier and more expensive so best suited to longer trips and rougher terrain. Plastic pulks are regularly used for shorter trips. They are little more than reinforced plastic sleds and can't be expected to take the same punishment as a fibreglass pulk but they are much lighter and considerably cheaper.

Skis for speed and safety

When people talk about 'skiing' to the South Pole it may sound a little more glamorous than the reality which tends to be a low-speed, high-exertion grunt pulling a heavy sledge. Nonetheless, using cross–country style skis with wax or **skins** attached – which grip when you push back and slide on the forward motion – still tends to be faster than simply walking. Skis also spread your weight over a greater area making soft snow easier to cross and reducing the risk of falling into a crevasse. Snow shoes are sometimes carried as well for trickier terrain.

Sleeping system inside the tent

Whatever the time of year you choose to travel, it will be cold when you go to sleep. At least Antarctica is a dry environment leaving you free to use down sleeping bags – which generally have the highest warmth to weight ratio – without fear of damp reducing their efficacy.

You will probably sleep in at least your thermals and a hat and probably on top of a couple of sleeping mats. Something that will cover your eyes is useful too since it probably won't be dark for long.

'Be cool. Bizarrely, the most important thing about skiing to the South Pole is staying cool, the moment you get too warm and start to sweat the moisture goes into your clothes and freezes and then you get hypothermic, so you must spend all day adjusting your layers in order to stay cool. My favourite bit of clothing to help with this is a little down vest, you can take it on and off quickly and easily to make big adjustments to your temperature.'
– Hannah McKeand, who holds the record for the fastest solo woman to the South Pole

Clothes to keep you warm
To keep warm during different levels of activity, a system of layers is your best bet:

- Base layer – one or two thin layers close to your skin that will help move sweat away so that you don't get wet and thus cold.
- Insulation – warm mid-layers tend to be made of fleece, pile, down or a synthetic down equivalent.
- Outer shell – the priority for your outer layer is windproofing. It won't get wet but waterproofs offer good wind protection and shouldn't get too clammy in the dry environment.
- And finally – a super-size down jacket to throw over the top of all of that will be a welcome addition whenever you stop.

For other parts of your body:

- Head and face – Balaclava, hat, neoprene face mask and goggles should help when the wind picks up. A furry hood is great for trapping warm air in front of your face. If it is going to be really cold, then be warned that fake animal fur can stick to skin.
- Feet – Unlike other cold environments where climbing rock and ice requires stiff boots with rigid soles, skiing in Antarctica you just need footwear that is warm. As such, Antarctic boots can be surprisingly comfy. Common choices are what can only be described as large, soft 'moon boots' made by the likes of Sorel and Baffin, and the old-fashioned looking felt and canvas boots made by Norwegian company Alfa.

Glove Choice
by Mike Thornewill

Skin layer
A thin, basic and inexpensive poly-propylene lightweight 'contact' glove.

Working glove
Must be windproof and have a surface that easily sheds snow. Choose lightweight, breathable and a comfy fit. This layer must not be bulky because it has to slide easily inside large over-mitts. A little bit of grip on the palms is helpful, but too much is not. For an idea of thickness, consider a cycling glove.

Over-mitt
Go very large and very warm. Must be breathable (although avoid Gore-Tex because it does not breathe well at cold temperatures). A fleece lining is ideal but avoid down filling as it retains moisture.

Extra large snowmobile gloves work particularly well. I buy synthetic snowmobile mitts from 'Weaver & Devore' for around 35 Canadian dollars.

Just don't let them blow away …!

Mike has completed coastal expeditions to both the South and North Poles. You can read more at: www.polarchallenge.org. Weaver & Devore are at: www.weaverdevore.ca.

Stove for cooking dinner and melting snow

Through melting snow, a stove is your route to water. It also delivers hot meals and a hot tent – or at least one that isn't frigid. A multi-fuel stove is the standard choice in Antarctica as they perform well in the cold. It is common practice to have them mounted permanently on a plastic or wooden board so that they can remain fully assembled in your pulk for swift set-up at tea time and to avoid them melting a hole in the ground while in use.

'Always sleep/ski with your MSR fuel pumps in your pockets close to your skin to keep them warm. Helps keep the rubber seals good and prevents fuel leaks.'
– Antony Jinman,
leader on the International Scott Centenary Expedition in 2012

Tent for shelter

If you are travelling by vehicle then you may be able to carry the big pyramid tents that look like tipis and were so beloved of the early explorers – often called 'Scott tents' for that very reason. They are wonderfully roomy compared to most expedition tents, can be heated by a stove or two in the middle, and are robust against winds despite their appearance.

If it has to fit in your pulk then you will probably take a much smaller tunnel or dome tent.

- Dome tents – shaped like igloos – are sometimes used and are strong against wind from any direction.
- Tunnel tents – shaped like a cylinder split down the middle and laid flat – are a more popular option as they tend to be roomier. They are weak if wind catches them from the side but can usually be pitched to avoid this since the wind in Antarctica flows fairly consistently away from the Pole.

And don't forget to take ...

Don't forget the following items:

- a pee bottle to avoid having to go outside in the cold at night;
- something warm to put on your feet as an evening treat;
- sunglasses and sun cream for that never-ending sun;
- a good eye mask and a dark coloured tent to absorb the most heat from the sun and give some respite from its illumination;
- a fully loaded MP3 player to deal with monotony;
- solar panels strapped to your pulk to charge your electronics;
- your nation's flag to fly when you get there.

'People wonder why their goggles mist up ... Always put them on last, and don't bend down and breathe out at the same time!'
– Fiona Thornewill,
joint first British woman to ski to both Geographic Poles

A Day in the Life of a South Pole Explorer
by Felicity Aston

Felicity was part of the first British women's crossing of the Greenland icecap, has skied 400 miles across Siberia's frozen Lake Baikal, and entered the first all-female team in the Polar Challenge race to the Magnetic North Pole. She has spent two and half years living and working in Antarctica and led a team of Commonwealth women to the South Pole in 2010. She recently became the only woman to have walked solo across Antarctica.

'Can you remember what you were doing 40 days ago? Take a moment to think about it. Now, imagine that you had been doing exactly the same thing all day, every day from that day to this. If the idea sounds like your idea of hell (or a sure route to insanity) then skiing to the South Pole probably isn't for you. An expedition in Antarctica is all about mental, rather

than physical, strength. The need for relentless willpower begins from the moment you open your eyes in the morning and have to force yourself from the warm sanctuary of your sleeping bag into the supercooled air of the tent. Stepping outside and exposing yourself to the full brunt of the Antarctic climate is the second exercise in self-discipline of the day. It doesn't matter if you are with a team or by yourself, as you lace your ski-boots and prepare to plunge yourself into the cold that waits outside you will have the same thought screaming through your head, "What am I doing??" Especially as you know it will be at least another 10 or 12 hours before you will have shelter again.

Within minutes of being outside, the cold will begin to numb your toes and fingers, forcing you to wriggle your digits furiously as you pack your tent and equipment into your pulk, stopping occasionally to punch the air and stamp the ground in an attempt to coax warm blood into your extremities. Eventually, when everything is packed, you can strap on your skis and face the horizon, a completely flat division of land and sky that will look exactly as it did yesterday and exactly as it will look again tomorrow. Monotony is an even greater enemy than the cold and the struggle to keep your mind busy is as unrelenting as the need to keep warm. Several times a day you will think longingly of the warmth and comfort of home and ask yourself again, "Why am I doing this??"

But, as you gaze upward at a sky full of rainbows, catch the sparkle of ice crystals suspended in the air around you or stumble across the delicate curve of a sastrugi, you will be filled with an all-consuming wonder at what is before your eyes – a wonder made all the more potent by the knowledge that only the privileged few have ever witnessed the scenes that are now so familiar to you. At those moments it will feel as if you are gliding on pure air; as if the world contains no challenge you could not tackle; and I guarantee that, at last you will have an answer to your question – you will know exactly what it is that you are doing and why.'

Read more at: www.felicityaston.co.uk

Costs

The biggest and generally unavoidable cost for getting to the South Pole is the flights. The companies that facilitate expeditions down south, of which the primary operator is Antarctic Logistics & Expeditions (ALE), offer a host of different packages.

- Return flight to, e.g. Chile or South Africa – £1,000.
- Return flight to an Antarctic camp – £7,000+.
- To the Pole and back – £25,000+.
- Drop-off at Hercules Inlet or Messner Start including flight to Antarctica and a pick up from the Pole – £30,000 to 35,000+. This price is per person and includes food, a guide and re-supplies. You don't have to take them but it's no cheaper if you don't.
- Drop-off at Berkner Island or McMurdo Sound and a pick up from the Pole – £60,000 to £150,000. Flights to further flung destinations like these are charged by plane not per person and are based on flight time and payload. You may be able to reduce the costs for the longer flights by sharing a plane with another expedition.
- Kit: £2,500–£6,000+. Skis, pulks, tent and stove can be hired but could easily cost £1,000–£2,000 if bought new, as could the many layers of clothing and sleeping equipment. You will buy or hire a satellite phone and EPIRB on top of that too.
- Food and fuel: £300–£1000+. This will vary depending on the length of your trip and how you source your food, e.g. complete ready-made ration packs off the shelf or a cheaper combination with supermarket food.

Lowest total cost – £36,000
An all-inclusive Messner Start trip with cheap flights to South America, hiring and borrowing as much kit as possible.

More typical total cost – £70,000 each
Self-guided Berkner Island to South Pole with some new kit but no re-supplies, and splitting the flight cost with team mates.

Training

Skiing to the South Pole is largely a long slog. It does not require running a mile in five minutes or performing 40 chin-ups but it does need you to walk for many hours a day pulling a heavy pulk.

Here are some basics:

Dragging tyres to build strength
This is the quintessential training method of the polar traveller. Tie a bit of rope around an old tyre or two (or three, or four), attach it to your waist and start walking. Tyres aren't as heavy as laden pulks but, laid flat, they create a lot of friction and thus give a similar effect. You can get a proper pulk harness, use an old climbing harness or wear a rucksack with a good waist belt. Bags of sand and large vehicles (brakes off) are possible alternatives.

Learning to ski efficiently
It is easy to learn and difficult to master. Improving your technique should make life easier but failing to do so is unlikely to scupper your chances. A training option for those who don't live in Scandinavia is to try roller skiing.

Adapting to the cold
It is questionable whether ice baths, sitting in a giant freezer or sleeping with the windows open in winter will actually help your body prepare for the cold but they might be interesting or useful experiences.

'I believe no one has ever given a better advice than Roald Amundsen for getting to the South Pole: "Victory awaits he who has all in order – people call it good luck. And failure always follows he who has neglected to take the necessary measures. People call it bad luck."'

– Erling Kagge,
the first person to walk to both Poles and summit Mount Everest

First Steps

1. Give yourself a taster at home – Spend a day dragging a tyre around a field in winter then spend a night camping in the snow to see if you enjoy it.

2. Consider your options – Joining an event or organised tour requires a lot of money but, beyond that, most people could sign up tomorrow. The company should tell you everything you need to know and you can focus on getting fit and learning to stay warm in the cold.

3. Go ski touring – Particularly important if preparing for a longer haul, a ski tour will get you used to travelling on skis and being in a cold environment. Scotland and Scandinavia are good options. Build up to multi-day trips carrying your own kit, ideally with a pulk.

4. Do more of the same – Skiing to the South Pole will probably be longer, colder and harsher than what you have experienced so far but not categorically different. So just keep going. Improve your skiing and camp craft, get more experience in the cold and build your strength, and you will soon be ready for Antarctica.

'There are so many people who say they want to do this and that, but there are so many excuses: "Maybe next year". If you have a dream to visit the Pole (or somewhere else) you must say to yourself that "Yes, this is something I will do" and set a date.'
– Børge Ousland,
who has skied solo with a kite to the South Pole and across the Antarctic continent

Easier, Harder, Different

- An unsupported, unassisted return journey by foot from the coast. Several teams have been queuing up to do this in time for the centenary of Captain Scott's attempt but, as yet, it's never been done.
- Cross Greenland. It's closer to home, considerably cheaper and offers a lot of great opportunities for genuine polar travel without too many of the extremes.
- Climb Mount Vinson, the highest mountain in Antarctica thus one of the Seven Summits. Or just climb one of the many other great but less popular peaks down there.
- Forget the Pole and do a 'low budget' Antarctic expedition with a return ticket to one of the camps (£10,000–£12,000+) to complete a round-trip with your own itinerary.
- Cycle there. There are myriad bicycle designs for travelling on snow and ice. Perhaps it would be possible to get to the South Pole on one?

Resources

- Adventure Stats – Statistics and records for all South Pole expeditions. North Pole and mountaineering stats too – see: www.adventurestats.com.
- Antarctic Logistics Center International (ALCI) – Offer flights from South Africa to the Novo runway and other services – see: www.alci.co.za.
- Antarctic Logistics & Expeditions (ALE) – Company providing support and logistics for expedition. Twinned with Adventure Network International (ANI) – see: www.antarctic-logistics.com.

How to Climb an Unclimbed Mountain

'Listen to your instincts and know when to turn back
as well as when to press on. Above all enjoy it.'
– Sir Chris Bonington,
veteran of many Himalayan expeditions and significant first ascents

Setting the Scene

Even in the 21st century, the world abounds with unclimbed mountains. Some are well-known as the highest yet to be climbed, others appear on checklists still to be checked and many more are just out there waiting to be discovered. While some will require technical climbing skills, plenty are simply off the beaten track and never had anyone on their slopes. As such, the pursuit of a first ascent is a realistic challenge for both the experienced mountaineer and the well prepared amateur.

Statistics

USP:	Being the first to stand on a summit.
Difficulty:	Moderate to very difficult.
Cost:	£2,000–£5,000+.
Hurdles:	Finding them, falls and avalanches.
Duration:	Two weeks+.
Purest style:	Unguided and independently organised.
Who's done it?:	Thousands.
Glory potential:	Low to high.

Background

People have undoubtedly climbed on mountains for millennia but it is in more recent history that peak bagging has become an objective in itself. Although some had started viewing mountains as a challenge sooner, it was an 11-year period in the mid-19th century known as the Golden Age of Mountaineering which saw intense activity on the previously unclimbed peaks of the Alps and began a craze that continues to this day. Climbers soon began to look further afield to the Caucasus, Rockies and Andes before finally setting their sights on the Himalaya and surrounding ranges in the late 19th and early 20th centuries. Everest was first climbed in 1953, and K2 the year after. By 1964, all 14 mountains over 8,000m had been climbed.

In the decades since, the major focus of mountaineering has shifted away from exploration and first ascents to the development of a multi-faceted sport and pastime. The sport has many different streams including rock, ice and mixed climbing, and alpinism and broader mountaineering. The motivations for climbing vary too – improving skills, trying new and different routes, or ticking off lists of the best and highest.

But despite the years of increasing popularity, in the 21st century there still remain hundreds, if not thousands, of unclimbed mountains. They are scattered around the world and often remain unclimbed less by virtue of their difficulty to climb and more due to politics, their remoteness or simply that no one has ever had a go.

'Many climbers want to know what they are likely to encounter before they invest time, energy and money in planning an expedition to a remote massif. They want to know how to get to the foot of the mountain, they want to know that the ice and rock will be climbable, and they want to know what the descent from the summit is like. In short, they want a guidebook. Which is why, in the 21st century, hundreds of virgin peaks still await their first ascents.'
– Paul Deegan,
who has been on expeditions to five continents including to a previously unclimbed mountain range in Central Asia

Introduction – How Do You Know if it's Unclimbed?

It may come as a disappointment to discover that there is no single, definitive list of mountains of the world that are yet to be climbed. Records of unclimbed peaks in certain ranges exist, as do lists of the highest, but there is nothing that could be considered comprehensive.

This is for a number of reasons:

1. Not every ascent of every mountain in history will have been recorded.
2. In less recent reports, where good maps and GPS may not have been available, it may not always be clear exactly which mountains were actually climbed, at least not without some detective work.
3. Different expeditions from different countries with different purposes will all record their expeditions in different places and perhaps different languages.

So while it is quite possible to research a given area and find out who has climbed what and when, there is no grand database that stores all of this information in one convenient place.

The fact is that you may never know for certain whether you are the first person to reach a summit, just as you may reach the top to discover a man-made pile of stones waiting for you. This is both the bane and beauty of planning an expedition to make a first ascent.

It may be a hassle but this mystery loans a little extra excitement to the challenge. The production of a complete list would remove some of the magic and invariably result in a ticking exercise for those that way inclined. Instead, you have to earn your reward through research as well as sweat.

However, finding a peak is just one small part of the process. To get to the top and back down safely, you need to be a good mountaineer. As such, much of this chapter is dedicated to the fundamentals of mountain climbing.

Climbing talk

Climbing is filled with a lot of jargon. Most of the terms are defined in the text below but some of them define concepts which it will be useful to get your head around before reading further:

- Protection – General mountaineering term for equipment used to secure yourself to the mountain. You can gain some security in the event of a fall by attaching yourself to this equipment with a rope. Also called pro or **gear**.

- **Anchor** – Something to which you can attach a rope to take your weight. This could be, for example, a spike of rock or a piece of protection that you have placed.

- **Belay** – This is both an act and a position:
  - The act of paying out a rope to a climbing partner, ready to lock off the rope should they fall. You might say: '*I climbed whilst my partner belayed me*'.
  - The configuration of ropes and anchors from which someone carries out the act of belaying. This involves the belayer attaching themselves to the mountain so that they are secure enough to take the weight of a falling climber. In this instance, you might say: '*I set up a belay at the top of the mountain*'.

- **Pitched climbing** – Any climbing which involves belaying. It results in climbers taking it in turns with one person belaying while the other climbs.

Options – Styles

Guided by a company

It is quite possible to pay a company or individual to guide you up an unclimbed mountain. Greenland and the Himalaya are popular destinations for such trips. The advantages of this approach are:

- Much less experience and skill is required. Check with your guide but this may be as little as basic fitness and some camping experience.

- The guide will already have found the mountain(s) for you.

If your aim is simply to be the first person on top of a given mountain then this is a good way to do that.

Independently organising your own expedition

Organising an independent climbing expedition will involve some or all of the following:

- finding the mountains in the first place;
- arranging the necessary visas and permits;
- organising the logistics of getting yourself and your kit to the base of the mountains.

It is common to use a local agent to help with some parts of your planning.

This approach obviously requires more time, effort and experience than paying a guide. But it is closer to the exploratory spirit of having truly climbed an unclimbed mountain in its fullest sense. As such, it is the assumed approach for this chapter.

'Don't seek or expect publicity, adulation or recognition. Climbing a virgin peak nowadays is a personal quest, and the fulfilment a private serenity to be shared only with your companions and loved ones. Always remember the words of Mallory: "Have we vanquished an enemy? None but ourselves. Have we gained success? That word means nothing here. Have we won a kingdom? No and yes. We have achieved an ultimate satisfaction ... fulfilled a destiny. To

struggle and to understand – never this last without the other; such is the law ..."'
– Martin Moran, British mountain guide and exploratory climber

Alpine or expedition climbing style
Traditionally there have been two broad approaches to mountaineering:

- **Expedition style**: The traditional approach with larger teams shuttling lots of supplies up and down the mountain, sometimes fixing ropes in place for team mates to follow. This suits larger mountains where there is a need to slowly acclimatise to the altitude.
- **Alpine style**: Climbers are self-sufficient, keeping supplies and equipment to a minimum so they can carry it all themselves, and climb quickly to minimise the time spent on the mountain. The alpine style works well for pairs and small groups on mountains that can be tackled in a few days.

These two styles are really at either end of a spectrum with all sorts of approaches sitting somewhere between the two.

Itinerary for climbing a remote mountain
Every mountaineering expedition will follow a different schedule but this is what a typical itinerary looks like after arriving in-country:
1. Travel as far as you can by vehicle.
2. Carry the necessary supplies onwards using pack animals, porters or big rucksacks. (You might be able to skip these two steps if you get dropped off by helicopter or plane.)
3. Find a suitable base camp where you can store your supplies, pitch your tents reasonably comfortably and have access to water.
(Depending on how far away your summit is, Step 4 is optional):
4. Continue the process of shuttling equipment further up the mountain, establishing advance base camps until the summit is within striking distance.

---

5. Take the necessary supplies – be it for a single day's climbing or to include a night or two bivvying – and go for the summit.
6. Return to base camp.
7. Repeat Steps 4 and 5 as appropriate.
8. Reverse the journey to civilisation.

Options – Routes

This section deals with how to actually find mountains that have yet to be climbed.

Remote mountains off the beaten track

Most unclimbed mountains will be reasonably remote. If a mountain is conquerable from road to summit and back again within a day then wherever you are in the world the chances are that it has already been climbed.

Remoteness can mean a far-flung destination, for example:

- Antarctica;
- Kamchatka;
- Greenland;
- Various Arctic islands.

But it also includes the harder to reach regions of well-known destinations such as Alaska, the Himalaya and the Andes.

'Look at Greenland. Compared to other parts of the world it's a perfect location. You can be at base camp beneath an unclimbed summit within 24 hours of leaving the UK.'

– Paul Walker, who offers guided first ascents in Greenland through his company Tangent Expeditions

Neglected mountains with more attractive neighbours

Climb Ben Nevis, the highest mountain in the UK, on any day of the year and you will meet dozens of other walkers. But look across at its closest neighbour, Càrn Mòr Dearg, and you will see far fewer.

This pattern repeats around the world. Certain mountains gain a reputation for being the biggest, best or most beautiful and attract lots of attention to the neglect of everything else in the area.

Find those honeypot areas and move your finger a little further across the map. Avoid the biggest, highest, most accessible area and go for the slightly smaller and more obscure.

The smallest, lowest and least-climbed range in Bolivia
by Tim Moss

Bolivia has four **cordillera** (mountain ranges). Three of them have peaks over 6,000 metres. One of them does not.

The Cordillera Quimsa Cruz, also known as Tres Cruces, also happens to be the smallest of the ranges which probably explains why it gets the least visitors. But it was for these same reasons that we decided to go there.

Sarah Griffin, who led our team, found that only a handful of British expeditions had visited the range. None of the peaks was entirely unclimbed but many had yet to see any Britons on top so we packed our Union Jacks and flew to South America in search of summits.

See: www.quimsacruz.info.

Mountain ranges with a political back story

Many mountainous areas of the world are in, or have been in, politically unstable areas. There is not a lot you can do if politics makes a country inaccessible but you can monitor areas for improvements and capitalise on developments.

Some possible examples include:

• The Former Soviet Union: Largely off-limits to visitors until the

1990s, many ex–Soviet states in Central Asia still have peaks waiting to be climbed. The Tien-Shan in Kyrgyzstan and the Altai mountains in Russia and Kazakhstan are two such examples.

- Jammu and Kashmir: A mountainous region in northern India, largely part of the Himalaya. It has slowly been reducing its restricted areas over recent years allowing access to many new peaks.
- The Wakhan Corridor: Afghanistan is largely out of bounds for the foreseeable future due to the ongoing conflict. However, several recent expeditions have visited a remote strip of the country known as the Wakhan which is bordered by the Hindu Kush mountains and removed from much of the trouble.

Visiting a potentially dangerous area, like Afghanistan, is not something to be done lightly, particularly not just for the sake of climbing a lump of rock. Always check travel advice such as that from the Foreign and Commonwealth Office (FCO). But do some research first before automatically ruling out a country based on its reputation alone.

Climb a bureaucratic or holy mountain
Some mountains of the world remain unclimbed because governments do not allow access, either for bureaucratic or religious reasons.

For example:

- China – The People's Republic is home to several high mountain ranges and many of them contain unclimbed peaks. However, it is often difficult to obtain permits to climb them.
- Bhutan – The highest unclimbed mountain in the world, Gangkhar Puensum (7,570m), lies in Bhutan. However, the Kingdom allows very little climbing at present as such mountains are considered sacred. Similar situations exist for some mountains in Tibet too.

You might not be able to change the rules but you can keep trying and be ready when the rules change.

First national or winter ascent

There are some alternative 'firsts' to being the first to a summit:

- First for your country: Less glory but still some satisfaction to be had from making the first ascent for your country, if only as a nod to a bygone era of exploration.
- First winter ascent: A more merit-worthy option might be becoming the first person to climb a mountain in winter. It is not always the case but the lower temperatures and shorter days will usually make a winter climb much harder.

New routes up old mountains

Far more common than making a first ascent is climbing a new route on a mountain that has previously been summited.

That typically means:

- approaching from a different side, e.g. the north side rather than the south;
- tackling a notable feature such as an unclimbed face or new ridgeline.

Most people will naturally take the easiest route they can find to the top of a mountain so the alternatives tend to be harder. But if you want more of a technical climbing challenge then new route opportunities exist on all but the most popular mountains of the world.

'On more technically demanding, steeper peaks, focus on one move at a time. There is no point in worrying about the next 5,000 feet if you can't do the next move. Looking too far ahead can be overwhelming.'
– Leo Houlding,
a world class climber, alpinist, base jumper and adventurer

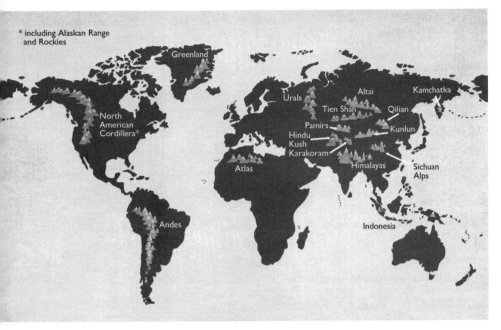

Map 7: World map showing major mountain ranges

Practicalities

Where do you sleep?

Where you sleep may vary depending on the stage of your trip but will include one or more of the following:

- Mountain huts – Less likely in remote areas, there is still a chance you will pass simple wooden huts during your approach to the mountains. Tea lodges are common in the Himalaya.
- Tents – The standard accommodation in the mountains is tents. You may have the relative luxury of a larger, more spacious tent for your base camp in which you can stand up straight and get your whole team inside for dinner. The rest of the time you will typically be in a smaller, two- or three-person tent.

255

- Bivouacs: When weight needs to be kept as low as possible, you may opt to sleep outside without a tent. This also allows you to sleep on small ledges where a tent would not fit.

'Pick the right partner i.e. not only someone who is capable of doing what is planned, but someone you will get on with. You are much more likely to take the right decisions if they are taken harmoniously.'
– Simon Yates,
who has nearly 30 years' experience on high mountains and is best known for climbing Siula Grande in Peru

What do you eat and drink?
The food you eat will usually vary through the different stages of an expedition:

- Local food for base camp – You need food you can transport, that will keep for a long time, and can be cooked on camping stoves. Whatever is available locally should do. For example: rice, pasta and potatoes; dried meats, tinned fish and vegetables; and packets of sauces and herbs.
- Snacks on the move – Snack foods like flapjack, dried fruit, nuts and chocolate are typical while walking and climbing.
- Mountain food – Higher up the mountain, weight and space become factors. For short trips you may rely on snack food. Dehydrated rations are common when cooking as they pack a lot of calories for their weight and are quick and easy to prepare.

Once you reach the **snow line**, water will come from melting snow in a pan with your stove. Anywhere below that, lakes and rivers will be the most likely source. Where necessary it can be purified by boiling or using chlorine tablets, iodine or various different devices.

Where do you go to the loo?

You will be toileting in the great outdoors. When you are up high or experiencing lower temperatures, it can be cold and require a lot of effort to extricate yourself from your sleeping bag and tent in the middle of the night for the sake of a quick wee. As such, a **pee bottle** is often carried.

You want a wide-mouthed bottle that is clearly labelled to avoid confusing it with your water bottle. Women can get a funnel device to help with this such as a SheWee or Pee Zee (actual names). Once full, the bottle is best kept inside your sleeping bag to stop it freezing – it will act like a hot water bottle for a while – and disposed of appropriately in the morning.

How do you know where to go?

Being unclimbed, there will be no guidebook or paths to follow. You will have to stand at the bottom and look for a route up that is accessible and safe, then adapt it is as necessary on your way.

You can use the following to help:

- Maps, photographs and satellite images – Useful for planning your initial approach but not much help once actually on the mountain. Old expedition reports may contain photos and you can print 3D images from Google Earth.
- **Ridges** – These often provide the easiest access to a summit as exemplified by the 'classic' routes up many popular peaks. They are usually obvious to find and follow, and less susceptible to avalanches.
- **Gullies** – Also called **couloirs**, they tend to be steep but comparatively easy to climb. They are your best bet after ridges and often provide an easily traceable route up a mountain. However, gullies also act like funnels for falling snow and rocks so you need to be aware of what is above you.
- Rocky buttresses and steep ice – Typically the hardest options but sometimes the only ones available.

'All mountains are being weathered constantly by the elements, but they do not experience this equally on all sides. In the northern hemisphere, the southern side of mountains go through much greater swings in temperature. Northern aspects will stay frozen more consistently than southern sides, which often freeze during the night and then thaw in the warmth of the day's southern sun. This freezing/thawing action splits rocks, leading to greater erosion and more loose stones and scree.'

– Tristan Gooley, author of *The Natural Navigator*

How long do you actually spend climbing?

It is generally preferable to spend as few days and nights on the slopes of a mountain as possible. The sooner you are down, the sooner you are away from danger and discomfort.

The result is that climbing days can be quite long. On snow, climbers tend to start before sunrise, sometimes in the middle of the night, to maximise the colder time of day when the snow is more stable underfoot.

Eight hours would be a short day and 16 hours would be long but anything up to 24 hours or more is possible. These longer days are usually interspersed with quieter periods, resting at base camp or waiting for good weather.

How long will it take?

The quickest you are likely to travel to a remote mountain range, climb some peaks and get home again, is two weeks. It will take longer if your mountains are harder to reach, you want to climb more than just one or two, and as they get higher because you will need time to acclimatise. Three or four weeks is more likely but it can be twice as long.

The climbing tax man

Winner of the prestigious Piolet d'Or (golden ice axe) award, described by Chris Bonington as 'one of our greatest mountaineers' and voted the 'Mountaineer's Mountaineer', Mick Fowler is a leading figure in British mountaineering.

He has climbed many new and hard routes in the remote ranges of Pakistan, China, India, Peru and the Yukon, to name a few.

He is not a full time, professional mountaineer, however. He is a tax man. He works for HM Revenue and Customs and can only tackle climbs that fit in with his 30 days' annual leave.

When to go

Climbing is possible somewhere in the world at any time of year but tends to be easier in certain periods. Weather is the determining factor and the variables will include:

- Temperature – High mountains are cold places at the best of time so most ranges away from the equator will be more easily climbed in the warmer months. However, even Everest has been climbed in winter and the transition to a warmer season can lead to unstable snow conditions.
- Precipitation – Down low, lots of rain can mean high rivers blocking access to mountains. Higher up you will get snow instead and too much of that can make progress slower and harder.
- Stability – Unpredictable weather can make planning and timing difficult.

These are some broad rules of thumb for peak periods:

- May to October – Most high mountains including those in Asia, Central Asia, and North America, and the parts of the Andes close to the equator.
- November to March – Patagonia and Antarctica.

What if something goes wrong?
Rescue from a mountain is difficult at the best of times and being in a remote area will make it harder.

If you get in trouble half way up a climb, then rescue will almost invariably start from within your team. This might include:

- re-tracing your steps back to base camp;
- **abseiling** where walking is not possible;
- supporting an injured person or carrying them with a makeshift stretcher. This is very hard work without a large group and may simply not be possible on steeper ground;
- an alternative is trying to lower them with ropes.

Once down, you will probably need to reach an appropriate rendezvous somewhere between base camp and civilisation for one or more of the following options:

- pick up by plane or helicopter if you are lucky enough for that facility to be available and there to be somewhere for it to land;
- collection by vehicle as close as it can get to your base camp;
- being carried out of the mountains on horse-back or other pack animal; or
- in the worst case, walking or being carried all the way to the nearest settlement.

Difficulties

Snow slopes, rock faces and steep ice
Although common parlance sees the ascent of any mountain described as a 'climb', the reality is that much of the time you will be walking and scrambling rather than actually climbing with ropes. However, it is these latter times that will often be the more difficult and dangerous.

Big mountains present a variety of different obstacles including:
- Snow slopes – Usually quite easy to climb but can become dangerous

when the snow starts to melt making falls and avalanches more likely.
- Rock faces – There may be times when you need to climb steep sections of rock which will require skill and present the risk of a fall from a false move or loose rock.
- Steep ice – Sometimes it may be necessary to tackle sections of hard ice. This can be physically demanding over long periods. The condition of the ice – how solid and consistent it is – will also affect the difficulty and danger of this.

What's the difference between scrambling and climbing?

Getting to the top of a mountain can require a variety of different climbing styles. Here is a basic overview of the broad categories:

Type	Description	Typical equipment	Rope usage
Scrambling	Easy climbing up short sections of rock where the risk of falling is low.	None.	None.
Walking on snow	Easy walking on snow. Typically found on slopes, **gullies** and **ridges**.	Crampons and one ice axe.	Either unroped or tied to a team mate.
Moving together	Method offering a degree of protection whilst allowing fast movement than pitched climbing. Used on easy to moderate ground where the consequence of a fall would be serious but the risk is manageable.	Basic rock or ice protection. Crampons and axes too if moving on snow and ice.	Roped to team mates all climbing at the same time. First climber secures rope to protection which is removed by last climber.
Rock climbing	Steep sections of rock where walking or scrambling are not possible. Can be very difficult.	Mountaineering boots if cold. Rock shoes if warm. Various anchors to attach a rope to the rock.	Tied onto the mountain. One person climbs whilst the other belays.
Ice climbing	Found on steep glaciers and where water has frozen over rock. Can be difficult when steep and/or the ice is very hard.	Crampons and two ice axes. Anchors that you can secure to ice.	Tied onto the mountain. One person climbs whilst the other belays.
Mixed	Some sections will have both ice and rock, and be too cold or impractical to use rock shoes and bare hands.	Crampons and two ice axes, even when climbing on rock. Anchors for both rock and ice.	Tied onto the mountain. One person climbs whilst the other belays.

'Failing on unclimbed stuff is par for the course. Sometimes it works first time and at others it takes a few goes to get the climb done. It is all part of the experience. And if we fail, it's usually for a good reason.'

– Andy Parkin,

artist and climber who explores the mountain ranges of the world looking for first ascents, adventure and images

Acute Mountain Sickness (AMS)

Most unclimbed mountains are of sufficient height to warrant some thought to altitude and its effects on your body.

The higher you get, the less oxygen there is in the air. The effects of this range from:

- making any exertion feel twice as hard;
- constant headaches;
- reduced appetite;
- interrupted sleep.

Right up to:

- loss of rational thought;
- fluid on the brains or lungs (known as cerebral and pulmonary oedemas respectively) which can result in death.

Your body can slowly adapt to the lack of oxygen but circumstances can limit the amount of time to do so and some people simply do not adapt well.

Adjust to thin air

A basic rule of thumb for climbing above 3,000m is to end each day no more than 300m higher than where you started and to take a day off for every 900m you ascend.

Everyone is different, however, so you should monitor yourself and your team mates. Simple tests such as the **Lake Louise Score** measure your symptoms on a scale.

Some symptoms – like shortness of breath and a mild headache – are common but should pass. If they persist then you should allow longer for your body to acclimatise. If they get worse then the treatment is immediate descent.

There are a few other things that you can do to help ensure optimal acclimatisation, such as:

- drinking plenty of fluids;
- not over exerting yourself until you have adjusted to whatever height you're at;
- climbing high during the day and sleeping low at night;
- using Diamox – the brand name for the drug Acetazolamide – which promotes breathing and gets more oxygen into the blood. However, some argue that this simply masks the problems rather than dealing with them.

These things should only be done in addition to following a gradual ascent programme, not instead.

For more advice on dealing with altitude, visit: www.thebmc.co.uk.

'We live increasingly busy lives with, for many, decreasing job security. In days of yore, going on an expedition involved greater commitment. These days, one of the biggest single factors for failure to reach that desirable summit is lack of time. With the trend towards "quick hits", the schedule for so many parties allows only one major attempt on the peak. Mountain weather is fickle, and another week at base camp could be just enough to give perfect conditions for that second, or third, attempt. You might also consider matching the venue with your time-scale for a greater chance of success.'

– Lindsay Griffin,
who has undertaken many exploratory expeditions to remote ranges
and made dozens of first ascents

Cold temperatures and varied activity levels
The height of a mountain, combined with the winds often experienced up high, can make climbing a cold experience. This is exacerbated by:

- the need to keep weight down – meaning you will probably carry the thinnest sleeping bag and least layers that you can get away with;
- switching between intense bursts of exercise which make you sweat – like hauling yourself up steep sections of rock carrying a heavy pack in the midday sun – and long periods of sitting still, perhaps on snow, while belaying your climbing partner.

You can minimise the amount you sweat by taking off layers before you start moving. Even if it makes you feel cold at first, you need to learn how quickly you will warm up. This sentiment is often summarised with the saying: 'Be bold, start cold'.

Getting caught out in bad weather

A bad forecast or bad weather at the start of a day is unlikely to put you in any danger – you can simply choose not to climb that day. Of more risk is continuing in spite of such warnings, perhaps eager to summit, and being caught in a storm whilst up high.

It is feasible to get weather reports if you have a method of communicating with the outside world otherwise you will be relying on your own observations. Many mountaineers carry watches with barometers so that they can monitor changes in pressure.

Taking a fall

At height, there is always the risk of taking a fall. This can happen both when you are climbing – perhaps struggling on a difficult section or taking a slip on a steep slope – and also during a careless moment such as tripping when going for a wee at night in a precarious location.

You can help minimise the risk with a few basics:

- maintaining vigilance with your footwork at all times;
- double checking knots and other equipment;
- only climbing routes well within your ability while in a remote area.

Touching the void

Siula Grande is a 6,344-metre high peak in the Peruvian Andes. Its west face was first climbed in 1985 by Simon Yates and Joe Simpson who succeeded where several others had failed. However, it is their subsequent descent of the same mountain which has entered mountaineering legend.

Simpson broke his leg on the way down and had to be lowered on a rope by Yates. Inadvertently lowered over the edge of a cliff,

Simpson was unable to climb back with his hands which by then were frost-bitten. He was also too heavy for Yates to pull up and was in fact dragging Yates down towards the cliff edge. Yates was left with little choice but to cut the rope and let his climbing partner fall.

Freed from the rope, Yates was unable to find his team mate. He was in a bad state himself after the long climb and had to descend to base camp alone, certain that his friend had died in the fall.

But Simpson survived. His harrowing three-day crawl over snow and rock, slipping in and out of consciousness from pain and a lack of food and water, is recounted in the best-selling book and film *Touching the Void*.

Falling snow, rocks and ice

Popular skiing and climbing areas have avalanche forecasts but this is less likely for the world's more remote mountains. That means you need to learn how to assess the risk yourself.

There are certain things that you should consider when assessing a slope for avalanche risk. These include:

- recent weather patterns and particularly a change in temperature or heavy snowfall;
- the angle of the slope. Around 30–45 degrees is most prone;
- which way the slope faces. Varying sunlight and wind exposure will make it less stable;
- the shape of the slope. Convex slopes tend to be more prone than concave.

Just as important as the environmental factors is the condition of the snow itself. You can assess this from a safe position on or near the slope by:

- digging into the snow and looking for warning signs such as multiple layers of differing hardness or colour;

- testing a small section of snow by digging a hole at the bottom to see how easily it falls beneath your bodyweight.

Avalanche and snowpack assessment, as it is known, are complicated arts about which even the most experienced mountaineers will keep learning.

In addition to falling snow, falling ice and falling rocks are other hazards you might encounter.

Falling into a crevasse

Crevasses are cracks that appear in glacial ice which threaten to swallow careless or unfortunate climbers. To aid safe travel across glaciers, teams tie ropes between each of their members so they can drag out anyone unlucky enough to take a fall.

Glaciers covered in snow are known as 'wet' and typically present more risk to climbers as it is often impossible to see where a crevasse lies. In contrast, you can often see crevasses many metres away on their dry counterparts.

Crevasse rescue techniques are well documented in mountaineering books and online. They are reasonably straightforward to learn and it would be foolhardy to head into a glaciated area having not practised them.

Getting carried away with 'summit fever'

It is not uncommon for people to get carried away when a goal is in sight. However, pressing onwards to the summit late in the day is particularly risky in mountaineering because:

- you may have limited daylight;
- weather windows can sometimes be narrow;
- if you tire then a single lapse in concentration can be disastrous;
- most accidents on mountains happen during the descent and working extra hard during the ascent may exacerbate this.

As such, it would be wise to remember that the summit is only the halfway mark and give some consideration to your descent when making decisions about how long to keep climbing. Some people agree a fixed time at which to turn back, regardless of how close they are to the top.

'Be prepared to back off. Staying alive is success.'
– Alan Hinkes,
the first Briton to climb the fourteen 8,000-metre peaks
(the highest in the world)

Getting permission to climb

Since remote mountains have a tendency to be in contentious areas, near international borders or in national parks, it is often necessary to obtain some form of permit to climb on them. Sometimes this is a straightforward process, but, unfortunately it is not always easy or indeed possible.

You can find out what you need by:

- scouring the internet. SummitPost.org is a good resource for this;
- reading the reports of expeditions who have visited the area recently;
- contacting local agents or mountaineering groups.

Applications can take time to process so plan ahead.

Kit

Stiff mountaineering boots

Mountaineering boots are much like normal hiking boots except they tend to have:

- Better insulation – Sometimes they even have a removable fleece bootie inside.

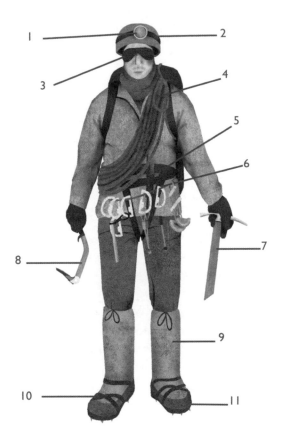

1. Head torch – for hands-free illumination.
2. Helmet for protection from falling debris.
3. Sunglasses – tight fitting to avoid snow blindness.
4. Rope – coiled neatly to avoid tangles.
5. Harness.
6. Protection – ice screws, nuts, cams and other equipment that can securely affix rope to snow, rock and ice.
7. Mountaineering ice axe.
8. Ice climbing axe. (N.B. you wouldn't usually carry these two axes at the same time)
9. Gaiters – waterproof to keep snow out of boots.
10. Crampons – metal spikes for walking and climbing on ice.
11. Boots – stiff soled and made of leather or plastic.

Fig. 7: Typical mountaineer

- A rigid sole – Useful for climbing, allowing purchase with just the edge of the boot, but particularly important for fitting crampons, described below.

There are two main types of mountaineering boot:

1. Leather – Generally better for lower mountains where it is not so cold and for more difficult climbing as they allow better precision.
2. Plastic – Not dissimilar to ski boots, they tend to be warmer so better for higher, colder mountains.

Other footwear in the mountains
You might take some other things to put on your feet as well as mountaineering boots:

- Something more comfortable – Mountaineering boots can be heavy and uncomfortable for long periods for walking. Light walking boots, **trail or approach shoes** (tough trainers) and sandals are common additions and useful for river crossings.
- Climbing shoes – It is relatively rare to undertake difficult rock climbs on a first ascent but in such instances a pair of climbing shoes might be taken. They look a little like ballet shoes – small, thin and tightly bound – have grippy soles and allow delicate foot placements. They have very little insulation though and are not comfortable for walking.
- Skis and snowshoes – If you are going somewhere with a lot of deep snow then you might consider snowshoes or skis. They make travelling easier and spread your weight over a wider area to reduce the risk of falling into crevasse. Skis are more popular in part because they allow for faster and more exciting descents.

Crampons for moving on snow and ice
Crampons are sets of metal spikes that you strap to the bottom of your

boots. Basic crampons will allow you to walk across snow and ice without slipping. The more advanced variants are used on harder ice and more technical climbs as they typically have more and stronger teeth, and more robust attachments to the boot.

Boot and crampon ratings

Boots can be categorised on a rating between 0 and 3 to signify the purpose for which they are designed and the crampons with which they are compatible. Crampons are similarly rated 1-3.

Rating	Boot description	Rating	Crampon description
B0	Light and flexible walking boots that won't reliably take any crampons.		
B1	Flexible but stiff soles. Used for walking but not climbing. Takes C1 crampons.	C1	Flexible crampon. Allows walking on snow and ice. Fits B1–3 boots.
B2	Semi-rigid boots. Designed for mountaineering but not harder ice or mixed climbing. Takes C1 or C2 crampons.	C2	Semi-rigid crampons. Allows easier level ice and mixed climbing. Fits B2 and B3 boots.
B3	Fully rigid boots. Designed for mountaineering including steep ice and hard mixed climbing. Takes any crampons.	C3	Fully rigid crampons. Allows steep ice and hard mixed climbing. Only fits B3 boots.

The higher the number, the more expensive and heavy the equipment tends to become.

Ice axe for many tasks beyond climbing

An ice axe is a key piece of equipment for a mountaineer. You might typically associate them with the overhead swinging motion of a climber on steep ice but there are many other uses, including:

- **arresting** (stopping) yourself should you take a fall on a snow slope;
- support when walking uphill through snow;
- digging snow and/or burying the axe to create an anchor off which you can abseil or belay a climbing partner;
- cutting out sections of snow to check its condition and avalanche risk.

There are many types of ice axe which sit on a spectrum between two extremes:

1. General mountaineering axes – Long, straight shafts that are good for arresting, walking uphill and creating anchors but hard to use for climbing steep ice.
2. Ice climbing axes – Short, curved axes that allow easier overhead swinging but are less good for arresting and making anchors.

Equipment for climbing

There is a huge range of equipment available for climbing and climbers often take great pride in collecting a large **rack** of gear, as it is known.

However, the most pertinent pieces are:

- Harness – This is tied round your waist and attached to a rope. It also has loops on either side onto which you can clip other equipment so it is easily accessible.
- Rope(s) – Mountaineering ropes are typically 50 or 60m long. The ropes are **dynamic**, meaning that they stretch a little under strain which makes the impact of a fall less painful. They are used for abseiling (lowering yourself), attaching yourself to team mates, and tying onto protection.
- Protection – There are many types of protection but some common ones include:
- Nuts – small metal wedges you lodge into gaps in the rock.
- Camming devices – spring-loaded devices that can be slotted into a gap and then expanded once inside. Usually just called cams.
- Slings – loops of cord or tape that you can wrap around spikes of rock.
- **Ice screws** – metal screws you bore into ice.

Helmet to protect yourself

A hard plastic helmet is usually worn any time you are using ropes, axes or crampons. It offers some protection from:
- falling snow, ice, rocks and equipment;

- impact following a fall;
- the sharp points on the axes and crampons you and your team mates are carrying.

Kit for performing a crevasse rescue

The basic requirements for rescuing someone from a crevasse include:

- a rope (hopefully already tied to the person that's fallen in);
- some protection – ice screws or similar – to anchor yourself to the glacier and avoid anyone falling further into the crevasse;
- something to act as a pulley to make it easier to haul the person out of the crevasse. Karabiners will suffice although you can take pulleys specifically for this purpose;
- something that will lock the rope so that you can pull it in one direction (up!) and not have it fall back down again. You can get a special piece of equipment for this or use **prusik loops**. These are short loops of cord that you can wrap around a rope to achieve the same effect.

Layers of clothing to deal with a range of conditions

Climbers use multiple thin layers of clothing rather than one or two thicker layers as it allows more clothing combinations to cope with a wider range of conditions.

These layers are typically split into:

- **Wicking** base layer – This should be tight fitting and worn next to your skin. Wicking refers to the ability to quickly remove sweat which is important because wet clothes are much colder. Synthetic fabrics do this best although merino wool is also popular.
- Insulating mid layers – Fleece, pile, and down and synthetic equivalents to keep you warm. You might carry several such layers.
- Weather proof shell layer – Protection from the elements. Goretex, Paramo and Event are common waterproof layers. Although rain is usually rare high on mountains, it can happen lower down and these

materials are also good for blocking wind and shedding snow. Alternative **soft shell** garments offer wind and rain protection to a lesser degree but breathe better meaning your sweat can escape more easily.

Tent and bivvy bags for shelter at night

You will need one or more of the following:

- Base camp tent – Weight and weather are less of an issue low on a mountain so, if you have a separate tent for base camp, then you can afford a larger, heavier one.
- Mountain tent – When you have to carry a tent yourself, the most desirable attributes will quickly become low pack size and weight while maintaining strength against high winds. Dome tents (sometimes called **geodesic**) are the most popular as they tend to be a strong design with efficient use of space.
- Bivvy bags – A large cover for your sleeping bag, usually waterproof, that offers some extra warmth and wind protection.

Sleeping bag and mattress

Down sleeping bags are usually preferable as they are so much lighter for their warmth than synthetic equivalents and high mountains tend to be dry.

Because of the need to keep weight down, it is common to carry a slightly lighter sleeping bag than would normally be ideal but wear clothes and a hat at night to compensate.

Sleeping mats are important for warmth as well as comfort, particularly when sleeping on snow or ice. There are a few types:

- Solid foam – Big and bulky. You usually have to strap them to the outside of your rucksack which might be awkward for climbing but they are cheap and indestructible.
- Self-inflating – Thin mattresses containing a less dense foam material that expands with air. These tend to be smaller, lighter and warmer than the solid foam option. They are more expensive though and there is a risk of puncture.

- Down- and synthetic-filled mattresses – These are like a warmer version of a lilo. They are similar to the self-inflating options but offer even better insulation and are more expensive still. They also take a couple of minutes to inflate by hand.

Equipment for communicating with the team and the outside world

You can climb a new mountain without any communication equipment but here are some options you might consider:

- **UHF and VHF radios** – Also known as walkie-talkies, these might help communicate between camps or belays over short distances with line of sight. VHF radios are more powerful with a longer range but a little heavier and more expensive and sometimes require permits. The acronyms stand for Ultra and Very High Frequency.
- Mobile phone – Most remote mountain ranges will be well out of range for mobile masts but don't always make that assumption, especially once you are on top. The author picked up signal at 3,000m on the summit of a previously unclimbed Siberian peak.
- Satellite phone – A satphone should get a signal in all but the steepest sided valleys.
- **EPIRB/PLB** – An emergency beacon might also be a consideration.

Either take enough batteries for these gadgets to last the duration of your trip or take some means of charging them such as a solar panel.

'Ensure you and everyone with you are clear of the objectives on a rolling basis. Know your collective limitations, find appropriate solutions, pin your ears back and remember to look around and enjoy the panorama.'
– Neil Laughton,
who has climbed the highest mountain on each of the seven continents

Rucksack to carry all of the above

Mountaineering rucksacks tend to:

- be tall and narrow to allow your arms room to move while climbing and not get stuck in tight sections. They lack external pockets for the same reasons;
- have a few straps dangling or an option to tie them away neatly so they don't catch on your axe or crampons;
- be as light as possible whilst still being tough enough to withstand being dragged over rocks.

It's not uncommon to take a large rucksacks, perhaps 60–80 litres, during a walk to base camp, then switch to a small pack, perhaps 30–50 litres, while climbing.

And don't forget to take ...

Don't forget the following:

- hats and gloves and spare hats and gloves;
- hat and cream to deal with the strong sun, sunglasses to avoid snow blindness from the reflective snow, and goggles if you anticipate bad weather;
- maps, compass, GPS and Google Earth satellite imagery printouts;
- a probe for testing snow and avalanche risk and **avalanche transponders** which help find people buried by snow;
- survival bag for when you are not carrying overnight kit;
- first-aid kit and the training to use it properly;
- a head torch or two with spare batteries;
- a multi-fuel stove that works well in the cold and will burn whatever fuel you find locally.

'Do not overload yourself with excessive equipment and supplies, but do take plenty of resolve and as

much humility as you have. Always remember that getting back tired, safe and happy is the final goal, and that exploration is always worthwhile even if you do not reach a summit. Good luck and enjoy.'
– Roger Payne,
who has made over 20 expeditions to the high peaks of the world
including first ascents on four continents

A Day in the Life of a Mountaineer
by Andy Kirkpatrick

Andy Kirkpatrick has been described as a climber with a penchant for the cold, the hard and the difficult. He specialises in winter expeditions and climbing big walls – huge vertical faces that can take several days to ascend. He has climbed the notorious El Capitan in Yosemite over 15 times, spent two weeks climbing the West face of the Dru in winter – one of Europe's hardest routes – and had several winters climbing in Patagonia. He has written three books, produced several DVDs and gives regular motivational speeches.

'Ernest Hemingway said that mountaineering was one of the only sports, the rest being just "games". But he was a tourist and really hadn't a clue what he was on about. Mountaineering is no sport.

Mountaineering is total war and total peace. Mountaineering is love and hatred, of yourself and your partners. Mountaineering is hope and despair, up and down, stop and go. Mountaineering is life and death.

The life of a mountaineer is the life of a fantasist and dreamer, believing that with dedication, focus and a good weather forecast they might climb the mountains and routes of their dreams. For most this is their overriding passion; every waking hour spent climbing these mountains within the mind, every hold touched, every ice field traversed, every little chink in the climb's armour sought out. The climb rehearsed over and over and over. In doing this the dreamer begins to believe that perhaps this one could come true.

And so one day the climb begins, and if you're lucky that dream does indeed come true, but more often than not it doesn't — well not unless you keep your dreams and mountains small — so don't worry too much about it.

The best mountaineer is an Olympic athlete, a horrible thing to be. A person with no room for anything or anyone but the pursuit of gold. But a medal or a summit is an empty trinket without the colour of life. So my advice when it comes to how far you allow yourself to slip under climbing's spell is the same as the instinct all us monkeys are born with, and that's to get a grip and never let go.

There is much romance written about mountains and mountaineering, but mostly these are the rose tinted views of the tourist like Hemingway who sees only a postcard view. To understand mountains you must commit everything. To spend some time below, on, or if you're lucky, on top of a mountain is to know that there is no romance, only desire, fear and relief - and in between each, a drop of the most precious peace. To know the dragon you must sleep on its back, but if you dare you'll gain a mighty reward.

To know a mountain and what mountaineering is, is to know what it takes it gives back. But ultimately there is nothing there but you, what you bring, what you take, and what you leave behind.'

To read more about Andy and get his books and DVDs, visit: www.andy-kirkpatrick.com.

Costs

- Flights and transport: £600–£2000+. This will be influenced by how far you have to fly and how easy the base of your mountain is to reach. Lots of pack animals or sherpas can be expensive, and chartering a plane or helicopter even more so.
- Visas and permits: £50–£1,000+. Some unclimbed peaks require expensive permits and other times you won't need anything besides a tourist visa.
- Equipment: £1,000–£4,000+. For less difficult mountains you can avoid much of the expensive climbing equipment but certain items – like tents, boots and sleeping bags – are unavoidably expensive.

- Supplies: £5–£15/day. Ration packs can be expensive but locally sourced food is often very cheap.
- In-country agent: £0–£1,000+. Not always necessary but often useful for complicated itineraries in difficult areas.
- Communications: £0–£400+. Satphones, EPIRBs and solar panels.

Lowest total cost – £2,000
Fly to Central Asia with a tourist visa, hire horses for a day's walk to base camp, avoid technical climbing and rely on supermarket food.

More typical total cost – £5,000
Fly to the high mountains of Asia, pay an agent to arrange permits and logistics, and get dropped by helicopter to climb technical peaks relying on ration packs.

Sample budget: Kyrgyzstan
by Tim Moss

My first mountaineering expedition was to the Tien Shan mountains of Kyrgyzstan in 2003. Not including equipment, the entire expedition cost around £1,000.

Here is a rough overview of our budget:

- Flights to Kyrgyzstan: £500
- Accommodation: £75
- In-country transport: £75
- Local agent and food at base camp: £150
- Food: £100
- Insurance: £150
- Visas and permits: £50

A more recent expedition to the Russian Altai mountains – which required horses on the walk to and from base camp but no new equipment – totalled £1,300 per person.

Training

Rock climbing indoors and out
Learning about climbing will be a necessary step for scaling big mountains:

- Indoor climbing: Basic rope and climbing skills can be learnt on indoor walls. Most walls offer beginners' courses and there are often clubs you can join. There are plenty of climbing handbooks which can be useful for learning different rope techniques and best practice.
- Outdoor climbing: Climbing on real rock with real weather will always be better training than a sanitised gymnasium so take opportunities whenever you can. Start with **single pitch** climbs which are no longer than a rope's length, then move to longer **multi-pitch climbing** where climbs happen in several stages. It is also important to learn about placing protection in what is known as **traditional, or trad, climbing**.

Most first ascents will not require lots of elaborate climbing manoeuvres. As such, training is less about becoming an expert rock climber and more about learning efficient rope work and safe practice in a variety of environments.

To get a sense of what it could be like on a big mountain, practise tying your knots in the shower wearing gloves with the lights off.

Getting used to a mountain environment and learning good camp craft
As well as needing to know specific techniques like avalanche assessment and abseil methods, you also want to develop a general sense of outdoor savvy. This includes things like:

- how fast you travel on different terrains and how much ground you can cover in a day;

- route finding without a map and navigation when visibility is only a few yards;
- keeping your wits about you at the end of a long day when it is cold and dark, and you are tired and wet;
- efficient bag packing so you know your gloves are at the top when you need them and can access your first aid kit quickly should the need arise.

The way to get this experience is simply by spending time in a mountainous environment, walking, climbing and camping.

Winter and Alpine mountaineering
Big mountains invariably involve travel on snow and ice. British winters in North Wales, the Lake District and the Highlands are a great place to get experience of that. You could start with an introductory winter skills course.

Some basic skills to learn include:

- walking in crampons;
- performing an ice axe arrest;
- different methods for climbing snow slopes;
- setting up belay anchors in snow.

You will also need to move onto more advanced skills such as:

- glacier travel and crevasse rescue;
- **moving together** and the need for efficiency and swiftness.

Working towards qualifications
You don't need any qualifications to go mountaineering but the courses are an excellent way to learn the fundamentals, even if you just do the training and don't end up taking the assessment.

Here are some that may be useful:

- Summer Mountain Leader (ML) – Basic training for leading groups in the British mountains including navigation.
- Winter Mountain Leader (WML) – Covers skills for mountaineering on snow and ice, including some rope work and avalanche assessment.
- Single Pitch Award (SPA) – Introductory climbing including setting up anchors and belays.
- Mountain Instructor Award (MIA) – Covers more advanced climbing on longer routes.

Getting hill fit

Mountaineering is not a high-intensity activity. It tends to be an endurance event. Apart from those attempting the hardest routes, most mountaineers don't undertake strict training regimes. The best training is simply getting out in the hills for long walks with a heavy pack.

'Research hard and well, balance the risks and retreat only when you can sleep easily knowing that you tried your best.'
– Mick Fowler,
winner of the Piolet d'Or Golden Ice Axe award and voted the 'Mountaineer's Mountaineer'

First Steps

1. Start by walking and wild camping in a National Park to get a taste of long mountain days and practise camp craft.
2. Sign up for a climbing course, join a club or a go to a local wall to learn some basic ropework and climbing skills.
3. Build up to climbing outdoors and in the mountains.

4. The next step is winter mountaineering. A course in Scotland is a good place to start.

5. Book a cheap flight to the Alps to teach yourself about glacier travel and the importance of travelling fast and light. Perhaps you will have met more experienced climbers who will take you out, otherwise you could hire a guide or attend another course.

6. Consolidate your experience with more time spent in the mountains, in winter conditions and on the continent when you can. Meanwhile, keeping read up on mountaineering techniques and perhaps work towards some qualifications.

7. Now pick a country or mountain range that appeals. Read past expedition reports from the area, dig around online and contact local companies to ascertain some possible targets then start planning.

'Get The Information. In other words, find out the local knowledge from local based people and people who have climbed on the mountain before, or attempted it. If people have failed or had problems, why is that? Obviously, all info must be from a reliable source and viewed in context of the conditions at that time. Knowing options for escape and descents is vital.'
– Andy Cave,
who has climbed many new and hard routes around the world and written two award winning books

Easier, Harder, Different

- Climb the highest of them all - Gangkhar Puensum (7,570m) – in Bhutan. Unfortunately, permission to climb high peaks in the Kingdom has not been granted since 1994 so you may have to wait a while.

- Find the unclimbed peak with the greatest prominence – height from base to summit – rather than altitude. Adam Helman devotes an entire chapter of his book *The Finest Peak* to the search for this mountain.
- Do the opposite of tackling an unclimbed peak and go for a classic instead: the Matterhorn in the Alps; the Caucusus' Mount Elbrus; Mount Washington near Seattle or any of the hundreds of popular peaks around the world.
- Climb the 22km-high Olympus Mons which remains unclimbed by virtue of being the highest mountain on Mars.
- Instead of a first ascent, try a first descent – skiing a route that has never been done before.

Resources

- The American Alpine Journal – Good resource for researching past ascents, particularly in the **Greater Ranges** and Americas – see: www.americanalpineclub.org.
- The British Mountaineering Council (BMC) – Medical and equipment advice, insurance, grants and local climbing groups – see: www.thebmc.co.uk.
- International Mountaineering and Climbing Federation (UIAA) – Articles on equipment, technique and medical advice – see: www.theuiaa.org.
- Jonathan Conville Memorial Trust – Heavily subsidised Scottish and Alpine mountaineering courses – see: www.jcmt.org.uk.
- Royal Geographical Society Expedition Report Database – Thousands of expedition reports covering most mountain ranges of the world – see: www.rgs.org/expeditionreports.
- The Alpine Club – Expedition report database, Himalayan Index of mountains and a library of mountaineering books and journals – see: www.alpine-club.org.uk.
- Summit Post – Large database of expedition reports and information on different mountains, routes and ranges including weather and permits – see: www.summitpost.org.

Training programmes and qualifications come from the following associations:

- Mountain Leader Training Association (www.mlta.co.uk);
- Association of Mountaineering Instructors (www.ami.org.uk);
- British Association of International Mountain Leaders (www.baiml.org);
- British Mountain Guides (www.bmg.org.uk).

Special thanks

Thanks to Thom Allen and Michael Halls-Moore.

Did I Miss Something?

I have tried hard to include as thorough and accurate information as possible but I welcome input to improve for the future.

Omissions – Is there something I should have included or failed to answer?
Corrections – Do you think I got something wrong?
Feedback – What can I do better?

Please send your comments, feedback and suggestions to: feedback@thenextchallenge.org.

You can check my website for any corrections or amendments, at: www.thenextchallenge.org/books.

One Tiny Step

So, you have read the book and filled your mind with information and ideas.

What next?

Information can be empowering but it can also be daunting. *So much to learn! So many questions!* You may feel like it will take you forever to find all of the answers but I will let you in on a little secret: nobody has them.

People go away on an expedition and come back time and again without knowing all the answers. It is important to research and plan but there comes a point at which the correct step forward is action.

Things will go wrong. That is the nature of expeditions. You will make mistakes and you will learn from them – but if you never begin, then you will never know what you are capable of.

The first step need only be a small one – ordering a book, emailing a company, booking a flight – just be sure you take it.

If you think that I can help you with an expedition, then please get in touch. All emails come directly to me, and so far, I have replied to every one.

Email: tim@thenextchallenge.org.

Acknowledgements

Writing this book has been a long and hard process but a deeply satisfying one too. I am very fortunate to have been helped so much along the way by such a variety of people.

This list will not cover them all but I am certainly thankful to the following:

The contributors who put up with my persistent questions: Sam, Louis-Philippe, Alex, Helen, Chris, Rachel, Ben, Scotty and, most of all, Andreas. Also, Tom Brearley and Robbie Briton.

The 'Day in the Life' authors: Charles, Sarah M, Sarah O, Al, Skip, Felicity and Andy.

The illustrators, Jim Shannon, Rebecca Peacock and Ted Hatch.

All those who kindly contributed the advice you see quoted throughout this book. And Cath Bruzzone for all the advice you've given me.

My proofreaders: Jamie Abbey, Thom Allen, Michael Halls-Moore, Jonathan Bartlett, Tom Allen, David Pearson, Nancy Williams, Lucy Bruzzone, my mum, and my Proof Reader In Chief – Laura – whose influence is apparent on every page of this book.

I scoured the internet endlessly during my research but I owe a particular thanks to www.adventurestats.com and www.oceanrowing.com for their impeccable records.

Finally, amongst the many other people that I could mention, I would like to give a special thank you to all those who have followed my website over the last three years, emailed me about your expeditions and otherwise given me the encouragement to continue with what I have been doing.

Glossary

Abseiling – Method of lowering oneself using a rope. Used for descending sections of mountain too steep for walking, e.g. back down a route up which you have just climbed.

Acute Mountain Sickness (AMS) – Collection of symptoms experienced as a result of the lack of oxygen at altitude. Sometimes just called altitude sickness.

Aft – Back of a boat. Also called the stern.

Alpine style – Self-sufficient style of mountaineering with a focus on travelling fast and light.

Anchor (climbing) – Something to which you can attach a rope to take your weight.

Antiemetic – Drug used to combat motion sickness.

Arresting – Method of stopping oneself from falling down a snow or ice slope with an ice axe. A tumbling or sliding mountaineer would 'perform an ice axe arrest'.

Auto pilot – Equipment used to automatically steer a boat.

Automatic Identification System – Tracking system used on boats.

Avalanche transponder – Electronic gadgets which indicate the location of team members. Carried in areas with a high avalanche risk so that you can find a team mate should they get buried by snow.

Bar bag – Small bag that attaches to the handlebars of a bike for easy access whilst cycling. Also called a handlebar bag.

Barneo – A temporary Russian base that is set up every year on the sea ice about 60 nautical miles from the Geographic North Pole. It has an ice runway and helicopters at its disposal and is thus used as a stepping stone for many expeditions. Sometimes spelled 'Borneo'.

Bedouin – Technically an ethnic group but a term now commonly used to refer more broadly to any Arabic desert-dwelling nomads.

Bedu socks – Woollen socks made by Bedouin for walking in deserts, they have long thin hairs which are supposed to keep scorpions away.

Belay (position) – A configuration of ropes and protection from which someone carries out the act of belaying.

Belaying (act) – Paying out rope to a climbing partner, ready to hold them if they take a fall.

Bivvy bag – Waterproof cover for a sleeping bag. See Introduction chapter.

Black water – Waste water.

Blue ice runway – A landing strip made of ice.

Boom – The horizontal beam running perpendicular to a ship's mast. Adjusted to maximise the wind in the sails.

Bottle cage – The metal or plastic holder on a bike's frame that carries water bottles.

Bow – Front of a boat.

Broach – Excessive rolling of a boat to one side as a result of waves or wind.

Cape Arktichevsky, Ward Hunt Island and Cape Discovery – Locations on the coast of Russia and Canada commonly used as start points for full distance North Pole expeditions.

Capsize – A boat getting rolled over and upside down.

Cassette – The stack of cogs on the back wheel of a bike.

Catamaran – Boat with two hulls.

Chain whip – A tool used to grip the cogs on a bike while removing the cassette.

Chart – Map of the sea.

Cockpit – Place from which a boat is steered.

Cordillera – Another word for a mountain range.

Couloir – French word for gully.

Crevasses – Large cracks in the ice of a glacier.

Cruising ships – Boats designed for long, slow passages.

De-salinator – Machine that removes the salt from sea water to make it drinkable.

Dynamic rope – A type of rope that stretches a little. Used by climbers to lessen the impact of a fall.

Electrolyte – Group of minerals that your body needs to function properly. They are lost through sweat and can be replaced by a varied diet, unrefined salt and hydration supplements.

EPIRB/PLB – Emergency beacon. See Introduction chapter for details.

Expedition style – Traditional approach to climbing mountains involving large teams and large volumes of kit to lay a mount under siege.

Gear – Colloquial name for climbing protection: equipment used to secure a rope and a climber to a mountain.

Geodesic (dome) tent – Tent shaped like an igloo. See Introduction chapter for details.

GPS – Global Positioning System – Used at its most basic to provide current coordinates but can also store maps, plot routes and calculate times and distances.

Greater Ranges – The high mountains of Asia such as the Himalaya, Hindu Kush and Tien Shan.

Gully – Like a vertical ditch on the side of a mountain. They tend to fill with snow or loose rocks and can often provide an easy route of ascent.

Head – Name given to the toilet on a boat.

Heel – The leaning or rocking of a boat.

Hobble – The act of tying a camel's legs together to stop it running away at night or when unattended.

Hose-clamp – Adjustable device for holding things together. Small, cheap and useful for emergency repairs to a bike.

Ice screw – Device for securing a climber or a rope into thick ice.

Immersion suit – An all-in-one dry suit that covers you from hood to booties to help protect from hypothermia and the ravages of the sea while keeping you buoyant and visible.

Jackline – Rope that runs around the deck of a boat to which you clip on.

Jury rig – Makeshift mast and sail combination.

Katabatic winds – Gravity-assisted winds that flow from the South Pole outwards.

Knockdown – A boat being tipped onto its side such that the mast is horizontal to the water.

Knot – Measurement of speed. One nautical mile per hour. Abbreviated to kn, kt, or kts.

Lake Louise Score – Self-assessment test for measuring the symptoms of Acute Mountain Sickness.

Last Degree – The distance between the 89th degree of latitude and the 90th where the Geographic North and South Poles are located.

Leads – The stretches of open water that appear amidst sea ice on the Arctic Ocean.

Lee cloth – Material used to keep sailors in their beds as a boat rocks.

Live-aboard – Term used to describe those who live on a boat.

Master link – A spare section of bicycle chain that allows you to remove and fix your chain without using tools. Also known as a power link or quick link.

Mayday – Distress signal.

Monohull – Boat with a single hull.

Montane desert – Arid environment at high altitude. Some areas of the Himalaya fall into this category.

Moving together – Method of climbing or scrambling using a rope but without stopping to belay.

Multi-fuel stove – Stove that burns several types of liquid fuel. See Introduction chapter.

Multi-hull – Boat with more than one hull such as a catamaran or trimaran.

Multi-pitch climbing – Type of climbing that involves ascending several lengths of rope (known as pitches), taking it in turns to belay and climb with a partner.

Multi-tool – Like a pen knife for bikes. Typically a collection of Allen keys, screw drivers and other useful tools for adjusting your bike.

Nautical miles – The standard measurement for travel at sea. Also used in the polar world. It is equal to 1.15 miles.

Odometer – Simple computer that uses a magnet attached to the wheel of a bike to calculate speed, distance and time.

Pan-pan – Signal used at sea to indicate urgency.

Parasail – Another name for a kite used with wind to propel a skier over ice.

Patriot Hills/Union Glacier – An Antarctic base camp with an ice runway which is run by Antarctic Logistics & Expeditions (ALE).

Pee bottle – Bottled used to urinate inside a tent or sleeping bag and avoid going outside in bad weather or at night.

Pitched climbing – Any climbing which involves belaying. It results in climbers taking it in turns with one person belaying while the other climbs.

Pitchpoling – An end-over-end capsize of a boat which usually results from surfing too fast down a wave.

Port – Left side of the boat when facing the bow.

Pressure ridges – Large blocks of ice that rise up from the pressure of moving ice on the Arctic Ocean.

Prusik loop – Short loop of cord that can be tied around a rope to grip it when bearing weight. Used during crevasse rescue and for ascending a rope.

Pulk – The sled full of equipment and supplies that you drag behind you.

Rack – Name given by climbers to their collection of climbing equipment.

Radar detector – Electronic equipment that detects large objects in the vicinity.

Radar reflector – Picks up incoming radar signals and sends them back, amplified, to increase the likelihood of a small vessel appearing on someone else's radar. Also called a transponder.

Rally raids – Long distance off-road driving races, sometimes competitive, sometimes just for fun.

Ration packs – A package with sufficient easily prepared meals, snacks, and drinks for a single day's activity.

Recumbent – A bike that puts the rider in a reclined position, closer to the ground. They spread the rider's weight onto the back as well as backside and tend to be faster than upright bikes by virtue of improved aerodynamics.

Ridge – Long, thin line of elevated rock or snow leading to or between mountains.

Rigging – The combination of masts and sails on a boat.

Rudder – Blade beneath a boat used for steering. Controlled with a wheel on most cruisers.

Sastrugi – Ridges of compact snow formed by wind in Antarctica that can make dragging a pulk frustrating work.

Satellite phone – Like a moblie phone but which transmits via satellites rather than phone masts. They can be used anywhere on the planet with an open view of the sky.

Sea ice – The frozen ocean on which North Pole expeditions are largely conducted.

Semi-desert – region with many desert-like properties but which does not meet the exact criteria for desert classification.

Single pitch climbing – Type of climbing that can be completed from bottom to top with a single length of rope.

Skin – Attachment for skis that gives traction without impeding forward movement.

Snow line – The point on a mountain above which snow does not melt.

Soft shell – Type of outer garment that offers some protection from the elements but sacrifices complete waterproofness in favour of better breathability.

Sport climbing – Climbing where artificial protection is available such as metal bolts drilled into a wall.

Sportive – Large, organised cycling event.

Squall – Small and sudden localised storm.

SSB radio – Method of communicating between boats over large distances. Also called HF (High Frequency) radio.

Starboard – Right side of the boat when facing the bow.

Swag bag – Heavy cotton bag used to protect yourself from creatures and the elements when sleeping. Common in Australia.

Tarpaulin – Large sheet strung between trees to provide shelter. See Introduction chapter.

Trade winds – Another name for prevailing winds.

Traditional (or trad) climbing – Method of climbing in which the climber places their own protection against a fall. An alternative to sport climbing.

Trail or approach shoes – Names given to a collection of shoes similar to trainers but a bit tougher and with better grip.

Tropical cyclone – Large area of low pressure containing lots of storms.

Tuareg – The nomadic inhabitants of the Sahara in North and West Africa.

UHF radio – Ultra High Frequency. Technical name for walkie-talkies.

Unassisted – An expedition can be called this if it is entirely self-sufficient and does not use external help such as having a plane drop off supplies. The term 'without resupply' is often used too.

Unsupported – An expedition can be called this if it works under its own steam and does not make use of things like animals or motors.

Vapour barrier liner – A waterproof liner that goes inside your sleeping bag to prevent your body's moisture from reaching the bag.

VHF radio – Very High Frequency. See Introduction chapter.

Wet rations – Pouches containing instant, ready to eat meals. Unlike their dehydrated 'dry' counterparts, they do not require water and can be eaten cold. See Introduction for more on this.

Wicking layer – Garment that quickly removes sweat. See Introduction chapter.

Wind vane self-steering – Simple mechanical method of maintaining direction on a boat.

Some other titles from How To Books

MAKE & MEND
A guide to recycling clothes and fabrics

REBECCA PEACOCK AND SAM TICKNER

This book shows how, with a little knowledge and creativity, you can make a wide range of fantastic items from those old clothes and fabrics you can't bear to throw away. Whether it's a cushion cover from a coat, a tote bag from a torn dress or a neck tie from a negligee, this book will show you how to make it. Packed full of projects, from aprons to curtains, bags to jewellery, we show you how to turn a pile of scraps into wearable, beautiful and personalized items. Each project offers a step-by-step guide to making successful pieces.

ISBN 978-1-905862-79-5

LIKELY STORIES

Fabulous, inspirational, chuckleworthy and deeply instructive Tales about creative writing as told to the author by his ubiquitous Guru

HUGH SCOTT
Whitbread winning author

Originally published as articles in the *Writers' Forum* magazine, these tales tell of the author's adventures when he meets his Guru, a fabulous and wise Being who appears in many guises and who guides his pupil in the sometimes bewildering ways of creative writing. Each story covers an aspect of creative writing such as character, dialogue, atmosphere, writers' block, vocabulary, etc.

ISBN 978-1-84528-461-8

POCKET WEDDING PLANNER

ELIZABETH CATHERINE MYERS

In this short easy-to-read guide a professional wedding planner gives you the benefit of all her experience and advice on organising a fabulous wedding. Use this book to plan your wedding and you will keep the romance in your very special day, without the stress and the costs spiralling out of control. In fact, you are likley to save hundreds if not thousands of pounds.

ISBN 978-1-84528-485-5

HOW TO COOK YOUR FAVOURITE TAKEAWAY FOOD AT HOME

The food you like to eat when you want to eat it – at less cost and with more goodness

CAROLYN HUMPHRIES

Why do we eat takeaways? Because they taste great and mean we don't have to slave over a hot stove for hours. But the downsides are they cost a fortune, and are full of excess fat, salt and sugar so can be pretty unhealthy. What if you could have the best of both worlds? This book gives you great-tasting, very quick to prepare, healthy versions of your favourite fast foods using simple, fresh and frozen ingredients that put pounds back in your pocket, not on your waistline. It includes Indian, Chinese, Japanese, pizzas, pasties and good old fish and chips.

ISBN 978-1-905862-93-1

A GUIDE TO MODERN GAMEKEEPING

Essential information for part-time and professional gamekeepers

J C JEREMY HOBSON

This book is a comprehensive gamekeeping manual for those enthusiastic amateurs who spend their spare time running a small DIY syndicate shoot, and for those who are professionally employed on a full-time basis. It shows the reader how to perform all the tasks required of the modern gamekeeper, including how to rear and release game and it advises on many aspects of habitat improvement and conservation. It also covers important and sometimes controversial issues, such as public access on private land, the need for predator and pest control, and many other aspects which need to be considered by keepers, be they part-time or professional.

ISBN 978-1-84528-497-8

CHOOSE THE RIGHT WORD
An entertaining and easy-to-use guide to better English – with 70 test-yourself quizzes

ROBIN HOSIE & VIC MAYHEW

Light-hearted does not have to mean lightweight. *Choose the Right Word* sets out the commonsense, if sometimes confusing, rules of the English language without resorting to the tedium of technical terms that are understood only by professional grammarians. It is a valuable source of reference for people whose grammar may have become a little rusty over the years, and the quizzes help them to measure progress at their own rate. This entertaining, reliable and easy-to-use guide to better English features guidance on grammar rules and when they can be bent; spelling and pronunciation tips; fun facts; and around 70 test-yourself quizzes.

ISBN 978-1-84528-499-2

EVERYDAY CURRIES
How to cook your own tasty curry dishes at home

CAROLYN HUMPHRIES

Curries are amongst our favourite foods but few of us go to the trouble of making our own, preferring to resort to cook-in sauces or takeaways. But curries don't have to be complicated to make. In fact, they are really easy to cook at home, and a great way to serve delicious meals with a variety of fresh ingredients, lots of healthy vegetables and stacks of flavour. This book focuses on Indian curries, but for those who enjoy Thai, Malaysian or Chinese curries, there are plenty of those in here, too.

ISBN 978-1-905862-92-4

How To Books

are available through all good high street and on-line bookshops,
or you can order direct from us through Grantham Book Services.

Tel: +44 (0)1476 541080
Fax: +44 (0)1476 541061
Email: orders@gbs.tbs-ltd.co.uk
Or via our website
www.howtobooks.co.uk

To order via any of these methods please quote the title(s) of the book(s)
and your credit card number together with its expiry date.

For further information about our books and catalogue,
please contact:

How To Books
Spring Hill House
Spring Hill Road
Begbroke
Oxford
OX5 1RX

Visit our web site at
www.howtobooks.co.uk

Or you can contact us by email at
info@howtobooks.co.uk

Like our Facebook page **How To Books & Spring Hill**

Follow us on Twitter **@Howtobooksltd**

Read our books online **www.howto.co.uk**